The Restoration Court Stage

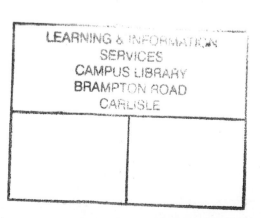

DIANA

The Restoration Court Stage
(1660=1702)

WITH A PARTICULAR ACCOUNT OF
THE PRODUCTION OF *CALISTO*

By

ELEANORE BOSWELL

London

GEORGE ALLEN & UNWIN LTD

RUSKIN HOUSE   MUSEUM. STREET

To

FRANCESCA FRAZIER

χάλκεια χρυσέων

Preface

THIS study is based principally upon materials, hitherto unpublished, from the Accounts of His Majesty's Office of Works and the records of the Lord Chamberlain's Department, both preserved in the Public Record Office. I have drawn upon various other classes of documents there, and have also made use of printed sources, but I have by no means gone through all the material which might possibly bear on my subject. I have sought to present the archives I have used completely and accurately, although it is indeed difficult to maintain strict vigilance through thousands upon thousands of manuscript pages, and my work on them is offered merely as a step towards the discovery of the whole truth.

For the Restoration period, the most important records of the Office of Works are the Accounts Ordinary and Extraordinary (Works 5), which begin in 1660 and are almost complete, only the books for 1680–81, 1692–93, 1696–97, and 1698–99 being missing.[1] Documents belonging to this Office can be examined only by special permit, a fact which I suppose explains their neglect by stage historians, but thanks to the permission very readily granted me by the Board, I have been able to make a thorough search of the books for Whitehall, and

---

1. There are duplicates of some of the early books in the British Museum, and there are also in the Record Office a book of warrants and a book of contracts, Works 6/1 and 5/145. The Declared Accounts in the Exchequer are practically useless.

have collected a few items from the Accounts for other royal residences. Unfortunately, the Windsor accounts were kept separately, and so far as I can discover are not extant.

Many years have elapsed since the first extracts from the Lord Chamberlain's Books found their way into stage history, and it is, perhaps, rather surprising that this mine of information is not yet worked out. A few volumes have been quoted extensively by R. W. Lowe, Dr A. Thaler, and others, and all the entries pertaining to music were excerpted and printed by H. C. De Lafontaine in *The King's Musick* (1909). More recently Professor Allardyce Nicoll has published a large collection of items from the Miscellanea (LC. 5) and the Theatre Books (LC. 7) in an appendix to his *History of Restoration Drama* (1923),[1] but even this leaves much room for further work. Professor Nicoll himself would probably be the last person to claim that he had exhausted his sources, and indeed, many important entries relating to the Court stage are omitted. In those that are printed, omissions are seldom indicated, even when they affect the sense of a passage; there are minor inaccuracies of transcription, and an occasional misleading summary of a warrant.

On page 342, for example, he prints: "(*g*) (Cancelled order.) Warrant to deliver for use in the Cockpit 'Six Turky worke chayres for ye Stage two Spanish Tables Six tynne Candle sticks Six Little tynne Candlesticks ... one greate Chayre to bee vsed vpon ye stage.'

1. The revised edition of 1928 contains no new documents, but I have used it for page references throughout.

Dec. 31, 1666." He adds the reference (LC. 5/138, p. 261) and a note of another entry of the same warrant dated "Feb. 3, 1667, probably 1667/8, in L. C. 5/139, p. 9," where "two 'Turkey workc carpetts' and green baize are ordered as well." Turning to the first book, we find the warrant entered twice, on page 261 where it is deleted, and on page 264 with the date 28 February 1666/7. They are marked "for yᵉ Theatre" and "for yᵉ stage at Whitehall," but there is no mention of the Cockpit, and they have nothing to do with it. The omitted words are "for sizes," that is, a particular size of candle known by that name. The entry dated 28 February 1666/7 adds "two Turky Worke Carpetts." Other entries in LC. 5/139 show that the warrant there cannot possibly be for any other year than 1667/8, and the amount of green baize is specified as "as much . . . as will couer the stage."

Among the provisions for *Calisto*, Professor Nicoll (p. 320) writes: " (*g*) Warrant for ribbons to hang on the curtain. Jan. 15, 1674/5," from LC. 5/141, p. 102. The warrant there entered [1] calls for "Such a quantity of fferrett Ribbon to Hang the Curtaine vpon in the Theatre at Whitehall as shalbe sufficient And also Eight Dozen of White Tynne Plates to put over the sconces in the said Theatre." It does not seem necessary to add further instances, and in giving page references to Professor Nicoll's extracts — for any accidental omissions of which I wish to take this opportunity to apologise — I have not noted errors in his text.

The Lord Chamberlain's Books which I have used

1. It is also entered in LC. 5/64, on f. 117ᵛ.

are as follows: the Registers (LC. 3), of which little use has previously been made,[1] the various kinds of warrant books and original warrants in the Miscellanea (LC. 5), the Theatre Books (LC. 7), which are chiefly eighteenth century and contain little to my purpose, and the Great Wardrobe Accounts and Bills (LC. 9), which, although very valuable, seem to have been totally neglected.

Another hitherto unexplored source of information is the Lord Steward's Department. The principal records of the Board of Green Cloth are Entry Books (LS. 13), and the chief accounts are the Cofferer's, to be found among the Declared Accounts; but more about the Court stage is to be learned from the Creditors (LS. 8), i. e. accounts of extraordinary and special expenditures. Although the entries are often rough and incomplete, they supply the dates of many Court plays.

Other records used are the Declared Accounts of the Treasurer of the Chamber, Master of the Revels, Great Wardrobe and Master of the Robes, as preserved in the Audit Office and Pipe Office (AO. 1 and E. 351); the Accounts Various and Enrollment Books in the Audit Office (AO. 3 and 15); State Papers Domestic and Treasury Books so far as they are calendared; and the Patent Rolls (C. 66).

Very little about the Court stage is to be found in the British Museum manuscripts, at least by using the catalogues, but the Herculean task of searching the uncalendared letters there might yield much. My most important printed sources will be found in the list of authorities, but many of the books one would use for a

1. I published an annotated list of these in the *Bulletin of the Institute of Historical Research* for June, 1929.

general account of the stage are useless for the Court. The most valuable are the Reports of the Commission on Historical Manuscripts, the diaries of Pepys and Evelyn, and the plays themselves. Much remains to be done in the exploration of the uncalendared State Papers, both domestic and foreign, and of letters and diaries either unprinted or inadequately indexed; and there is still a chance that some obscure corner of the Exchequer will yield up further payments for plays.

In quoting from the above records, I have retained the spelling and punctuation, but have not attempted a type facsimile. I have taken no note of trivial errors and corrections *currente calamo*, and have expanded the contractions for *-es* or *-is*, *-rum*, and *-bus*. Important deletions are printed enclosed in square brackets, autograph signatures are in italics, and anything which I have interpolated in a quotation is in italics enclosed within square brackets. In quoting warrants, I have almost always omitted the purely formal opening and concluding phrases,[1] and have given the date, which is usually written out at the end of the warrant and is often in regnal years, in the modern form. For most of the entries there is a brief marginal note of the nature of the warrant; this I have omitted except in the rare cases where it contains additional information. Where the same warrant is entered in two or more places, the particular entry quoted is placed first in the list of references.

Webb's plans for the Hall Theatre and design for its proscenium, and his drawings of the scenery for *Mus-*

---

1. Such as "These are to pray and require you," "and this shall be your sufficient warrant, Given under my hand and seal," and the like.

tapha are in the Duke of Devonshire's collection at Chatsworth, and I am deeply indebted to His Grace for permission to reproduce them, as well as to his librarian, Mr Francis Thompson, who has very kindly examined the originals for me. Professor A. E. Richardson, of University College, London, has taken great pains to explain to me many technicalities of the construction of the Hall Theatre, Mr Thomas Mitchell has criticised my account from the architect's point of view, and Mr E. C. Northover has drawn a scale plan of the theatre and a conjectural view of the interior. The costume sketches were made by Miss U. M. Ellis-Fermor, who has not only rendered invaluable aid in working out the designs from the original bills, but has discussed with me a very large part of the whole study. Professor Charles Sisson has given me constant aid and advice, and read the entire book in manuscript. To all of them I owe sincere thanks for the great amount of time they have bestowed on my problems and their generous contributions to this book. It is an equal pleasure to thank Sir Edmund Chambers for reading and criticising the manuscript, Mr Hilary Jenkinson for making special arrangements for my work at the Record Office, and Miss Margaret Dowling and Mr Stuart Murrie for reading the proofs. Lastly, I wish to take this opportunity to acknowledge my debt to the American Association of University Women, who made possible, by the grant of their European Fellowship, the completion of my work, begun through the generosity of the friend to whom it is dedicated.

E. B.

DECEMBER, 1931

Contents

ILLUSTRATIONS

LIST OF AUTHORITIES [1]

ADAMS. *Shakespearean Playhouses.* By Joseph Quincy Adams. 1917.

ADAMS, DRAM. RECORDS. *The Dramatic Records of Sir Henry Herbert.* By Joseph Quincy Adams. 1917.

BAPST. *Essai sur l'Histoire du Théâtre.* By C. Germain Bapst. 1893.

BELL. "Contributions to the History of the English Playhouse." By Hamilton Bell. *The Architectural Record* (New York). 1913.

CHAMBERS. *The Elizabethan Stage.* By Sir Edmund Chambers. 1923.

CIBBER. *An Apology for the Life of Mr. Colley Cibber. Written by Himself.* Ed. by R. W. Lowe. 1889.

DASENT. *Nell Gwynne.* By Arthur I. Dasent. 1924.

DE LAFONTAINE. *The King's Musick.* Ed. by H. C. De Lafontaine. 1909.

DRYDEN. *The Works of John Dryden.* Scott's ed. rev. by Saintsbury. 1882.

EVELYN. *The Diary of John Evelyn.* Ed. by W. Bray. 1850.

EVELYN, GODOLPHIN. *The Life of Mrs. Godolphin.* By John Evelyn. 1848.

HIST. MSS. *Reports of the Royal Commission on Historical Manuscripts.* 1870–.

HOTSON. *The Commonwealth and Restoration Stage.* By J. Leslie Hotson. 1928.

KEITH. "John Webb and the Court Theatre of Charles II." By William Grant Keith. *The Architectural Review.* February, 1925.

LANGBAINE. *An Account of the English Dramatic Poets.* By Gerard Langbaine. 1691. B. M. copy with mss. notes, C. 28. g. 1.

LAWRENCE. *The Elizabethan Playhouse.* By W. J. Lawrence. 1912, 1913.

---

1. This list contains only important works to which reference is made in the footnotes in an abbreviated form, here given before the title.

LUTTRELL. *A Brief Historical Relation of State Affairs from September 1678 to April 1711.* By Narcissus Luttrell. 1857.

NICOLL. *A History of Restoration Drama.* By Allardyce Nicoll. Rev. ed. 1928.

NICOLL, THEATRE. *The Development of the Theatre.* By Allardyce Nicoll. 1927.

PEPYS. *The Diary of Samuel Pepys.* Ed. by H. B. Wheatley. 1893–99.

REYHER. *Les Masques Anglais.* By P. Reyher. 1909.

RUGGE. *Mercurius Politicus Redivivus.* By Thomas Rugge. B. M. Add. Mss. 10116, 10117.

SECRET SERVICE ACCOUNTS. *Moneys Received and Paid for Secret Services of Charles II and James II.* Ed. by J. Y. Akerman for the Camden Society. 1851.

SHEPPARD. *The Old Royal Palace of Whitehall.* By J. E. Sheppard. 1902.

SPENCER. *Shakespeare Improved.* By Hazelton Spencer. 1927.

SPIERS. "An Autograph Plan by Wren." By W. L. Spiers. *Annual Record of the London Topographical Society.* Vol. II. 1902.

SPRAGUE. *Beaumont and Fletcher on the Restoration Stage.* By A. C. Sprague. 1926.

WALPOLE SOCIETY. *Designs by Inigo Jones for Masques and Plays at Court.* Ed. by Percy Simpson and C. F. Bell for the Walpole and Malone Societies. 1924.

WHITE. *John Crowne: His Life and Dramatic Works.* By A. F. White. 1922.

The Restoration Court Stage

Introduction

MACAULAY once referred to the period immediately following the restoration of Charles II as "those scandalous years of jubilee." For him, the glare of scandal threw all other qualities into obscurity too deep to be pierced. But Macaulay was, as became a leader of his day, essentially respectable, — culottic, Carlyle would have called it, — and neither could nor would understand the temper of the sixteen-sixties. Indeed, I am not sure that Carlyle, the evangelist of the heroic, could have analysed any more impartially than Macaulay an attitude and point of view fundamentally reactionary. The Restoration was not for the nineteenth century. But the generation which grew up during or immediately after the Great War can, I think, appreciate better than the Victorians, or even the Edwardians, the disintegration of both ideals and artificial standards, the reversal of relative values, the thirst for excitement, and the *carpe diem* philosophy of Charles and his contemporaries.

The Restoration period has had, and survived, its detractors and its apologists; it still lives for those who will take the trouble to exhume it from its parchments, and it still awaits a literary historian who is at once an expert in archives and psychology. The workings of the Restoration mind deserve more careful and scientific study than has yet been given them, and although the balance was beginning to shift, the Court still qualifies as one of the chief fields of investigation. As Sir Ed-

mund Chambers has pointed out, with the advent of
the Tudor sovereigns the Court became the centre of
the artistic and intellectual life of the country.[1] This is
still true in the days of Charles II, but other groups
are forming — the coteries of the Coffee Houses, the
Royal Society — which in the eighteenth century will
transfer that centre to the upper middle class. By the
end of the seventeenth century the Court, while no
longer the inspiration, is still the end of intellectual and
artistic endeavour.

It was inevitable that emphasis should fall on the
arts. The exile-wearied Charles might study chemistry,
attend dissections, or discuss astronomy for a time, but
though intellectual pursuits were stimulating, they were
also exhausting, and above everything Charles must be
amused. He wanted a more superficial excitement,
something he could toy with for an hour or two and
then drop. Hence the collections of *objets d'art* so ad-
mired by Evelyn, the long line of royal mistresses, the
horde of household musicians, — hence the predominance of the theatre.

The perennial carnival established in London by the
return of the Court brought about the immediate re-
habilitation of the theatre. Yet from the first it was a
new and different theatre, albeit many of the actors,
most of their plays, and even some of their playhouses
dated from pre-Commonwealth days. Much has been
written about the importance of Elizabethan survivals
on the Restoration stage, and very true it all is; but the
resuscitated theatre was, in a way that it had not been
before, a plaything of the Court; it was no longer a na-

1. Chambers, I, 3.

tional institution. In this matter it is difficult to frame a nice equation. We can no longer pretend that after 1642 "the rest is silence," even so far as public performances are concerned; the old, comfortable convention of a definite end and new beginning has been demolished.[1] Furthermore, there are traces of considerably greater citizen support of the Restoration theatre than has usually been allowed. The plays themselves run rapidly through the last phases of a change begun long before the Civil Wars. To quote Sir Edmund Chambers once more, the Elizabethan play was a "psychological hybrid" between the romance and erudition of the Court and "robust popular elements of farce and melodrama."[2] The Restoration play has lost most of the popular element, the Court element has been transformed into wit and sophistication, and romantic realism has given way to its antithesis, the escape-motif of the heroic play.

On the whole, I think it would be as true a generalisation as most to claim that the theatre in the second half of the seventeenth century was essentially a Court theatre, and on that basis this study might be extended to embrace the whole history of the stage. Certainly the rather narrow limits I have set are arbitrary and require definition.

By the Court stage, then, I here mean theatrical performances at Court, principally in royal residences where there was a theatre or some regular provision for acting. Practically, I am very largely limited to performances at Whitehall by lack of documentary material for the other palaces. I have, perhaps with little rea-

1. See Hotson, ch. i.   2. Chambers, *loc. cit.*

son, excluded performances during progresses and trips (such as the King's visit to Dover in 1670), the barn-actors at Newmarket (evidently a local troupe), and plays given before the King at the Universities and in private houses. I have also ruled out royal attendances at public theatres. On the other hand, I have included what little I could learn of amateur acting at Court, and of the theatres at Windsor and Kensington. Within these bounds, I have attempted to discuss the theatres themselves, what was acted in them, by whom, and how produced. I have chosen the production of *Calisto* for fuller treatment in the first instance because of the unique set of documents pertaining to it, but also because in some ways it marks the culmination of the Court stage.

It is unavoidable that the first fifteen years of the period should fill most of my pages. Of the nineties there is exceedingly little to be said: there are definite indications that plays were still acted at Court, but diligent search for details has been almost fruitless. Charles is the tutelary genius of the Court stage, and when he is gone its slow collapse becomes a rather melancholy spectacle. Again, I have sometimes devoted several pages to a comparatively trivial matter when it is one over which there has been controversy or misunderstanding and on which I have found conclusive evidence. But I have made no attempt to go into the more literary phases of the subject, and there are many points in the account of *Calisto* which might be treated in even greater detail.

PART I

Court Theatres

I

COURT THEATRES

WHEN the players were summoned to Court in Tudor days, they acted in the great hall of the palace, or sometimes, on less formal occasions, in the presence-chamber. In course of time, the development of the masque called for even greater facilities than those offered by the hall, and the temporary masquing-house was invented, which in turn gave place to Inigo Jones' imposing Banqueting House at Whitehall. Plays, however, did not require so much space or such elaborate staging, and thus it came about that a remodelled cockpit remained the only Court theatre up to the Civil Wars.

The interregnum afforded ample opportunity for the exiled King and his friends to visit the Court theatres of Italy and France, and when at long last they reassembled in Whitehall, they brought back with them new ideas and new standards in Court entertainments. It is true that the Cockpit in Court had to serve for a time, but in a few years Charles II contrived to build the Hall Theatre, and there is reason to believe that he also carried out his plans for a theatre at Windsor. Such scant records as there are make it difficult to tell whether William III built a permanent theatre at Kensington, but in any case it is safe to say that the Restoration period saw the highest development of the Court theatre

in England. I have included here notes of other rooms
in the palaces where plays were occasionally acted or
entertainments given, taking shelter behind the definition of a theatre as "a place where public representations are seen." But it is the real Court theatre that
matters, for I believe it to be both a cause and an effect
of the importance and significance of the Court stage at
this time.

THE COCKPIT IN COURT

Thanks largely to Professor Joseph Quincy Adams,
the history of the Cockpit in Court has been familiar to
scholars for more than a decade,[1] but since there are still
some debatable points to be cleared up, it may be well to
review its story. The original building, a real cockpit,
was built by Henry VIII, and is readily discernible in
early maps of Westminster. It seems to have been first
used for plays by Prince Henry, at the beginning of
the seventeenth century, and is presumably the "New
Theatre at Whitehall" of Heywood's *Speech* addressed
to their Majesties on the occasion of its opening in the
winter of 1632–33.[2] Whether or not this reconstruction is shown in certain plans preserved at Worcester
College, Oxford, is one of the problems which require
further discussion, but before plunging into the controversy it may be worth while to pause a moment over
the name Cockpit.

Professor Adams and Mr A. I. Dasent, in his *Nell
Gwynne*, have successfully disentangled the Court playhouse from the Cockpit Theatre in Drury Lane, the

1. Adams, pp. 384–409.   2. *Ibid.*, pp. 394–395.

Royal Cockpit at the end of Dartmouth Street to the south of St. James' Park, and the congeries of buildings at Whitehall that went by that name. The whole heterogeneous mass of lodgings, tennis court, playhouse and chapel,[1] lying between "the Street" and the park, and south of the Holbein Gate, were constantly referred to and even marked on maps as "the Cockpit." Such phrases as "a sermon in the Cockpit" might well lead commentators astray, and even Professor Adams comes to grief over "the Cockpit in St. James' Park." This he says is the exclusive appellation of the real cockpit, but in contemporary records the phrase is repeatedly used of the theatre, and is, of course, more literally true of that than of the Dartmouth Street structure.[2]

It will be recalled that Mr Hamilton Bell first published the plans of what is now generally accepted to be the Cockpit in Court from the original manuscript at Worcester College, Oxford,[3] and that Professor Adams identified the plan with the theatre shown on the so-called Fisher Survey of Whitehall which dates between 1663 and 1670. Adams assumed that the plans represent a remodelling done by Inigo Jones in the winter of 1632–33, but Mr William Grant Keith has since argued that the plans are the work of John Webb and that the reconstruction took place after the Restoration.[4] While accepting Mr Keith's identification of the drawings as Webb's, I am convinced that they are pre-Restoration by the absence of any corresponding entries in the de-

1. Work on the "new chapel at the Cockpit" is recorded in Works 5/1.
2. See also the section on Cock-fighting in Appendix G.
3. In *The Architectural Record*, New York, March and April, 1913.
4. Keith, pp. 49–55.

tailed Accounts of the Office of Works, which begin in June, 1660, and I believe Mr Keith's argument can also be disproved on other grounds. He assumes that the Faithorne map published in 1658 depicts Whitehall as it was at that date, but the most cursory examination of the map shows that this is far from true, and the delineation there of the old Henry VIII cockpit, still unsquared, proves nothing at all.

Inigo Jones' sketch of a scene, marked "for yᵉ Cockpitt for my lo Chãberlin 1639," constitutes a more formidable argument. This scene has been accepted as for *The Queen of Arragon*,[1] although Mr Keith has pointed out that it shows an arched proscenium, whereas the other scenes for that play are evidently intended for a rectangular frame, and has suggested that it might be for Davenant's *The Siege*.[2] When *The Queen of Arragon* was acted at Court, it was in the Great Hall, where *Florimène* had been staged,[3] and so far as we know Jones and Webb always used rectangular proscenia for that stage.

We may therefore leave *The Queen of Arragon* out c account, but the writing on Jones' sketch remains puzzle, and I am at a loss for a theory to cover all th points. Professor Nicoll has already called attention t the similarity of the proscenium here sketched to

1. Walpole Society, p. 131; A. Nicoll, *British Drama*, note on illustration where the play is erroneously stated to have been produced at the Cockpi in Drury Lane.
2. Keith, p. 52. Mr Keith errs in thinking the "Citti of releue" was "to b modelled in relief, and not entirely rendered in paint on a canvas flat." A relieve was a flat, partly cut out to show the back-cloth some feet be hind it, and was a stock device of perspective.
3. Adams, Dram. Records, p. 58. The public production was at Blackfriar:

theatre plan by Jones recently discovered at Worcester
College,[1] and suggests to me that this may be the plan
of the Cockpit in Drury Lane. Davenant may have
produced *The Siege* there in 1639, and certainly if any
private theatre at that date had a Palladian proscenium,
it would have been Davenant's.[2] But this is purely conjectural, and leaves the way open for two very pertinent
queries: what had the Lord Chamberlain to do with the
Cockpit in Drury Lane; and why, if Davenant had such
an elaborate stage as early as 1639, did he blow his
trumpet so loudly over the scenes for *The Siege of
Rhodes*, and why were the first Restoration theatres so
much simpler? Furthermore, although the Cockpit in
Drury Lane was used after the Restoration, it was soon
abandoned. But to be taken into account on the other
side is the fact that French comedians acted *Le Mariage
d'Orphée et d'Eurydice* there in 1661, with scenes and
elaborate machinery.

Tempting as such speculation is, it is like unto the
flowers that bloom in the spring, and I must return to
the Cockpit in Court. If the Jones sketch does not belong to the Cockpit in Drury Lane, I can only suggest
that it may not represent any actual theatre or production. It is very roughly drawn, and may have been submitted to the Lord Chamberlain as a mere indication
of what might be done in a reconstructed theatre. If
the Palladian treatment of the Cockpit had proved
unsatisfactory, there may have been talk at this time of

1. Nicoll, Theatre, p. 134.
2. It occurs to me that this plan may have been made for Davenant's projected "opera house" in Fleet Street.

rebuilding it, and it is even possible that the Jones theatre plan was worked out for a new Court theatre which never materialised. In any case, this rough sketch is far too slight evidence on which to reject Webb's Palladian design or even to argue a second reconstruction. Finally, the Restoration records make no mention of scenes and are entirely compatible with the Webb plans.[1]

Turning, then, to 1660, we find that the first work was done in November and apparently on short order, as witness an item of ten shillings paid to John Davenport, Master Carpenter, "for money laid out by him to ye workmen at ye Cockpit for their extraordinary paines."[2] The work over which they were so diligent consisted in:

makeing of v large boxes wth seuerall degrees in them at ye cockpitt and doores in them, taking vp the floore of ye stage and pitt and laying againe the floore of the stage & pitt pendant, making of seuerall seats round and in ye pitt making of two ptitions in the gallery there for the Musick and players setting vp a rayle & ballisters vpon the stage making two other seats for ye gentlemen Vshers a [sic] Mr Killigrew cutting out a way and making a paire of Stayres cont. [blank] stepps to goe into ye Gallery ouer the stage & incloseing the said stayres wth a doore in it Cont. about one square, making of two new doores goeing vnder the degrees and bourding vp one doore vppon the degrees, setting vp xj squares of ptitioning vnder the degrees wth vj doores in them.[3]

---

1. There are at Chatsworth three drawings for back scenes, of a palace, an army, and a prison, which, as Mr Keith has pointed out (*op. cit.*, p. 55), fit the central arch of the Webb elevation of the Cockpit. These may, of course, be post-Restoration, but I think they probably represent the original scenery made in 1632–33.

2. Works 5/1. Davenport was appointed Master Carpenter of his Majesty's Works for life, by letters patent dated 21 July 1660, at 12*d.* a day (AO. 15/8, p. 295).   3. Works 5/1.

In the same month the matlayers were paid for "new matting some of the seats of ye degrees in ye Cockpit and the seats & floore where his Matie: sitts there, . . . new [*matting*] seuerall other seats and the flatt belowe the stage of the cockpit."[1] Apparently this was all that was necessary to make the theatre usable, and there is no mention of scenes. It is difficult to say whether "the gallery . . . for the Musick and players" refers to the square aperture shown on the Webb elevation or to part of the spectators' gallery. These reparations seem to be fairly conclusive evidence that the Cockpit was not used before November, and that Pepys' earlier references must be to the Cockpit in Drury Lane.[2]

When Albermarle entertained the King with *The Silent Woman* at the Cockpit in Court on 19 November,[3] the little theatre must still have been very bare, for not until the twenty-fourth did Manchester, the Lord Chamberlain, write to the Master of the Great Wardrobe:

These are to Signifie To Your Lordshipp,[4] his Maties pleasure that you provide for the Cockpitt as much Greene Manchester Bayes lyned wth Canvas as will Cover the Stage and twenty faire gillt Branches wth three Socketts in each for Candles and Six Sconces for the Passages that are darke, all these things to bee ready upon Munday, and send Workemen wth them to bee put up by the direction of Clement Kinnersly [5] for his Maties Service Munday night.[6]

---

1. Works 5/1.
2. On 18 August, 11, 16, and 30 October.
3. Pepys, 20 November; Hist. Mss. V, 200. A prologue was written for the occasion by Sir John Denham.
4. The Earl of Sandwich.
5. Groom, and later Yeoman of the Removing Wardrobe.
6. LC. 5/60, p. 63; 5/118. 120 yds. of baize, price £13, and 100 ells of can-

The upholsterer's bill merits quotation:[1]

For the Cockpitt att Whitehall	
For nailes and Iron buttons for the Stage	13.4
For Rings and tape	3.0
For a Curtaine rodd eight ffoote Long	4.0
For makeing a false Case of baies lyned wth Canvas wth large button holes to be placed upon the Stage and to take of at pleasure and for other worke don there	4. 0.0
For hookes staples & buckrome employde about a Crimson velvett Canopie & for altring & mending the s^d Canopie	13.6

The canopy was, of course, for the King's dais.

A further effort to light the theatre is recorded in a warrant of 29 December 1660, for "A Couple of faire brass branches for lights to bee used at the Cockpitt for Playes."[2] In the Wardrobe Accounts these are called "amplissim' globe Branches," and there is a further entry "pro Elocatione Consimił Branches dum ał ffact fuẽr," bringing the total cost up to £61.[3] Evidently they were handsome, and one is tempted to conjecture that they were for the stage.[4]

It was not the way of Restoration Court officials to make a thorough job of a thing and have done with it, and putting the Cockpit in order for plays ceased only a short time before the abandonment of the theatre.

vas, price £6.13.4, were supplied (LC. 9/104 and 9/378; LC. 9/104 and 9/377); and no branches, but 5 prs. of sconces, which were gilt and cost £15 (LC. 9/104).

1. LC. 9/381; 9/104; 9/378. John Casbert or Cassbert, upholsterer, did much work in the Court theatres.

2. LC. 5/60, p. 85.   3. LC. 9/104.

4. More sconces were supplied in August, 1662. (LC. 5/60, p. 344; LC. 9/105; 9/378. The same bill is repeated in LC. 9/106.)

Decoration of the auditorium was effected for the season of 1661–62, if I am correct in so interpreting an item in the Great Wardrobe Account from Michaelmas, 1661, for one year.[1] £69.9.11 are there charged "pro iiij^c iiij^{xx} iiij^{or} virg' Dimi' Bayes Seperał color' vsitat circa Cockpit Suspendeñd Lobbies et ad tegeñd Cathedr' Sedił et Pulviñ." The upholsterer's bill for that year adds to the recovering of the stage the making of two curtains and covering of seats.[2] The size of these curtains is not specified, and they may have been either for windows or for two of the doors in the proscenium.

In January, 1661/2, carpenters were employed in making new doors and stairs, boarding up two windows, and effecting various minor improvements.[3] I incline to think these windows were the two behind the stage, shown on Webb's plan. Much more perplexing are the windows mentioned in the April Account, when the Clerk entered in his book "making shutting windowes for ye Cockpit playhowse 4 fo^t. 3 iñ: wide & 4 fo^t. 10 iñ: high in 4 leaues."[4] Here I can only conjecture, and with considerable hesitation, that they were for the music room in the proscenium, for which they seem to be the right size.

The autumn of 1662 saw renewed activity at the theatre. The boxes were strengthened with battens,[5] and two new chimneys were built.[6] That the Palladian façade was still in place seems to be suggested by a new order for baize, to cover the stage and "to hang over the

1. LC. 9/105.   2. *Ibid.*; 9/380.
3. See p. 240.   4. Works 5/3.
5. *Ibid.*, September.   6. *Ibid.*, November.

Doares there."[1] This is, of course, an exceedingly slight clue, but taken in conjunction with the 8 foot curtain rod and the two curtains above mentioned, it at least establishes a possibility which there is no evidence to disprove.

By far the most interesting of the extant records are those relating to provisions for the tiring-room. A warrant, dated 10 December 1662, from the Lord Chamberlain to the Master of the Great Wardrobe specifies delivery to the Yeoman of the Revels, for use in the Cockpit playhouse in St. James' Park, of the following items:

. . . for the upper tyring roome in the Cockpitt the walles being un-fitt for the rich Cloathes, One hundred & tenn yards of greene bayes at three shill foure pence the yard One looking glasse of twenty seaven Inches for the Weomen Comedians dressing themselues. Twenty chaires & stooles three Tables two stands sixe Candlesticks two peeces of hangings and great curtaine rodds to make partitions betweene the Men & Weomen two paire of Andirons Two paire of Tonges two fire shovells & bellowes One Lanthorne & one Iron Pann, one proporty Bedd wth a redd Taffata Coverlet & taffata Curtaynes & quilt & one Couch.[2]

The Yeoman of the Revels, John Carew or Carey, seems himself to have supplied these needs: he submitted a bill for them, headed "Iohn Carew Yeoman of the Reuells his Bill for money disbursed since October 1660."[3]

1. On 13 November 1662. LC. 5/60, p. 385; 5/137, p. 175; Nicoll, p. 341.
2. LC. 5/60, p. 390; 5/119; Nicoll, p. 341. Also given, omitting the bed and couch, in LC. 5/137, p. 177.
3. LC. 5/119; LC. 9/105; 9/381. It continues:
   "The vpper Tyring howse in the Cockpitt
   The walls being vnfitt for the rich clothes
   iio yards of greene bayes at 3^s. 4^d per yard and ye Vpholsters   l. s. d.
   paines   18.16.8

This sounds very much like work done before the theatre could be used, and the warrant seems to have been drawn up from the bill: apparently Carew bought the things at his own risk and only after two years succeeded in getting the required authorisation to be reimbursed by the Great Wardrobe. At an unknown date he also supplied three silk curtains, presumably for the theatre, for which he obtained a warrant for payment on 20 August 1663.[1]

That year marks the last alterations to the playhouse as such. In January a new cistern was put up,[2] and the October carpentry includes a new pair of stairs going up from the upper tiring-room into the leads.[3]

Although plays were probably acted there until the end of 1664, the Cockpit seems to have received no fur-

---

a Looking glasse of 27 inches by reason the woemen have great difficulty in theire dressing and such a glasse too big to bee brought euery night from their howse	9. 0.0
20 chaires and stooles at 8ˢ the peice one with another	8. 0.0
3 Tables	1.10.0
2 Stands	0.10.0
6 Candlesticks	1. 4.0
2 peices of old hangings and great curtaine rods to make particōns betweene the men and woemen	6. 0.0
2 paire of andirons 2 paire of Tonges 2 fireshouells and bellowes Lanthorne &	1.10.0
Iron pan to putt coales in	0.15.0
a Property bed with red Taffaty couerlett and Taffaty curtains and quilt	8. 0.0
a Couch	3. 0.0
Summa Totalis 57.15.8.	

Thomas Killigrew"

This signature, which is autograph, is found only on the original bill in LC. 5/119.

1. LC. 5/138, p. 80. 2. Works 5/3.
3. Works 5/4; see p. 241.

ther attention from the Lord Chamberlain or the Office of Works. This absence of mention in the records is it-self significant, for it indicates that the theatre was not reconverted to its original use. There is additional evidence of this in later references. In the spring of 1670/1, Cockpit lodgings for the Duke of Buckingham were extensively repaired and partly rebuilt. The "vpper gallery & boxes lookeing downe into yᵉ Cockpit playhowse" were turned into "guardrobes," and there is also mention of some work in "a lower roome next vnto the pitt."[1] A careful study of the reparations made at this time might throw light on the history of the Cockpit group, but that the theatre was not yet replaced by another building is shown by an item the following November for work on the roof over the playhouse.[2] The theatre must have remained materially unaltered as late as 1672, for in the accounts for a new lantern at that date, the plumbers are said to have laid sheet lead "on the lanthorn at the cockpit, playhouse."[3] The Works Accounts contain no further entries for the theatre, and later Cockpit items refer specifically to the lodgings, gallery (i. e. the long passage from the street), or other parts of the group.

The exact date of the demolition of the Cockpit in Court is not known, but can be more closely approximated than has been realised. The theatre is shown in a prospect of Whitehall as seen from St. James' Park painted by Hendrik Danckerts between 1672 and 1677.[4]

1. Works 5/17, March, 1670/1.   2. Works 5/17.
3. Works 5/19. This lantern is shown in Danckerts' picture of Whitehall from St. James' Park.
4. Reproduced by Keith. For the date see above.

But in a picture of the Horse Guards by Van Wyck, who died in 1677, we find the site occupied by the same three-story brick building shown in Kip's view of London from St. James' Park (1710) and his view of Whitehall published in Strype's edition of Stow's *Survey*.[1] This brick building was in turn superseded by Kent's Treasury Building in 1732.

In view of the confusion which formerly reigned in regard to the name Cockpit and the extent of the buildings so called, a somewhat irrelevant note on this matter may perhaps be pardonable. In 1676, Charles made a grant of the Cockpit to Danby, and on the patent roll the property is described as abutting on Hampden House and garden to the south, the Tennis Court to the east, and St. James' Park to the north and west; and containing 210 feet in length, and in breadth, 140 feet at the south end and 80 feet at the north.[2] This definition of the property is repeated in a grant to Princess Anne in 1684,[3] and banishes forever our surprise at finding the King, the Archbishop of Canterbury, the Council of Trade, and various minor officials all lodged in the Cockpit after the Whitehall fire.[4]

1. Spiers.
2. C. 66/3185, No. 12.
3. C. 66/3245, No. 44.
4. However, the King ordered Wren to build at the end of the Banqueting House next the Privy Garden a council chamber and five lodgings for his own use: these were directly opposite the Cockpit and may have been called by that name (Luttrell, IV, 351).

THE HALL THEATRE

By far the most important event in the history of the Court theatre is the construction in 1665 of the playhouse variously known as "the theatre in the Great Hall," "The Theatre in Whitehall," or simply "the Hall Theatre." In view of the mass of information which presents itself to the investigator, the neglect and misunderstanding from which this playhouse has suffered is amazing. To mention only one of the more obvious sources, Pepys gives us due notice of it: on 20 April 1665 he wrote, "This night I am told the first play is played in White Hall noon-hall, which is now turned to a house of playing," and he later gives a full account of his first visit to "the new playhouse."[1] Even more explicit is a letter written by Lord Herbert: "There is to bee a great and publicke ball . . . in the great hall which now is turned into a theater . . . in lieu of the cockpit."[2] Yet Mr Keith has argued that although ballets and even plays were occasionally given there, "the temporary transformation of the Hall . . . did not constitute it a theatre in the strict sense of the term, nor was it ever so described in the records. One building . . . alone answers to this description at this period, that was the Cockpit."[3] Not only is Mr Keith wrong in his main contention, but the records again and again refer to "the theatre in the Great Hall," and the very documents he

1. On 29 October 1666. See p. 56.
2. Hist. Mss. XII, ix, pp. 54–55. Written 14 November 1666, when the theatre had been used very little because of the plague.
3. Keith, p. 51.

quotes change from "Cockpit" to "Theatre at Whitehall" at the time of its construction.[1] Professor Nicoll,
too, although he seems to recognise the existence of a
second playhouse, has confused documents relating to
the Cockpit and Hall Theatres. The credit for discover-
ing the latter is, I believe, due to Mr W. J. Lawrence; at
least he has several times referred to it in print, and very
kindly warned me of its existence when I first began my
investigations. And I am haunted by the impression
that I once met another reference to it, but have
searched in vain for the allusion.

The building in which the new theatre was constructed is not without its own interest. I have been
unable to discover the significance of Pepys' phrase,
"noon-hall": it was the great hall of the palace, and as
such is well known.[2] It lay between the Banqueting
House and the river, abutting on the northeast on the
passage leading to Whitehall Stairs, and was the middle
one of three buildings clearly and invariably shown in
early maps.[3] Morgan's prospect of Whitehall shows it
as a steeply gabled roof with a lantern in the centre,

1. Entries of the Theatre-Keeper's wages, in the Accounts of the Treasurer
   of the Chamber. Court officials never made unnecessary changes.
2. Accounts of it will be found in Sheppard, Dasent, and Vol. VII of the
   Annual Record of the Topographical Society.
3. The building next the Great Court comprised the Wine Cellar and, over
   it, the Guard Chamber; the one toward the river, shown with a flat,
   crenellated roof, was the Chapel. The three are shown on a map in the
   British Museum (dated 1700 in the Catalogue) which claims to show
   Westminster as it was about 1560; they appear in the Morgan and Ogilby
   map of Westminster, 1677, and the Norden map of 1732, which is an
   exact duplicate of the preceding so far as Whitehall is concerned. The
   Hall is shown in Hollar's 1660 drawing of Whitehall, and apparently in
   Kip's drawing of the palace in 1714; but see p. 56.

standing up just to the right of and below the Banqueting House. It is conspicuous in the Survey of Whitehall engraved by Vertue in 1747, which purports to represent the palace in 1680, but has been shown to fall within the years 1663 and 1670.[1] Vertue's uncertainty as to the date leads one to query his ascription of the survey to an otherwise unknown John Fisher, and a hitherto undiscovered entry in the Accounts of the Office of Works would seem to justify the sceptic. Among the charges for October, 1670, the Clerk wrote: "To Ralph Greatorex for 3 quarters of a years pains in surueighing & describing in vellom an Exact Grownd plott of ye whole house of Whitehall, Cockpit & parts adjacent 60: 0: 0."[2] Assuredly two such surveys would not be made within a few years, and it seems reasonable to conclude that Vertue's original was drawn by the famous instrument-maker, frequently mentioned by Pepys. On the other hand, had the survey been made after the building of the theatre, one would expect the structural changes then effected to be shown, whereas the Hall is treated in less detail than either the Cockpit in Court or the Banqueting House. It is, however, generally realised that the plan is not exact in all details, and it is also quite within the bounds of possibility that the work entered on the Accounts in 1670 had been done some years before.[3]

According to tradition, the Hall was a survival of Wolsey's palace.[4] At least we know that it was not new in Elizabeth's time, and the Clerk of the Works sometimes calls it "the old hall." This does not, of course,

1. Spiers.   2. Works 5/15.
3. I shall refer to it briefly as the Survey.
4. Dasent, p. 174.

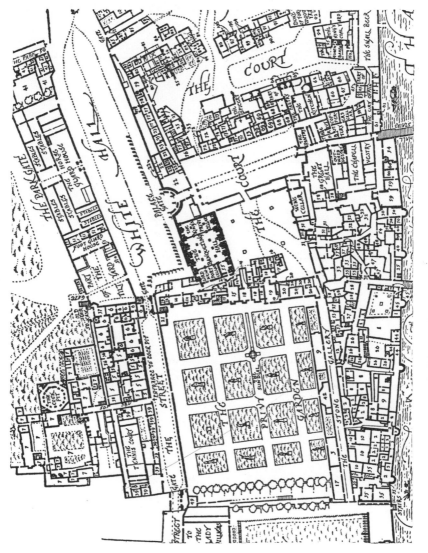

PART OF THE SURVEY OF WHITEHALL

establish any great antiquity, but its position between the Guard Chamber and the Chapel suggests that we have here the nucleus of the original palace. Burbage and his fellows acted here before their Sovereign Lady, and it was frequently used for plays by James I,[1] while even the masques were given in it when the Banqueting House was being rebuilt by Inigo Jones after the fire of 1619.[2] When Charles' care for the Rubens ceiling drove Court entertainments again out of doors, the Hall was once more called into service, and *Florimène* was staged there in December, 1635. The plan of the temporary theatre then fitted up is preserved in the British Museum,[3] and throws considerable light on the details of the later theatre.

I have already called attention to the fact that the Cockpit in Court was not put into condition until November, 1660. But Charles did not wait until then for entertainment; in August he had rope-dancers in the Hall, which presumably at that date was not encumbered with a stage. Preparation for the performance was made by letting timbers into the walls to fasten the ropes to, and seats, perhaps even boxes, were provided for the spectators.[4] After this we hear no more of *divertissements* in the hall for some time, and that it was not equipped for them seems evident from the fact that in 1661 it was used for the King's Maundy.

The winter of 1662–63 marks the real beginning of its theatrical career under Charles II. In December a carpenter was set to work to build a stage and degrees for

1. Adams, pp. 387–389.   2. *Ibid.*; Reyher, p. 344.
3. Lansdowne Ms. 1171.
4. Works 5/1, August, 1660; see p. 241.

seats, of which we know only what can be gleaned from his bill, the important items of which are:[1]

> ... xviij squares iij q^rters & x foote of vpright worke & flooreing on the stage at x^s the square .... xxxix square & iij q^rters in the degrees & staires at xij^s ye square .... setting vp xij fo^t. Di': of railes & ballisters on ye said staires at vj^d ye foote .... xxvij foote of raile & termes[2] on ye stage at vj^d ye foote ....

Part, but apparently part only, of the degrees was covered with bulrush matting.[3] All this is exasperatingly vague, the only clear deduction being that the stage was 27 feet wide, since that is the length of the balustrade set upon it. Evidently the results were not altogether satisfactory, for in January the degrees for the musicians were enlarged, 182 feet of ledges for hangings put up, and the "state" or throne, which measured 125 square feet, enclosed with slit deal.[4] On the twenty-seventh of that month, the Lord Chamberlain sent a warrant to the Great Wardrobe for "Twelue tynne Candlesticks each to hold twelue candles & as much greene baies as will Cover the new stage that is erected in the great Hall."[5] The stage must have been built some four weeks earlier, and the delay in ordering baize is strange. No less than 156 yards were supplied, but the upholsterer's account shows that this di more than cover the stage: he charged "pro tegend ffundid et al sedes pro comœd in Regis aula magna."[6]

Where the aforesaid state was I do not know, but apparently it did not please the King, even when en-

---

1. Works 5/3; E. 351/3276. For the entire bill, see p. 242.
2. Uprights or posts.   3. Works 5/3.
4. *Ibid.*   5. LC. 5/60, p. 404; 5/118.
6. LC. 9/106.

closed with slit deal, and in February the carpenters were again at work,

takeing downe the throne in y⁰ hall and makeing good the raile & termes on the stage there, & bourding vp part of the foreside of the stage wth slitt deale, making a foot pace at y⁰ vpper end of the hall Cont' j square & 40 foote, . . .¹

This sounds as if the state had been on the stage, but the Clerk of the Works had strange ideas of punctuation and style, and I do not think we can always take him absolutely literally. Such a position for the King's seat would be contrary to both common sense and precedent as shown by the *Florimène* plan and the Cockpit in Court. The further laying of mats completed the season's work,² and left the hall in fairly good shape, but, so far as I can ascertain, without provision for scenes.

I take it that Charles perceived in this somewhat primitive theatre greater possibilities than were offered by the small Cockpit with its formal, Palladian proscenium, for early in 1665 he determined to convert the Hall into a permanent theatre, equipped with scenery and befitting his Court. I have been unable to find the warrant authorising the work, but perhaps the loss is not great, for it would be formal and undetailed, and directed to Sir John Denham as Surveyor General.

The work was, however, under the direct supervision of John Webb, and although the King may have given some instructions, the theatre was probably planned by him. This, I think, is the only possible interpretation to put on his own statement (when he petitioned the

1. Works 5/3.   2. *Ibid.*

King against Wren's appointment as Surveyor General) that "At Whitehall hee made yor. Theater, and
thereby discovered much of the Scenicall Art, wch. to
others then himselfe was before much unknowne."[1]
Mr Keith interprets this as referring to the Cockpit,
which he thinks was remodelled at the Restoration,[2]
but Webb is giving a chronological list of his services to
the second Charles, in which the making of the theatre
comes last, after the preparation of Whitehall for the
King's return and his appointment as Assistant Surveyor at Greenwich in 1663. His claim to have made
known "much of the Scenicall Art" is a little puzzling:
his stage for the Hall Theatre is essentially the stage of
the Caroline masques and his own *Siege of Rhodes*, but
it is probably quite true that he was the only man then
living who had been intimately connected with the
earlier Court stage and had practical knowledge of its
workings.

Webb's responsibility for the Hall Theatre is further
demonstrated by the plans and designs for *Mustapha*,
which was acted there soon after its opening.[3] The plan
and elevation of the stage are marked, ". . . for the
Queens Ballet in the Hall at Whitehall 1665/ To be
vsed also for masques & Playes. 1. The Tragedy of
Mustapha." Now it may be that the Queen's Ballet
opened the theatre and was the performance Pepys
wished he could see on 20 April, although he definitely
calls it a play, and that, because of the plague, *Mustapha*

1. S. P. 29/251 *b*., fol. 120. The petition is undated, but calendared as 1668.
2. Keith, p. 50.
3. In the Duke of Devonshire's collection at Chatsworth.

did not follow until 18 October 1666, on which date Evelyn was present. But in any case, *Mustapha* must have been one of the first productions, and Webb's drawings must represent the original layout of the stage.

These plans are, of course, of the utmost importance for the study of the theatre, and I have further had the great privilege of consulting Professor Richardson, of University College, London, on technical points; yet withal, I confess to considerable diffidence in interpreting the somewhat cryptic Accounts drawn up by the Clerk of the Works. But these Accounts are the chief source of information on the Hall Theatre, and I have therefore reproduced *verbatim* in an appendix all entries pertaining to the Great Hall.[1]

When, early in 1665, Webb set to work to plan the "new" theatre, he had anything but a free hand to work out his ideals. The Hall was already there, and so solidly constructed that it could be altered but little. Moreover, Charles was doubtless short of money for this new extravagance, and it must therefore cost as little as possible. The outside measurements of the Hall have been stated by Mr Ernest Law to be 100 x 45 feet,[2] but he considered the passage to Whitehall Stairs part of the Hall; the inside measurements may fairly safely be taken from the *Florimène* and *Mustapha* plans as approximately $39\frac{1}{2}$ x 87 feet.[3] There remained in it the stage and degrees erected two years before; otherwise it

---

1. See pp. 241–271.
2. *Annual Record* of the Topographical Society, VII, 41.
3. The theatre as arranged for *Florimène* did not occupy the entire length of the Hall.

was unencumbered, and open to the high, hammer-beam roof, in which there was a lantern.

The main features of Webb's theatre are clear enough.[1] At the northeast end of the Hall he built a stage which extended from wall to wall and was 32 or 33 feet deep. Next the pit it was 5 feet high, then slightly canted for 17 feet, with the rear portion level at 6 feet. This construction seems to be typical of Webb's design, for it is the same used for *The Siege of Rhodes*. The proscenium, or frontispiece as it was called, was set at the very front of the stage, and the space over it to the roof boarded up. Over the stage Webb placed a heavily canted "floor," to serve as a grid for the scenes and probably also as a sounding board.

This stage was an entirely new structure, and that fact leads me to the conclusion that the previous one was at the opposite end of the Hall, for the carpenters began their work by

taking downe all the old degrees in the hall & raysing the old Stage there higher & cutting it shorter, making & putting vp 12 boxes and severall degrees round y[e] said stage . . . making a foot pace vpon the stage for the K and Queen wth a rayle about it.

The King's seat had to be well raised if he was to look down on a stage 5 feet above the ground, and this use of the old stage as the foundation of the dais, boxes, and degrees is a pretty bit of ingenuity. The footpace and rail would be in the centre, the degrees, with divisions to form boxes, around three sides to the walls.[2] I am somewhat at a loss how to dispose "2 large doorcases &

---

1. The following details, unless otherwise noted, are taken from Works 5/7 and the *Mustapha* plans.   2. Cf. Chambers, I, 203.

doores wth 4 stepps of staires goeing downe to ye stage where ye footpace was made for ye K & Queen to sitt in," unless they were set in the back line of the degrees, which might be several feet from the wall and serve as a partition to divide off a lobby at the back of the Hall. But in that case, the steps would have gone *up* to the dais.[1]

The space between the stage and the dais constituted the pit. The work done here is described as "making a pendant floor in ye pitt wth degrees at each end wth 16 seates in it." The degrees were, I think without doubt, ranged along the side walls as in the *Florimène* plan, for apparently the large diameter of an area was called the length even when it lay across a building.[2] Professor Richardson suggests that "pendant" means that the floor was laid on sleepers or joists, and the New English Dictionary gives one sense of the word as "supported above the ground on arches, columns, etc." On the other hand, Inigo Jones is quoted by the same authority as applying the word to a slanting roof, and various illustrations are given (some of which I confess I do not find convincing) in which it denotes a slope. I have already mentioned an item in the Works Accounts for the Cockpit, for laying the floor of the stage and pit pendant,[3] and I think this can only mean slanting. There were benches in the pit, as witness numerous entries for matting, but they could easily be cut to fit

1. Mr Thomas Mitchell suggests that the entrance at this end of the Hall may have been at first-floor level, and in that case, steps leading down to the dais would be perfectly logical.
2. Thus the 39 foot width of the stage is repeatedly called its length.
3. See p. 14.

the slope and nailed into place. It must be noted that the pit is here taken to extend across the entire building, whereas the term is later used in the same records for the space enclosed by the degrees along the sides, the dais, and stage. Its dimensions are then given as 28 x 18 feet,[1] and to these measurements I shall return later.

Across the end of the Hall above the degrees there was a gallery 7 feet wide, with three degrees, and at least part of it was divided into boxes. It was reached by a single flight of stairs, but where placed is not stated, nor is its elevation.

At the back of this gallery was the great stone window which must once have been one of the chief beauties of the Hall. Its noble proportions were, however, for theatrical purposes, only a source of annoyance, and it suffered many indignities. I take its original size to have been some 12 x 20 feet, but it is impossible from the available data to be sure. Part of it, presumably the lower part, had been boarded up in 1663, and the amount is given as 160 square feet, but this figure may stand for the wood used rather than the area of the boarding.[2] Curiously enough, nothing seems to have been done with the window when the theatre was constructed, but in 1666/7 it was provided with a curtain of fine blue canvas,[3] and later still more of it was plastered up.[4] There were other windows in the Hall, all of

---

1. Works 5/49, November, 1697.
2. Works 5/3, February, 1662/3.
3. Works 5/9 and 5/10. See pp. 246 and 247. It worked with an elaborate arrangement of weights and pullies.
4. Works 5/11. For later repairs and a new curtain in 1697, see Works 5/24 and 5/26; LC. 5/69 f. 148ᵛ, 5/152, p. 35; AO. 3/1141, p. 49; LC. 11/5.

which, according to the Works Accounts, were boarded up when the theatre was built. Later entries for repairs show that as a matter of fact some lights must have been left open, but they would easily be covered with hangings, and we need not pause over them.[1]

When we come to consider the doors and stairs which gave access to various parts of the theatre, we at once find ourselves on difficult ground. I have already mentioned stairs leading to the gallery, and the two doors with four steps going down to the King's dais. These must have been somewhere within the theatre, for "at the south of the hall," was a large ornamental doorway with double doors, specially made as task-work by one John Angier, "for a passage for the King into ye hall."[2] At the other end of the Hall there was a door opening into the passage to Whitehall Stairs, shown, in different positions, on both the *Florimène* plan and the Survey. After the stage was built, this door would be under it, and seems to be the one referred to in an entry for "lathing & plaistering on ye bourds at ye outer doore, vnderneath ye stage."[3] Perhaps with a view to preventing the public from using this entrance, " a boarded fence in ye passage to Whitehall bridge before ye Theater dore

1. There are no bills for curtains for these windows, but a bill for a stage curtain in 1686–87 ends: "For tape and nayles used in Six Windowes." (LC. 9/278.)
2. No such doorway is to be found on the Survey, but both this and the *Florimène* plan disagree with the Accounts, as well as with each other, and it is impossible to arrive at any satisfactory conclusion. There is a later entry of making a rail with a flap at "the K^s. doore" (Works 5/39, December, 1685), which I take to be the same one.
3. Works 5/9, January, 1666/7. This does not, I think, mean that the doorway was closed up, but refers rather to work done about the frame or in the thickness of the three-foot wall.

25 foot in length" was subsequently set up.[1] From an order of the Lord Chamberlain's,[2] we learn that there was an entrance from the "Chapel Chamber," presumably the "Outward Vestry" marked by the ghostly John Fisher, but there is no mention of it in the Works Accounts.

On the opposite side of the Hall there were at least two entrances, one from the Wine Cellar and one from the Guard Chamber over it. On this side also, there was a large recess or oriel,[3] and next to this must have come the stairs leading to the Guard Chamber.[4] I take it that "ye Theatre dore next ye guard Chamber," so frequently referred to in the records, was at the foot of these stairs;[5] but probably the "Lobby goeing into the kings Guardchamber"[6] was part of that structure rather than of the theatre.[7] The entrance from the Wine Cellar seems ordinarily to have been boarded up, and would, I should think, come under the degrees on that side, but it could be opened for special occasions.[8]

All this is confusing enough and difficult to visualise, but confusion is worse confounded by the building of a new "passage for the Queen to goe into ye Sceenes." It

1. Works 5/25, April, 1675. 2. See p. 183.
3. Shown in different proportions and positions, on both the Survey and the *Florimène* plan.
4. These may be the "great Stars." referred to in Works 5/43, November, 1689.
5. Works 5/25, April, 1675, *et passim.*
6. Works 5/28, December, 1677.
7. According to Works 5/21, January, 1673/4, there was also a passage from the Guard Chamber to the Chapel, — an apparent impossibility, — with a door in it into the theatre.
8. See Works 5/9, January, 1666/7; 5/30, February, 1678/9; 5/44, April, 1690; see also p. 53.

must be remembered that Webb labelled his plans, "for the Queens Ballet," and it is evident that convenience for royal performers had to be kept in mind. The new passage was formed by cutting off a strip of the Great Court by a brick wall 12 feet long, and must therefore have run along the side of the Hall. I think its position can be identified on the Survey as between the oriel and the porch.[1] The Works Accounts give many details of the cutting of doorways, and refer to stairs in the passage. An item of "working a bricke wall 9 inches thick to face between 2 walls" suggests that the recess or oriel was now permanently cut off; the passage touched the foot of the Guard Chamber stairs, or perhaps ran under them. We do not, however, know any specific levels, and a definite reconstruction would be purely conjectural.

Another piece of construction difficult to understand is the building of four tiring-rooms at the stage end of the Hall. It is clear that these were not on stage level, and Professor Richardson believes they were built over the passage leading to Whitehall Stairs. I incline, however, to think they were over the stage, as in the second Theatre Royal in Drury Lane, designed by Wren.[2] The carpenters' account for enclosing and flooring the rooms gives no details; my theory is based on the building of two chimneys. For these, stone trusses were let into the outside of the wall, and at first sight this looks as if the tiring-rooms were over the passage; but the brick-

1. This wall was built of rubbed brick, ornamented with a copeing and corbels, and had a window in it. The passage was paved with Purbeck stone, plastered, and roofed with pantiles.
2. See the drawing, reproduced in Nicoll, Theatre, p. 164.

layers in building the chimneys cut a way "through the stone wall at the north end of the hall." Had the rooms been outside, there would have been no need to cut *through* the wall, although space for the flue may have been cut out of its thickness. But again, there is no mention of cutting doorways, although the carpenters made "4 pair of staires leading vp to ye great stage and ye said Tiring Rooms," nor of roofing the new rooms. Finally, there is a later reference to "ye windowes behind ye sceanes and ye tireing roome." [1] That considerable care was taken over these rooms, no doubt with an eye to royal actors and actresses, is revealed by an order from the Lord Chamberlain to the Yeoman of the Revels, bidding him attend and consult with the Surveyor General "concerninge the convenient makinge the Attyreing-roome." [2]

When we look for special equipment for the stage, the Accounts fail us sadly. The space under the stage was divided into rooms "for severall necessary vses and Keeping of Provisions in," but there is no mention of traps or machinery of any sort. The joiners made a model of the scenes, and twenty-two frames and joined forms — the latter perhaps clouds — and the carpenters too made "severall frames shutting vpon ye said stage." Most unfortunately, Robert Streeter, the King's Serjeant Painter, put in a separate account for painting the scenery, instead of including it in the Works Accounts, but we know what they were like from Webb's designs for them, preserved at Chatsworth.[3] Streeter's

1. Works 5/24.   2. LC. 5/138, p. 425. See p. 75.
3. For further details, see pp. 149–150, 153–154.

bill must also have included the proscenium, which the
carpenters dismiss briefly as "making a frontispeece."
There are, however, two items in a later bill for scene
painting which seem to refer to the proscenium:

ffor new painting the figure of fame and Altering the posture 1:0:0
. . . Payd by him [*Streeter*] to ye Joyner for new putting together the
figure of fame.[1] . . .

Working on this clue, I believe I have found Webb's
design for the frontispiece among the Duke of Devonshire's drawings at Chatsworth, and His Grace's librarian, Mr Francis Thompson, tells me he has not the
least doubt that my identification is correct.

In the descriptive catalogue of the Inigo Jones drawings published by the Walpole and Malone Societies, in
the section on unidentified scenery, will be found the
following description:[2]

380. A Proscenium.
    The sides are composed of two three-quarter columns of the
Tuscan order, standing on pedestals panelled with bas-reliefs, the
shafts rusticated with plain blocks. These support an architrave,
broken forward over the columns and in the middle, where it is surmounted by a broken sweeping pediment which is partly covered by
an irregular trilobed cartouche panel, the frame of which is ornamented with Sirens and festoons of fruit; it is inscribed, "*Hi sunt de
pace triumphi Bella dabunt alios.*" On the top of the panel is a seated
figure of Fame blowing a trumpet; to its sides are attached draperies,
which hang in festoons over the frieze and are twisted round the side
columns. On the outside of both columns are bases of rusticated
masonry with semi-circular openings, above which are balconies,

---

1. Works 5/15, January, 1670/1.
2. Walpole Society, p. 137.

faced with panels containing bas-reliefs, and entered by doorways surrounded and surmounted by trophies of arms; near that on the right is the inscription, in Webb's writing, "*This dores were left out a way being made in ye Belconies A. A. for the Players to gett vpp into them vpon occasion.*" The front edge of the stage is a plain sill, without stairs descending from it, supported on coarsely rusticated masonry. On the right an enlarged detail of the blocking of the columns.

Pen and black ink washed with sepia and squared with black lead for enlargement, the squares being numbered. Splashed with scene-painters' distemper. $15\frac{3}{4}$ x $19\frac{1}{4}$ inches.

This drawing is almost certainly entirely by Webb's hand and the writing is his. The side piers, with their Tuscan columns, present an analogy with those decorated in the same way with a Doric order, used by Webb in his proscenium for *The Siege of Rhodes*, 1656. It is not improbable that the present design may have been made by him at a period several years after the death of Inigo Jones.

It seems extraordinary that the editors, while recognising the drawing as Webb's and postulating a late date for it, failed to compare it with the *Mustapha* scenery and stage plans in the same collection, which it exactly fits. As noted, the drawing is squared for enlargement, showing that the proscenium opening is 23 feet high and 25 feet wide, the uprights 3 feet 8 inches, and the horizontal part at the top a little less than 4 feet.[1] These are precisely the dimensions marked on the two stage plans.

Since the frontispiece was made by carpenters, and its uprights are shown on the stage plan as only about 2 inches thick, I am forced to conclude that the whole thing, with the possible exception of Fame, was painted on a flat wooden surface or on canvas nailed to the boards. (I may remark in passing that painting to represent stone was used extensively throughout the

1. The pediment and figure of Fame of course add considerably to the total height.

WEBB'S DESIGN FOR THE FRONTISPIECE OF THE HALL THEATRE

palace.) I am rather worried about Fame, who was put together by the joiner: was she merely a flat piece of jigsaw work?

The most interesting part of this not very beautiful design is the unsuccessful attempt to combine proscenium doors and windows with a typical masque frontispiece, for I can interpret the note about the "Belconies" in no other way. The matter is decidedly perplexing, for in the first place, the space between the column and the wall is only 3 feet or a trifle more,[1] and a doorway some $2\frac{1}{2}$ feet wide would scarcely allow for the sweep of Restoration costumes, or even a bulky actor. But even more insuperable is the fact that the proscenium, according to the plan, was set only a foot from the edge of the stage, and if a heroine did manage to get herself into the balcony, it would be quite impossible for the hero, on the stage, to see or converse with her. And there is the further problem of what Webb meant by the note quoted in the description: if the doors into the balconies were left out, other access could not possibly be provided. It occurs to me that the note may be misplaced, and that the semi-circular openings may originally have been the tops of the doors in question, which were abandoned because they could not be reached from the stage, but their line left in the design for the sake of ornament. Obviously the balconies could easily be gained by stairs or ladders behind the proscenium, and in view of Webb's statement I think we must conclude they were sometimes used by the players, but they must

---

1. The *Mustapha* stage plan is inaccurate here, the columns being set too far to the side, although the space between them is correctly marked 25 feet.

have had far fewer possibilities than their prototypes in
the public theatres.

One other important provision was made by the carpenters, a "large seat wth severall degrees in it for y^e
musick." The *Mustapha* stage elevation shows that
this was placed behind the upper shutters, 12 feet,
6 inches above stage level at the front, and reaching
the back cloth at a height of about 14 feet. It would be
directly over the relieves, and, in an ordinary set, entirely invisible to the audience. But in the carpenter's
Account there is a further and most curious item, "making provision to draw ye Ovall Shutt^{rs} before ye musicke." This at once suggests an orchestra concealed
behind jointed shutters, under an oval projection at the
front of the stage, but in view of the *Mustapha* plans I
think it must be interpreted as meaning a pair of scenic
shutters representing clouds and forming an oval when
closed, which could be withdrawn to disclose the musicians.

A few further details are to be gathered from the
Works Accounts. The joiners made a "Compart seat
or Throne for the Queen," which I take to be part of
the setting for her ballet, since she was otherwise provided with a crimson velvet armchair on the royal dais.
Provision was made to "take vp and let downe the
Curtain"; the great chimney was rebuilt. Finally, matlayers covered with bulrush matting the backs and seats
of the boxes, the degrees in the gallery and seats below,
the steps and walls of the stairs, the tiring-rooms and
music-room, the degrees and seats in the pit, and the
floors and walls between and behind the scenes. This

completed the Office of Works' share in preparing the theatre. Some details of the labour and materials will be found in the appendix, but I cannot forbear to mention here that one Robert Little, carpenter, was given £5 "for his Extraordinary paines early and late in hastening the carpent^{rs} worke." The whole Account for the theatre comes to £737.11.2¼.

The theatre was not yet ready for use: an important part in fitting it up was played by the Great Wardrobe.[1] One of the earliest orders, apparently in preparation for the new theatre although the date may be mere coincidence,[2] was for "Indian gowns" for the musicians. The warrant, dated 18 March 1664/5, calls for

Habitts of sev^{ll}. colrd rich taffatas for foure and twenty Violins like Indian Gownes but not So full wth. short Sleeves to the Elboes & trimed wth. Tinsell about the Neck bottome & at the Sleeues. And also . . . twenty fowre Garlands of flowers of sev^{ll} sorts to weare upon their heads all of the fashion & manner as S^r. Henry Herbert Ma^r of his Maties Revells shall informe yor Lo^{pp} All wch pticul^{rs}. are to be deli^d unto Sr Henry Herbert for his Maties. extraordinary Service.[3]

The result must indeed have been extraordinary, but Charles, at least, seems to have found it pleasing, for he kept his musicians in taffeta for some years.

1. Since most of the Wardrobe records specify only the year in which certain work was done, it is sometimes difficult to tell, when the warrants are lacking, to what particular occasion the various items should be assigned, but I believe that everything provided for the Hall Theatre in the year 1664–65 (the accounts run from Michaelmas to Michaelmas) may be taken as part of the original equipment of the playhouse.
2. Similar costumes were provided by the King for the music at the two patent theatres. See a warrant dated 20 March 1664/5, from LC. 5/138, p. 45; 5/61, p. 225; and 5/119, in Nicoll, p. 341.
3. LC. 5/61, p. 224; 5/138, p. 46; 5/118; Nicoll, p. 341. The taffeta, 92⅝ ells, was supplied by Edw. Trussell, for £79.5.7. (LC. 9/108).

The furnishing of the King's dais is happily described in some detail, and we can form a fairly complete picture of the way Charles sat in state, quite as much a part of the show as the people on the stage. It will be recalled that the carpenters remodelled what the Clerk of the Works called a "stage for the K & Queen," with a footpace, and a rail around it. This was covered first with canvas and then baize, and a canopy of state set up over it,[1] very effectually blocking the view of those behind. The canopy was made of crimson velvet, trimmed with gold and silver fringe, with a tester and valance. To match it there were two great chairs of state and two cushions. Room on the dais must also, I think, be found for "a framed table wth turned feet 3 foot di long and 2 foot and a halfe broad" (made by joiners and included in the Works Accounts), for there was a "table Carp^{tt}" of yellow damaske, with fringe, and to match this, a "large long Cusheon of gold Colrd damaske trimed wth silke fringe & tassells." The same warrant calls for a pewter standish, but why the King should have felt any need for pen and ink during a play is difficult to conjecture. Probably the dais was also the place for which three very large standards, i. e. tall candlesticks to stand on the floor, were provided at no less than £10 a piece.

Turning to the stage, we find that it too was covered first with canvas and then with baize.[2] The only indica-

1. These and the following details will be found in bills in LC. 9/108, 9/378, and 9/382, and a warrant, LC. 5/61, p. 228, repeated in LC. 5/138, p. 49, and Nicoll, p. 342.
2. LC. 9/108, 9/378; 9/382. The baize, 80 yards, cost £10.13.4. The upholsterer's bill includes "hanging the two sides of the Masquing Roome," but there is no other mention of this.

tion of the lighting provided is the following item, in which the Clerk's Latin did not prove equal to the occasion:

pro nigris et albis plates, lucernis soder' wyres lynes, vitrio Muscoviae pulleys et pro divers alijs necessar' praeterea impens circa illa p novo Theatro apud Whitehall et pro dive˜s dierum opificio circa praemissa — xxxiiij^{li}. v^s. viij^d.[1]

Muscovy glass is common mica or talc, and I infer that out of these supplies were manufactured lanterns, three sides of the glass, with a white plate at the back for a reflector, and black ones top and bottom. Evidently they were hung on wires over pulleys, perhaps in rows behind the frontispiece and scenes, for there must have been a great many, to judge by the amount of the bill.[2] Probably for the stage were six large Turkey work chairs,[3] and the equipment of the theatre was completed by two necessary-stools with extra pans, six pewter chamber-pots, and three large trunks to keep costumes in.[4]

The theatre was now presumably ready for use. We hear nothing more of the Queen's Ballet, for it was a play, not a masque, which Pepys wished he could go to on 20 April, but there must have been time for several productions before the plague became serious, and Charles was not the man to neglect a new toy. But on 29 June the Court left town,[5] and plays were not re-

1. LC. 9/108. Perhaps also for the lights were "quatuor truncis et ligament' et . . . quatuor orbiculis — vj^s." (*Ibid.*)
2. One of the *Empress of Morocco* plates shows a large lantern hung with a rope and pulley in the centre of the stage.
3. LC. 9/108; 9/382. Cost £6: See p. 157.
4. *Ibid.*, LC. 5/61, p. 230; 5/138, p. 49; Nicoll, p. 342.
5. Pepys, on that date.

sumed at Whitehall until October, 1666, with the result
that at that late date the Hall Theatre was still regarded
as new.[1] The first play there of which I have found
mention was *Wit Without Money*, acted on 11 October.[2]
At that time there was still work to be done in the theatre. Seven branches or chandeliers were hung, presumably in the auditorium.[3] In the same month was
begun the practice of flooring over the pit for dancing,
at this time described as "Joysting & boarding a floore
ouer the pitt there Cont': about 6 square";[4] and on the
seventeenth the Lord Chamberlain ordered baize and
canvas to cover the stage "for her Ma[ties]: Daunceinge."[5]
A later entry shows that this floor was laid level with
the stage.[6] It is difficult to see how joists laid temporarily over the sloping floor of the pit and so graduated
as to bring the dancing floor level at 5 feet above the
ground could have resulted in any but the shakiest
superstructure, but the "safety first" slogan had not
been invented. The ball must, I think, have taken
place between the eighteenth, when Evelyn was an
unwilling spectator at *Mustapha*, and the twenty-ninth,
for on that date the theatre was visited, most willingly,
by Mr Pepys, who wrote of it:

... I away before to White Hall and into the new play-house
there, the first time I ever was there, ... By and by the King and
Queene, Duke and Duchesse, and all the great ladies of the Court;

---

1. See p. 22.   2. Rugge, II, f. 179.
3. Works 5/9. To them must, I think, be assigned an item in the Wardrobe
   Accounts, "For 7 doubled wyers cont 50[li]: of Wyer & for makeing of them
   4.00.00." (LC. 9/375; 9/382.)
4. Works 5/9. ·   5. LC. 5/138, p. 74.
6. Works 5/28, November, 1677.

which, indeed, was a fine sight. But the play being *Love in a Tub*, a silly play, and though done by the Duke's people, yet having neither Betterton nor his wife, and the whole thing done ill, and being ill also, I had no manner of pleasure in the play. Besides, the House, though very fine, yet bad for the voice, for hearing. . . . The play done by ten o'clock.

From this point, the records pertaining to the Hall Theatre may be roughly classified in three groups: alterations and innovations, replacements and routine repairs, and staging. It is not always possible or desirable to keep these groups distinct, but on the whole I shall now deal only with the first, reserving the others for full discussion later.

At first there is little work for the theatre. New seats are made for the music for a ball;[1] two new boxes are built for the Commissioners of the Treasury and the Vice-Chamberlain.[2] The Lord Chamberlain's books inform us that in February, 1667/8, "the turning dore in the Theatre" was covered with green baize. This door does not seem to have been newly made: in fact there is no trace of it in the Works Accounts. All that we learn about it is that it had "strings to draw it round," and took 12 yards of broad baize, a prodigious amount.[3]

Except for an apparently unexecuted order for a new box in the gallery,[4] we hear of no further alterations until the preparations for the Queen's Ballet (or "Grand Ballad" as it was christened by the Clerk of the Kitchen)

1. Works 5/9, February, 1666/7.
2. Works 5/10, February, 1667/8.
3. LC. 5/62, f. 16ᵛ, 5/118; 5/139, p. 9, 3 February, 1667/8; LC. 9/271, f. 15ᵛ. Price of baize, £1.13.0. Reyher, p. 38, notes that admission to the court masques was by "chaise tournante" or "tourniquet."
4. LC. 5/12, p. 280. There is no entry in the Works Accounts.

of February, 1670/1, if I am right in considering the provision of a cloth ceiling for the auditorium as part of those preparations. I do not know that the height of the Great Hall has ever been determined, but if we can trust at all to old maps and views, it was very lofty, and doubtless cold. Pepys had noticed, on his very first visit, that the theatre was "bad for the voice, for hearing." This first attempt to make it warm took the form of a great awning of sky-blue calico, 50 x 40 feet, laid on ropes painted to match, stretched across the Hall, an idea apparently borrowed from the Palais-Royal.[1] At the same time a ladder 26 feet long was made, permanent scaffolds were built above the ceiling, "to Goe rownd to hang vp ye branches," and a door was cut in the boarding over the proscenium, "to Come out of ye Clouds on the said scaffold."[2] Taking into account the fact that the stage was 5 feet or more above the ground and the proscenium some 35 feet high, I conclude that the ceiling must have been about 40 feet above the ground line of the buildings, but how they contrived to reach it with a 26 foot ladder remains a mystery.

In January the stage was enlarged by building it out over the pit and facing it with slit deal, with a little door. The enlargement seems to have been only a few feet for the area is given as about 300 square feet.[3] On the eleventh, the Lord Chamberlain ordered "Bayes" suitable to add to the covering of the stage, 3 yards

wide and the length (i. e. width) of the stage.[1] This had
to be laid twice,[2] for in February further alterations
were made: the stage was again enlarged about 100
square feet, and a section of it cut out, boarded and
railed, for a place for the Queen's music.[3] This seems
to be the same arrangement shown in Inigo Jones' plan
for the 1637 Masking-House.[4] There must have been
three orchestras in the masque, for the old music-seat in
the clouds was newly boarded about, and "a roome for
y^e Italian musitions Cont': one square $\frac{1}{2}$" was enclosed.[5]
If we may trust the analogy of the Jones plan, this
would be at one side of the pit, immediately below the
stage. Although I have relegated the stage lighting to
the section on staging, I must note here the first provision for footlights: "making a trough at y^e foote of
the stage for lights to stand in."[6]

Finally, improvements were made in the tiring-rooms
to fit them for the Queen and her ladies. A cloth ceiling
was put up in "ye Queens roome,"[7] and there was much
hanging of baize.[8] This work seems to have been for a second presentation of the masque, for on 14 February the
Lord Chamberlain ordered it to be ready "by Fridaye
Night next,"[9] (i. e. the seventeenth), whereas Evelyn
had attended a performance on the ninth.

For these performances, rails had been set up in the
Queen's Presence Chamber and the King's Guard-

1. LC. 5/62, f. 119^v; 5/63, p. 85.   2. LC. 9/272, f. 111^v; 9/381.
3. Works 5/15, February, 1670/1.
4. B. M., Lansdowne Ms. 1171, ff. 9^v–10.
5. Works 5/15, February, 1670/1.
6. Works 5/15, February, 1670/1. For stage lighting and scenery see
    pp. 160, 161, 152.   7. Works 5/15, February, 1671.
8. LC. 9/272, f. 112.   9. LC. 5/62, f. 121; 5/63, p. 91.

chamber and its stairs. This was the first of a series of experiments designed to keep people from crowding into the theatre,[1] an experiment which reached its final stage in April, 1675, with "railes with flapps to them att yᵉ Staire head going to yᵉ Kings Guard Chamber & in yᵉ guard Chamber & att yᵉ Theatree [*sic*] dore next yᵉ guard Chamber."[2]

The next important changes [3] made were for *Calisto*, and most of them can best be described in connection with that production,[4] but since two galleries were then built which remained a permanent feature of the theatre, it seems desirable to consider them now. They were along the side walls, supported by trusses let into the stone wall and into some of the windows.[5] Professor Richardson tells me that, although there is no mention of them, there must also have been upright posts for supports. Each gallery was 36 feet long and 4½ feet wide, with two degrees in it. They were boarded up in front, and boarded and plastered underneath. The end of one was partitioned off with a rail and flap, to form a box for the Countess of Suffolk. The warrant describes them as "ranginge with the Gallery at yᵉ End,"[6] so I conclude they were contiguous and reached by its stairs.

1. See Works 5/19, December, 1672; 5/21 January, 1673/4.
2. Works 5/25.
3. On 24 September, 1673 a warrant was signed for a new box for Lord Newport, "vnder the Box where now the officers of the Guard are to make a passage to come out that way." (LC. 5/140, p. 334.) Whatever this may mean, nothing was done. It is curious that of the few warrants we have for alterations in the Hall Theatre, several cannot be traced in the Works Accounts.   4. See pp. 200–205.
5. Works 5/24, December, 1674, where further details will be found.
6. LC. 5/141, p. 551; Nicoll, pp. 43, 321.

The year 1675 was an eventful one for the Hall Theatre, for in June, close upon the second production of *Calisto*, the theatre was altered for Scaramouche and his company. There is no warrant, so far as I am aware, for these preparations, and the Italians are not mentioned in the Works Accounts, but they are known to have acted at Whitehall that summer,[1] and later records show that special arrangements of the kind here described were made for their subsequent visits. First, the King's dais was altered by "takeing away the foote pace & the raile that encompassed y[e] Kings seat . . . & makeing 3 boxes there with 4 benches in each box."[2] A new entrance, the purpose of which is not clear, was made by "cutting way through y[e] Degrees on one side of y[e] Theater & makeing a paire of staires of 8 stepps to goe into the Theater with an hand Raile on each side the staires and bourding up y[e] End of y[e] degrees on each side y[e] staires Encloseing y[e] fore side of y[e] degrees on each side y[e] pitt & takeing downe y[e] Surveyours Box there."[3] It may be that the construction of boxes on the dais cut off any entrance from the back of the theatre, and that the new stairs were to give easier access to the pit,[4] but a later warrant to alter the theatre as it was for the Italians orders "that y[e] doore be opened as the Act[rs] then went in at."[5]

At this time, an additional staircase to the gallery was constructed, and lastly some important changes were

1. See p. 121.
2. Works 5/25, June.
3. Works 5/25.
4. These stairs may have led to the door into the Wine Cellar.
5. LC. 5/141, p. 528; Nicoll, p. 342.

made on the stage. The entry reads: "Setting up ye 2 portalls vpon ye Stage removing ye Bosketts and Setting up the Architectures in there places."[1] The "Bosketts" and "Architectures" I take to have been certain scenes already made,[2] but the "2 portalls" are new, and can, I believe, be no other than proscenium doors set, this time, immediately behind the proscenium instead of in front, between it and the first pair of wings.[3] In November the dais was restored to its former state and the theatre arranged for a ball. The carpenters also took away "two boxes from amongst ye Sceanes," of which there had been no previous mention.[4] It scarcely seems possible that they were the "portalls," but they might be some other part of the setting.

The year ended with the construction of a new ceiling — not a cloth one this time — "that ye Voyces may ye Better be heard, & alsoe to make the roome Warmer."[5] This ceiling was made of boards, lathed and plastered, ornamented with soffit, ogee, and cyma mouldings (called "suffeete," "O. G.," and "scymore").[6] Provision was made for hanging the branches by putting quarters under the ceiling to reinforce it, and the beams were painted. This is the only work for the Hall Theatre for which there is a contract.[7]

1. Works 5/25.   2. See p. 152.
3. *Cf.* p. 52.
4. Works 5/26; LC. 5/141, p. 288.
5. LC. 5/141, p. 267.
6. Works 5/25, Extraordinary Account; 5/26, November and December, 1675.
7. Works 5/145, p. 101. The work was done by John Cell. For other work done that year, see Works 5/25, April and May; and *cf.* LC. 5/141, pp. 196, 201.

After this comes a very quiet year, with no new work of importance.[1] I have already commented on the fact that there are no corresponding Accounts for two warrants to build new boxes, and it is evident that the Clerk of the Works was not impeccable. In February, 1676/7, he passes over in complete silence an order to alter the theatre for the French comedians as it had been for the Italians.[2] Yet the work must have been done, for in May the carpenters pulled down "the Boxes [?on] the throne in ye Theater," and made the King's seat as it was before, and also closed up several doors and put benches there.[3]

Again in December of that year, 1677, the theatre was arranged for a company of French comedians, "after ye same manner as it was for ye Italian Players."[4] This time, in addition to removing the throne and making boxes as before, the dais was extended forward half way across the pit. The Account reads:

makeing a new box for his Maj^{tie}. tenn fo^t. long for awarder [sic] into the Pitt 8 fo^t. wide, laying a new floore with Ioysts and bourds on each side of the kings Box 8 fo^t. wide and tenn fo^t. long and putting up 5 benches on each side: and putting up 2 railes before the said benches, & bourding upp with slitt deale before the benches, lengthening the degrees in y^e Lord Chamberlaines and Lord Treasurers lodgs [sic] 3 fo^t. $\frac{1}{2}$ long^r. then they were before.[5]

This custom, as it had now become, of altering the King's seat is very curious and perplexing. I have looked in vain for any helpful analogy in contemporary French theatres, and since the King remained in the same posi-

1. But see Works 5/26 and 5/27, February, May, and November, 1676.
2. LC. 5/141, p. 528; Nicoll, p. 342.   3. Works 5/28.
4. LC. 5/142, p. 160; Nicoll, p. 342.   5. Works 5/28.

tion in relation to the stage, it is difficult to see what concern the comedians could have in the matter. Professor Sisson has suggested that the two new boxes beside the King's were for ambassadors, performances by French and Italian actors being in the nature of diplomatic functions; but the ambassadors seem always to have had their own box in the theatre,[1] and I confess the argument does not seem to me very convincing. I incline to think the practice originated in some forgotten Franco-Italian theatrical tradition, and venture to hazard the suggestion that it found favour with Charles because it enabled him to gather his mistresses around him within talking distance, for he finally had his seat so arranged even when there were no foreign actors at Court.[2]

No further alterations seem to have been undertaken until the following November, when the carpenters made "2 Portholes with 2 dores in them betweene yᵉ Seeings each ii [= 11] foote high & 4½ foote wide."[3] Since at this time the Italian players had just arrived for another visit,[4] I conclude that these were the portals we have already heard of, and the theatre was evidently still arranged à la française, for the February Account includes "takeing away pte of the Kings Box and takeing away 2 other Boxes . . . setting up 2 seates in the Kings Box."[5] This was, however, only a partial restoration to the original arrangement: there is no mention of replacing the throne.

1. See pp. 100, 238.   2. See also pp. 237, 238.
3. Works 5/30.   4. See p. 123.
5. Works 5/30.

The records for 1680–81 are missing. A warrant to prepare the theatre for a play on 15 November 1681 instructs Wren to make "the place where His Ma^te Vsually Sitts Convenient for ye Chaires to bc placed as formerly,"[1] but no such alteration was made that month. Scarcely any work was done in the Theatre that year, but in November, 1682, several boxes were removed and the King's throne set up in thcir place, with three new benches at one side of it.[2]

In November, 1683, a few changes were made "for Mr Abell to represent his Musick."[3] John Abell was one of the King's band of violins,[4] but nothing is known of this performance. For it, "the Passage . . . coming vp from ye Cellar doore" was opened, and the music-seats and desks enlarged.[5] The theatre may at that time have been arranged for dancing: it had been fitted for a ball on 15 February 1682/3,[6] and there is no entry of the removal of the dance floor until the following February, when preparations were made for *Valentinian*.[7]

For some time there had been but few plays at Court, and consequently there are very considerable gaps between the entries for the theatre in the Work Accounts. In the autumn of 1684, however, the arrival of the French players belonging to the Prince of Orange lifted for a little the melancholy which seems to have settled over Whitehall.[8] The King's throne was not removed,

1. LC. 5/144, p. 140.
3. LC. 5/144, p. 510.
5. LC. 5/144, p. 510; Works 5/37.
6. LC. 5/144, p. 360; Works 5/35.
7. Works 5/37; LC. 5/145, p. 14.
8. LC. 5/145, p. 90. See p. 126.

2. Works 5/35.
4. De Lafontaine, *passim*.

nor the special entrance called into service again, but
40 feet of rail, which I take to be a new balustrade
across the stage, was set up, and a new trough made for
the footlights. Other work was done which I can only
interpret as part of the setting of an unidentified play:
"cutting a hole & making a sight in y[e] doore putting a
shelfe vnderneath to slide vp and downe."[1] The next
month there is more work behind the scenes, probably
for the same players: "fixing two large balks each
14 fo[t]. long to fasten y[e] flying ropes in the Theatre and
making two scaffolds there abo[t]. 12 fo[t]. long a peice and
two foote wide."[2]

On New Year's Day, 1685, Charles decided he would
like his seat made as it had been for the French season
of 1677, and accordingly, gave what seems to have been
his last order for the Hall Theatre.[3] The old throne was
once more restored by James in preparing for a ball the
following October,[4] but meantime a new use had been
found for the theatre during the summer months when
there were no plays. It was converted, or part of it, into
an office for the "Clarkes of the Councell" — I suppose
the Privy Council — by altering some of the boxes to
accommodate books and papers, "fixing the screw for
the Seale," and matting some seats.[5]

The season of 1685–86 found the theatre once more
in demand. A new box for ambassadors and foreign
ministers was ordered but apparently not made;[6] other-

1. Works 5/38, September, 1684.
2. *Ibid.*, October.   3. LC. 5/145, p. 135.
4. Works 5/39.
5. Works 5/39, June and July, 1685.
6. LC. 5/17, p. 20; 5/146, p. 27; Nicoll, p. 342.

wise the frequent alterations for dancing and again for acting involved no new work beyond the making of an occasional rail or music-seat. In fact, throughout James' brief reign, although there were plays and balls aplenty, there was little new work,[1] but he concluded his commands for the theatre with a gesture of solicitude for his Queen. In January, 1687/8, the Clerk of Works recorded "making 11 new Steps of whole Deale over the old Sta^{rs}. going into the Hall Theatre for her Maties: Chaire to goe downe easily, . . ."[2]

After the accession of William and Mary, there were many balls in the Hall Theatre, but few plays. For the first ball, music-seats were built "round the Sceens 11 foot high";[3] and for another, a new bank of seats, perhaps for musicians, was constructed by

putting vp 6 Seats in degrees One above another wth. Strings and bearers and footboards, & boarding vp the back with boards 3 fo^t. high above the Seats and making two Steps at each end to go vp to those Seats.[4]

The last work on the theatre was done only a few weeks before the Whitehall fire. In November, 1697, a new floor for dancing was made.[5] At about the same time, the scenes were mended — no new ones had been made in this or the preceding reign — new curtains for the stage and great window provided, and probably

1. In May, 1687, there is a rather unintelligible entry for "enclosing a place within the Scenes for the plays 16 foot long 2 fo^t.$\frac{1}{2}$ high and a flo^r. 3 fo^t:$\frac{1}{2}$ by 3 fo^t. and taking them downe againe" (Works 5/41).
2. Works 5/41.
3. Works 5/43, October, 1689.
4. Works 5/45, November, 1691.
5. From the description (Works 5/49), I conclude by a new method. See p. 271.

some new matting.[1] All this suggests that William was planning for the renewal of plays as well as for court balls, but if so, his intentions were frustrated by the fire of January, 1698. The numerous accounts of this disaster [2] fail to mention the theatre, but since it is never included in the short list of buildings which were saved, I think we may safely conclude that it was demolished, possibly blown up in the efforts to save the Banqueting House. To be sure, there is a building which strongly resembles early pictures of the Great Hall, in Kip's 1714 drawing of Whitehall,[3] but unless Kip was merely copying an older picture, this must have been a new building on the same site. Never again, however, was there a "Theatre at Whitehall": Streeter had put Fame, but no Phoenix, in his frontispiece.

OTHER APARTMENTS AT WHITEHALL

The Queen's Presence Chamber

Attention has more than once been called to the scandalous disparity between the plain apartments allotted to Catherine of Braganza and the luxurious suites built and rebuilt for the more distinguished of the King's mistresses. Unpretentious as they doubtless were, the Queen's apartments nevertheless included at least one room large enough for private theatricals. In October, 1662, the Clerk of the Works recorded that the month's work included

1. Works 5/49. See pp. 145, 271.
2. Chiefly letters in the Reports of the Historical Mss. Commission.
3. Reproduced in Sheppard.

WEBB'S DESIGN FOR A SCENE FOR *MUSTAPHA*

making a stage in yᵉ Queene [*sic*] Guardchamber about 18 foote long and 20 foote wide and encloseing the same rownd wᵗʰ whole deales & making a doore into it, making a footpace 12 foote wide & 16 foote long for the king & queene to sitt on.[1]

This may have been for the puppets which Pepys reports at Whitehall on the eighth of the month.[2]

Thereafter nothing more is heard of performances in the Guardchamber, but some four years later carpenters were employed in

making holes through the Seeling, in the Queenes presence, for the hanging vp of branches, making a seate there for the musick, Carrying foormes there, Incloseing a place there wᵗʰ: whole deale for a [puppet play] Drollery Cont': about 3 square, making a stage there 5 foᵗ: broad & 16 foᵗ: long wᵗʰ: a raile before it.[3]

Since the dimensions in these two entries suggest approximately the same sized room, I incline to think that "Guardchamber" was merely a slip of the pen and that both performances were in the Presence Chamber. There are no other entries in the Accounts which indicate plays there, but it seems to have been the room regularly used for the Queen's music, for there are several references to it in connection with borrowing musicseats for the Hall Theatre.[4]

The account of the preparations for the drollery is of considerable interest, in that it shows what kind of lighting was used for such performances and the general arrangement of the room. The "stage," in view of its

1. Works 5/3. The stage and footpace were removed the next month (*ibid.*).
2. See p. 116.
3. Works 5/9, October, 1666.
4. Works 5/25, 28, 35, 46.

dimensions, must be a dais,[1] and one wonders why a dais should have to be specially built in a presence chamber. It may be, however, that the permanent one was the "place" enclosed for the actors.

The Lord Chamberlain's Lodgings

A play was acted, perhaps by amateurs, in the Lord Chamberlain's lodgings in February, 1677/8. For this a "New stage" was erected, 2 feet high, 19 feet long, and 12 feet wide, according to the Accounts, which I take to mean 19 feet broad and 12 feet deep.[2] There was no scenery, for the carpenters put up "a Rayle ii foo^t Long 7 foo^t & half high for to hang a hanging vppon for ye Actors to goe behind. . . ."[3] Arlington was then Lord Chamberlain, but I have been unable to find out where his lodgings were.

St. James'

I do not know that attention has ever been called to the fact that after the Restoration plays were still occasionally acted at St. James' Palace.[4] *Pompey the Great*, the joint product of Waller, Buckhurst and Sedley, must have been acted there prior to 1664, for in that year it was published with an Epilogue to the King at St. James and one "to the Dutchess." We have more definite information about a performance of the *Queen*

---

1. The word is so used elsewhere in the Works Accounts.
2. The greater dimension is regularly called the length in the Works Accounts.
3. Works 5/29. The stage was taken down again.
4. For earlier plays there, see Adams, Dram. Records.

of Arragon, which, according to a newsletter dated 13 October 1668, was to be acted in the Guard Chamber at St. James' on the Duke of York's birthday,[1] and the same room may have served for a comedy on 6 April 1670. It is again a newsletter, written on the seventh, from which we learn that on the preceding evening, "their Majesties were diverted with a Comedy acted at St. James's by the little young ladies of the Court, who appeared extraordinarily glorious and covered with jewels."[2] I have examined the Works Accounts for St. James' at these two dates, but find no trace of the plays. The absence of such items creates at least a probability that there was no theatre there, and that plays were, perforce, somewhat informal and private.

WINDSOR CASTLE

When, in the summer of 1674, Charles wished to move his Court to Windsor, he encountered difficulty in the shape of Scaramouche. This celebrity, whose real name was Tiberio Fiorelli, had brought his company from Paris to entertain the English King the preceding summer, and apparently did so with such success that he was several times invited to return.[3] His 1674 visit is our immediate concern, for it occasioned the building of a stage at Windsor. Plays had been given there, in the hall, in the days of Elizabeth,[4] but evidently no permanent arrangements for acting had been made, for Charles found it necessary to erect a new stage. For

1. Hist. Mss. XII, vii, 59.   2. *Ibid.*, p. 70.
3. See pp. 118 119, 120, 121–122.   4. Chambers, I, 15.

this he chose St. George's Hall, the dimensions of which are 200 x 34 feet, and early in June, among other provisions for the removal to Windsor, the Lord Chamberlain ordered green baize.[1] It is doubtful, however, whether this warrant was executed. It was not until 8 July that he wrote to the Officers of the Works at Windsor, requesting them "to cause a stage to be Erected in St Georges Hall for acting of Playes before his Matie:"[2] The work then seems to have gone forward promptly, for on the twenty-seventh of the same month he again ordered baize. It is the marginal label of this warrant that tells us the stage was for "Scaramouchi," and the supplies ordered are "fifty yards of Bayes of three yards broad or One hundred of the other sort & a Canvas Sayle of 155 foote long & 40 foote broade for His Ma^{tes} Service within St Georges Hall at Windsor."[3] The sail is at first perplexing, but in view of the calico ceiling put up in the Hall Theatre at Whitehall in 1670,[4] I conclude that it was a temporary ceiling designed to lower the height of the room and improve the acoustics. The extreme length of the hall must have made for many difficulties, and one wonders, in vain, why it was chosen.

This stage probably continued to be used for some time, although there is no further mention of it in the

1. Warrant to Great Wardrobe, for "as much greene bayes as will Cover the stage that is to be made in St Georges Hall at Windsor," 2 June 1674 (LC. 5/15, p. 6).
2. LC. 5/140, p. 509; Works 6/1.
3. LC. 5/15, p. 20; 5/120. The tradesmen's bills show that 53 yards of broad baize at 3s. per yard, and 472½ yards of "Hall Canvas" at 12 pence per yard were supplied (LC. 9/112; 9/274, p. 243).
4. See p. 46.

records.[1] In the spring of 1683, Charles was again negotiating a return of Scaramouche and his troupe,[2] and this time he resolved to provide them with a proper theatre. On 20 April, the Lord Chamberlain wrote to the Officers of the Works at Windsor Castle:

> These are to signifie His Ma^{tes}. pleasure that you cause a Theatre to be forthwith made, in the White Tower in Windsor Castle where the Armory is: as soone as the Lord Dartmouth Master of Ordinance shall by His Ma^{tes} Command, haue removed all the Armes from thence & cleared the same: and that you make ye same Theatre in all parts as you shall receiue direction from His Ma^{te} vpon the place.[3]

The promise of Charles' personal supervision is extremely interesting and significant, especially as Wren was then Surveyor of the Works, and causes one to regret more than ever that the detailed Accounts for Windsor are not extant. That the theatre was actually constructed, seems clear from later references to "the Playhouse at Windsor." This phrase occurs in three warrants dated in July and August, 1688, when a troupe of French comedians were playing there, and Wren was instructed to prepare the playhouse for their use and make such alterations as they should direct.[4] And it may be that the same theatre was still in use in the middle of the nineteenth century. In the British Museum Newspaper Room is a bound collection of lace-bordered programmes, embossed with the royal arms, ranging in date from 4 January 1849 to 5 February

---

1. According to Cibber (II, 210), the King's Company acted in St. George's Hall sometime during Charles' reign.
2. See pp. 124–125.
3. LC. 5/144, p. 407.
4. LC. 5/17, pp. 60, 65. See p. 127.

1857.[1] Each one begins, "Royal Entertainment. By Command. Her Majesty's Servants will Perform, at Windsor Castle . . . ," and ends, "The Theatre Arranged and the Scenery Painted by Mr. Thomas Grieve." I like to think of Victoria sitting decorously in a theatre built by Charles II, devoting her royal attention, and perhaps even a ladylike tear, to a highly moral melodrama set by Mr Grieve.

KENSINGTON PALACE

Although William made Kensington his chief residence almost from the beginning of his reign, and it was the scene of many court balls, he does not seem to have had plays there until after the Whitehall fire. Unfortunately, the Works Accounts for all except the first three months of 1698 are missing, and it is impossible to tell where the first stage at Kensington was erected, or what it was like, except by inference from one warrant and one bill. On 10 May 1698, the Lord Chamberlain sent an order to the Great Wardrobe to deliver to Simon de Brienne (Housekeeper at Kensington),

the following Particulars for fitting up a Stage for a Performance of Musick before his Ma^{ty}. att Kensington. (Viz^t.) Seventy Six Yards of Green Bays a Yard and an half Broad, for covering the Stage, and for a Curtain. Also that four Ordinary Skreens of Six leaves each, be hired for that use, about Six or Seven foot high, and that an Upholsterer be imediately sent to fitt them up.[2]

One is left to wonder what kind of "Performance of Musick" could require a stage and such elaborate

1. N. R. No. 211.   2. LC. 5/152, p. 83.

preparations, for the next entries seem to refer to a different occasion.

In a book in which are entered tradesmen's bills for the year (beginning at Michaelmas) 1697–98, is an undated statement of money due to Richard Bealing, upholsterer, which begins:

> For a new Theater att Kensington.
> ffor 117 y^{ds}. of broad green bays to hang a stage & cover a floore of the same & to make traverse curtaines & 7 setts of full vallence crosse the Stage and to cover a raile to separate the room for musick and dancing before the King at $3^s.6^d - 20.9.6$.[1]

In the following June, John Churchill, carpenter, put in a bill for work "In making a Stage for y^e: play^{rs}: in y^e old presence."[2] His figures suggest a stage approximately $24\frac{1}{2}$ x 19 feet, with a balustrade across the front except where a flight of six steps 4 feet wide led down

1. LC. 11/5 (unpaged). It continues:
   "for portering the bays there — 3.6.
   for large pound rings for y^e curtains & tape used ab^t. y^e vallence and curtaines — 7.6.
   for nailes and thread used about them — 7.0.
   for 4 men 2 days each to do the worke there — 2.0.0.
   for 3 y^{ds}. of crimson Searge to cover a forme in y^t. room at $3^s.6^d$ — 10.6.
   for gilt nailes and tacks used about it — 5.6.
   for making a deep large curtaine to draw up & for O's plummetts and tape used about it — 7.6.
   for fine white thread fringe to put on the curtaines 10.0.
   for a String and tassel to draw it — 5.0."
   The total amounts to £25.6.0. The same bill is summarised in the Annual Account of the Great Wardrobe, AO. 3/1141.
2. Works 5/50, June, 1699. His charges, to cover workmanship and nails, were:
   "4 sq^r: 72 fo^{tt}: of loysting & rough boarding y^e floor at x^s. $p$sq^r: 02.07.02.
   40 fo^{tt}: of whole dealle bench & deske att iij^d p fo^{tt}:   00.10.00.
   20 fo^{tt}: of post & Raile att ij^d p fo^{tt}.   00.03.04.
   120 fo^{tt}. of battens for hanging att j^d p fo^{tt}.   00.10.00.
   6 whole dealle steps 4 fo^{tt}: going att xvj^d Each.   00.08.00."

into the auditorium, and a double row of music-seats in front of the stage. Apparently the walls were hung with tapestry in lieu of scenery. It is quite possible that this bill is for work done the previous year, and that this is the stage Bealing upholstered, but it would be exceptional to have the Account rendered so late. This stage has every appearance of being permanent, yet in November, 1700, Churchill included in another bill, "makeing convenance [*sic*] for y^e: Kings musick upon his birth day," and taking the work down again.[1] Nothing further seems to have been done during the remaining years of the reign.

GENERAL CHARACTERISTICS

At the beginning of this account, I suggested that the enforced sojourn of Charles and his friends at foreign courts helped to bring about a new and important phase in the Court theatre. This Continental influence — which, of course, found its fullest expression in the importation of French and Italian actors, and contributed to the development of both heroic tragedy and comedy of manners — took the form, so far as the playhouse itself was concerned, of a general tendency toward a larger and better equipped theatre, rather than the adoption of concrete details. The Cockpit in Court was too small, its Palladian proscenium too inflexible, to satisfy the Restoration. Movable scenery had become essential and brought with it new methods of stage lighting,[2] and had Charles' purse proved adequate,

1. Works 5/51.   2. See pp. 158–163.

doubtless would have brought spectacle and machinery. It may be argued that all these had been regularly employed in the Caroline masques: true, but twenty years elapsed between *Salmacida Spolia* and the Restoration, and most assuredly, Charles did not have the Twelfth Night splendours of his father's Court in mind when he planned for his own theatre.

But although the taste for all this must largely have been acquired abroad, the resultant theatre is almost entirely English. Webb's Hall Theatre is essentially the Great Hall arranged for *Florimène* by Inigo Jones. (It is, of course, superfluous to comment on Jones' indebtedness to Continental models, thus completing the full sweep of the circle.) But I do not mean to say that the masque stage necessarily represents Jones' own ideal of theatrical construction, for we cannot assume that he would approve of the same stage for both masques and plays, and his theories as an architect must often have conflicted with his obligations as Surveyor General.[1] However this may be, the important point here is that Webb's theatrical design so far as we know it, is taken directly from the masque stage, with the result that the Hall Theatre may be said to be Inigo Jones limited by the physical conditions of an already existing building.

Some few details, to be sure, can be traced directly to contemporary France. I have already said that the idea of a blue cloth ceiling to cut off the great height of the roof was borrowed from the Palais-Royal,[2] and have discussed at length the changes brought by the Italian

1. For an unexecuted theatre plan by Jones see Nicoll, p. 134.
2. See p. 46.

comedians.[1] But, as I shall have occasion to mention again, there is no trace of the *chambre à quatre portes*, no trace of such elaborate machinery and wealth of scenic effect as were the glory of the *Salle des Machines* and the *Opéra*,[2] while the Whitehall auditorium shows no analogy to the elliptical galleries and *parterre debout* of the French theatres.[3]

1. See pp. 49–50, 51–52.
2. See pp. 148, 154–155.
3. As described by Bapst, *passim*.

PART II

Maintenance and Production

II

MAINTENANCE AND PRODUCTION

GIVEN the theatres, our next concern is the use to
which they were put. This involves their general
upkeep, special preparations for performances, and
actual production, which in turn may be resolved into
actors, plays, and staging. At each step, too, there are
finances to be dealt with. This great mass of material
might, of course, be attacked in several different ways:
it has seemed to me that the method most desirable on
the whole is to consider who was responsible for each
part of the work, and to discuss in turn the various
offices and individuals who contributed to the making of
a Court play.

The Lord Chamberlain was and always had been the
official ultimately responsible for all Court entertainments, and the Master of the Revels, even in his heyday,
had been subject to this higher authority. We tend to
think of Herbert as the autocrat of the stage, and so he
was in many ways; but that the Lord Chamberlain was
actively concerned with theatrical affairs during the
years when Herbert was at the height of his power is
fully testified by extant records.[1] Herbert's efforts to
re-establish his authority after the Restoration are well
known, but this struggle was primarily for the control

1. I have collected all the theatre items from the Lord Chamberlain's Books,
1600-42, and they are about to be published by the Malone Society.

of the public theatres, and has little to do with the Court stage.

It is the Lord Chamberlain who, so far as we can judge, supervised the King's plays, taking into his own hands the power formerly delegated to the Revels. In the absence of any Revels Books it is dangerous to be dogmatic, but it is certain that the Lord Chamberlain gave orders not only to the various Revels officers,[1] but to the Office of Works, the Great Wardrobe, the Lord Steward's Department, and the players and musicians. In the following pages I have endeavoured to trace the different activities which he directed, and all orders and warrants may be taken to come from him unless otherwise specified.

THE OFFICE OF THE REVELS

The Restoration of Charles II marks the beginning of an interesting and as yet unwritten chapter in the history of the Revels Office and one which merits full discussion. But I must limit myself to an account of its activities at Whitehall and its finances as part of the Royal Household. This, however, involves a preliminary statement of who and what its officers were. In 1641 the Office comprised the Master, Clerk, Yeoman, and Groom, with a Clerk Comptroller shared with the Tents and Toils.[2] The same staff was re-established at the Restoration and continued throughout the century,

---

1. At the end of the century, the Lord Chamberlain claimed the right to appoint, *inter alios*, the Master and Yeoman of the Revels, the Master of the Revels in Ireland, the Theatre-Keeper, and the Poet Laureate (LC. 3/3, c. 1697).   2. LC. 3/1.

except that the Theatre-Keeper — apparently a new appointment — seems to have been considered a member of the Office, although he is not included in its accounts. A Scene-Keeper also appears for a short time, appended to lists of Revels Officers. The personnel of the Revels from 1660 to 1700 may be briefly stated as follows:[1]

MASTER

Sir Henry Herbert, 20 June 1660–27 April 1673.[2]
Edward Hayward, Deputy to Herbert, 23 December 1663–June 1664<.[3]
Thomas Killigrew, 1 May 1673–>24 February 1676/7.[4]
Charles Killigrew, 24 February 1676/7–1725.[5]

YEOMAN

John Carew or Carey, 25 June 1660–>6 August 1663.[6]
Henry Harris, 6 or 8 August 1663–1702<.[7]

---

1. Compiled chiefly from the Lord Chamberlain's Registers, for an account of which see my article in the *Bulletin of the Institute of Historical Research*, June, 1929. The first date is that of taking the oath of office; the second, of death or resignation. Where these are not known, I have used symbols: >1660 to mean before or in 1660, 1660< to mean in or after that year. I have omitted the Officers of the Revels in Ireland.
2. LC. 3/2 (over Thomas Killigrew, deleted); LC. 3/24, p. 149 and roll, 3/25, p. 115; 3/26, p. 151; LC. 7/1 at back of book. Herbert's only patent appears to be the reversion granted to him and Simon Thelwall in 1629 (C. 66/2512, no. 5). Thelwall was evidently a sleeping partner; his name appears in Herbert's suit against the players, but not in the LC. Registers. He was dead by 1668.
3. LC. 3/24, p. 149; 3/25, p. 115; 3/26, p. 151.
4. LC. 3/24, roll; LC. 7/1 at back of book. He obtained a patent for the reversion on 12 August 1659, which he surrendered on 25 January 1667/8 (C. 66/3097, no. 6).
5. LC. 3/3, f. 21; 3/4; 3/24 roll; 3/28, p. 51; 3/31, p. 92; 3/32, p. 95; LC. 7/1 at back of book. He had obtained a patent for the reversion on 6 March 1667/8 (C. 66/3097, no. 6).
6. LC. 3/2 (as Edward Carew); LC. 3/24 roll; LC. 7/1 at back of book.
7. LC. 3/24 roll; 3/25, p. 115 (where "John lang yeoman" has been inserted,

Peter Shuttleworth, Deputy to Harris, 17 August 1692–? [1]

CLERK COMPTROLLER

Alexander Stafford, > 1641–8 October 1666 < .[2]

John Pointz, Deputy to Stafford, > 15 August 1663–1 November 1665 < .[3]

John Lloyd, Deputy to ? Stafford and Pointz, > 8 April 1665–20 December 1670 < .[4]

Arthur Fleetwood, > 27 February 1673/4–> 29 June 1677.[5]

Thomas Francis, > 29 June 1677–> 8 March 1677/8.[6]

Lestrange Symes, 8 March 1677/8–21 September 1686 < .[7]

CLERK

John Green, 11 August 1660–20 December 1670 < .[8]

GROOM

George Johnson (? Junior), > 1662–9 September 1671.[9]

John Clarke, 24 October 1671–1701 < .[10]

THEATRE-KEEPER

George Johnson, Senior, 26 October 1660–> 10 February 1664/5.[11]

George Johnson Jr, 10 February 1664/5–> 10 November 1672.[12]

---

but this must be a mistake); 3/26, p. 151; 3/31, p. 92 (where he becomes "Gent"); 3/32, p. 95; LC. 3/3, f. 21; 3/4; LC. 7/1 at back of book. This may have been Henry Harris the actor.

1. LC. 3/32, p. 95.
2. LC. 3/1; AO. 15/8, p. 272.
3. Adams, *Dram. Records*, p. 130; AO. 3/908/29.
4. AO. 3/908. He obtained a patent for the reversion on 8 October 1666 (AO. 15/8, p. 272).
5. AO. 15/10, pp. 226–230.
6. *Ibid.*; LC. 5/53, f. 128.
7. LC. 5/42, p. 135; 5/53, f. 127; 5/143, p. 44. His patent is dated 15 May 1678 (C. 66/3202, no. 4).
8. LC. 3/33; SP. 38/19, p. 37; AO. 3/908/24.
9. LC. 3/24 roll; 3/25, p. 115; 3/26, p. 151; LC. 7/1 at back of book; LC. 5/14. See also Theatre-Keeper.
10. LC. 3/24 roll; 3/26, p. 151; 3/27, p. 113; LC. 7/1 at back of book. See also Theatre-Keeper.
11. LC. 3/24, p. 181.
12. LC. 3/24, p. 181; 3/24 roll; 3/25, p. 151; 3/26, p. 198; LC. 7/1 at back of book. There is a good deal of confusion about the two George Johnsons, but I think I have distinguished them correctly.

Philip Johnson, 10 or 15 November 1672->24 April 1678.[1]
John Clarke, 24 April 1678–1701 <.[2]

SCENE-KEEPER
John Bennett, 10 April 1665–?[3]

Wherein these officers, with the exception of the Yeoman and Theatre- and Scene-Keepers, found their *raison d'être* at Court is difficult to say. Yet the Master evidently had some duties there, for Hayward, when appointed Deputy to Herbert, included in a request for information the following:

> To know of Sir Henry what Dutie or attendance is required of mee at Whitehall, that I may not bee wanting therein, and charged with neglect, when time shall come to Demand my quarterly allowances and Wages . . .[4]

This was in July, 1663. Once, at least, Herbert seems to have come up from Ribbesford to attend at Court, for we find him engaged in the spring of 1665 in ordering and receiving Indian gowns for the musicians in the new Hall Theatre.[5]

The Master had his own seat in the theatre,[6] and apparently continued to earn it, for in 1678/9 the Lord Chamberlain issued the following order:

> I do hereby order that His Maties Comædians, and His Royall Highnesse Comædians do observe and obey such orders and directions as they shall from time to time receive from Mr Charles

---

1. LC. 3/24 roll (twice); 3/26, p. 198; LC. 7/1 at back of book.
2. LC. 3/24 roll (twice); 3/28, p. 51; 3/29 (resworn as James' servant, 26 May 1685); 3/31, p. 93 (resworn as William's servant, 2 June 1689); 3/32, p. 96; 3/3, f. 21; 3/4; LC. 7/1 at back of book. The reversion was granted to John Mortrem on 1 November 1689, and he may have served as deputy (LC. 5/149, p. 295).   3. LC. 3/24, p. 242; 3/25, p. 173.
4. Adams, *Dram. Records*, p. 126.
5. See p. 41.   6. See pp. 239, 254.

Killegrew Master of the Revells, to his Ma^te every night the said Comædians shall act at Court and alsoe that the yeoman and Groome of the Revells likewise observe His directions.[1]

When Killigrew became lax in these mysterious duties, the Lord Chamberlain wrote out another order, insisting that he

(according to ye right & duty of his place) doe attend at Court, every night whensoever Playes shall bee by mee Ordered to bee Acted there And that His Ma^tes Comædians, doe Obey, Such Orders & directions as they shall from tyme to tyme receiue from the said Mr Killegrew, And that he take care the Comædians doe come in good tyme.[2]

The most interesting point in this is that it is the Lord Chamberlain who orders plays; the Master of the Revels is clearly a subordinate officer with rather trivial duties.

Of the Yeoman we know a little more, although far from enough. His constant attendance was required, somewhere;[3] he employed three servants "to attend vpon the men and Woemen Comædians";[4] and sometimes received supplies for the theatre from the Great Wardrobe.[5] By far the most interesting of his known duties was looking after the tiring-rooms in the Court theatre. Carew, as Yeoman, seems to have been responsible for making the Cockpit tiring-rooms usable at the Restoration, for although the Lord Chamberlain sent a warrant, dated 10 December 1662, to the Great Wardrobe for what was needed, the bill for the same particulars was put in by the Yeoman, headed "Iohn

1. LC. 7/1, p. 8; LC. 5/143, p. 269; Nicoll, p. 293.
2. LC. 5/148, p. 19; LC. 7/1, p. 16; Nicoll, p. 298; 5 October 1687.
3. He made a successful claim to an extra shilling a day because of it. LC. 5/184, f. 132; SP. 29/75, no. 116.   4. LC. 5/138, p. 80.
5. LC. warrants to the Great Wardrobe, *passim*.

Carew Yeoman of the Reuells his Bill for money disbursed since October 1660."[1] That the tiring-rooms
were the Yeoman's particular charge is also shown by a
warrant addressed to him in the spring of 1665, when the
Hall Theatre was being constructed, bidding him

to repaire vnto S[r] John Dinham Kn[t] of y[e] Bath his Ma[tes] Surveyor
Gen[r]all and to advise with him concerninge the Convenient Makeinge the Attyreingroome in the New Theatre in Whitehall and that
you see that all things be fitt and Convenient according to y[e] Duty
of yo[r] Place and that yo[u] follow and take his directions for the doe-
inge of y[e] same till it be finished.[2]

Harris' patent, which, although he took office in the
summer of 1663, was not passed until 1 June 1667, describes his place as "yeoman or keeper of our vestures
or Apparrell of All and singuler our masks Revells and
Disguiseings And also of the Apparrell or Trappers of
all and singuler our horses ordeyned and appoynted for
our Iusts and Tournies."[3]

The Clerk-Comptroller and Clerk seem to have had
nothing to do with Court plays. The Groom, too, is
almost unheard of, unless, indeed, the Groom and the
Theatre-Keeper were one and the same.[4] Certainly the

1. See pp. 18–19. He seems also to have provided three silk curtains for the
   theatre, for which he was paid on 20 August 1663. (LC. 5/138, p. 80.)
   For Carew's difficulties over his perquisites, his resignation and Harris'
   appointment, see LC. 5/185, f. 10; SP. 44/13, pp. 288–289; SP. 29/75,
   no. 116; LC. 5/184, f. 132; LC. 5/185, f. 46; SP. 44/15, p. 85; AO. 15/8,
   pp. 363, 461, 495; SP. 44/15, p. 141; LC. 5/138, pp. 280, 369, 388;
   Nicoll, p. 329; C. 66/3090, no. 13.
2. LC. 5/138, p. 425.   3. C. 66/3090, No. 13.
4. The Groom is mentioned in an order to the Master (see p. 74), and
   figures in Herbert's accounts as Groom and Purveyor, but these are not
   to be relied on. There is also a warrant to deliver supplies for the comedians to the Theatre-Keeper and Groom of the Revels, which may refer to
   either one or two individuals (LC. 5/140, p. 407).

offices were twice held by the same man, but they are always separated in the Establishment lists, and in the absence of definite information it seems best to consider them as distinct.

The office of Theatre-Keeper may not have been newly created at the Restoration, for although George Johnson was sworn into the place on 26 October 1660, there is no patent or warrant for the appointment, but only a warrant for a signet bill to the Treasurer of the Chamber for payment of his wages.[1] The date of his death is not known, but he was succeeded by a son of the same name, whence much ambiguity in the records.[2] The father was dead by February, 1664/5, for on the thirteenth of that month George Johnson obtained a grant of the office of Yeoman of the Bows "in the place of George Iohnson his father dec̄d,"[3] and on 5 April 1665, the son secured a warrant for his wages as Theatre-Keeper, "to commence from the nativity of o^r Lord God last past."[4]

The younger George continued in his post until his death in 1672.[5] But among the State Papers is a rough draft and fair copy of the appointment of Henry Glover on 21 November 1666, as Keeper of the Theatre in Whitehall and of "Our Scenes, Machines, Engines, &

1. LC. 5/137, p. 270, 29 September 1662.
2. It is, for example, impossible to tell to which George Johnson the following warrant to the Gentlemen Ushers relates:
   "These are to require you to put George Johnson Keeper of the Cockpitt playhowse into Possession of those Lodgings in the Cockpitt that Mr Harris yeoman of the revells now possesseth." (LC. 5/138, p. 442, 26 May 1664.)
3. LC. 5/138, p. 396.   4. *Ibid.*, p. 399.
5. This shown by the payments of his wages, as given on pp. 276–277.

other things to ye same belonging." His wages of £30
a year were to be paid by the Surveyor of the Works,
"out of the money by Vs allowed for the makeing & en-
tertaneing the sd Scenes."[1] Glover seems to have been
a mechanic, or perhaps the Restoration equivalent of
stage-electrician, and his appointment probably did not
interfere with Johnson's. The only trace of him in the
Works Accounts is a bill, rendered by him in June, 1671,
for oil and cotton for lamps.[2] George Johnson Jr was
succeeded by Philip Johnson, who was in turn followed
by John Clarke, already Groom of the Revels, and this
veteran seems still to have been in office at the end of
the century.

The Theatre-Keeper is frequently designated in warrants to receive supplies from the Wardrobe and the
Green Cloth, and one of his duties was to clean the
playhouse. As a matter of fact, much of this seems to
have been done by the Office of Works and was charged
for in its accounts, but the Theatre-Keeper also made
good his claim to remuneration. His first warrant for
payment, dated 29 September 1662 and addressed by
the Lord Chamberlain to the Treasurer of the Chamber,
was for "the sume of six pounds for makeinge cleane the
stage Boxes and Galleries and alsoe the Branches in the
yeares 1660 and 1661,"[3] and he continued to obtain
similar warrants at intervals up to 1683.[4]

1. SP. 39/178, no. 173; SP. 44/23, p. 284.
2. See p. 251.
3. LC. 5/137, p. 235.
4. His further warrants may be summarised as follows:
  [29 June 1663]. For 1 year ending Lady Day 1663, £6. 3.0.

                                                      LC. 5/137, p. 377.
  11 May 1664. For 1 year ending Lady Day 1664, £6. 1.6.

The question of Revels finance presents more than one problem. The only extant Revels Accounts are those submitted by Herbert for the years 1660 to 1670 inclusive,[1] and the corresponding Declared Accounts, which are mere summaries of the first.[2] Some information is to be gleaned from the Exchequer Issue Books: they record the imprests advanced for the expenses of the Office (to be accounted for in the Revels Accounts), and the payments of the Exchequer fees on the Patents of the Master and Yeoman.[3] Imprests cease after

		LC. 5/138, p. 122.	
20 May	1667.	For 1 year ending Lady Day 1666,	£7. 3.0.
		Ibid., p. 235.	
20 May	1667.	For 1 year ending Lady Day 1667,	£8.14.0.
		Ibid.	
29 Mar.	1675.	For 1 year ending Michaelmas 1673,	£7.
		LC. 5/141, p. 150.	
1 Apl.	1675.	For 1 year ending Michaelmas 1674,	£7.18.0.
		Ibid., p. 151.	
9 Dec.	1676.	For 1 year ending Michaelmas 1675,	£7.18.0.
		Ibid., p. 491.	
9 Dec.	1676.	For 1 year ending Michaelmas 1676,	£7.16.0.
		Ibid.	
16 Aug.	1682.	For 1 year ending Lady Day 1679,	£7. 8.0.
		LC. 5/144, p. 231.	
16 Aug.	1682.	For 1 year ending Lady Day 1680,	£7. 8.0.
		Ibid.	
27 Apr.	1681.	For 1 year ending Lady Day 1681,	£6. 7.0.
		Ibid., p. 426.	
20 Apr.	1682.	For 1 year ending Lady Day 1682,	£6. 7.0.
		Ibid.	
18 Apr.	1683.	For 1 year ending Lady Day 1683,	£6. 5.0.
		Ibid.	

How much of this was ever paid I do not know; I have seen entry of only the first payment, and that in the Account for 1665–66 (E. 351/546).

1. AO. 3/908/24–33.
2. AO. 1/2047/28.
3. These fees are, of course, entirely distinct from the wages charged in the Revels Accounts.

19 June 1678,[1] but the Master continued to collect his
£10 *per annum* to the end of the century.[2]

Unfortunately, Herbert's documents, although detailed, cannot be accepted as at all indicative of what
was actually done by the Office. Long before the Civil
Wars, the astute Master had learned exactly what
would and would not pass the auditors, and thereafter
repeated his items *verbatim* every year. For example,
he consistently charged the Yeoman's wages and rent
allowance, although after 1663 these were separately
paid to the Yeoman by the Treasurer of the Chamber.[3]
Herbert charged his own ordinary attendance for those
ten years at no less than 1791 days, on the basis of daily
attendance from the last of October to Ash Wednesday,
with four days at Easter, four at Whitsun and twenty
during the summer. This brought him in £720.8.0,
and to it we must add £12 per year for extraordinary
attendance during October. How much of this was

1. During his Mastership, Herbert received £900 in imprests (E. 403/1762,
   ff. 37 and 89; 1763, f. 73; 1764, f. 58ᵛ; 1765, f. 78ᵛ; 1766, f. 23; 1769,
   ff. 15 and 41; 1770, f. 32); between 10 December 1674 and 19 June 1678,
   Thomas Killigrew had £1000 (E. 403/1784, p. 163; 1786, p. 119; 1789,
   p. 122; 1791, p. 125).
2. E. 403/1761, f. 80ᵛ; 1763, f. 84ᵛ; 1769, f. 108; 1775, p. 86, 1778, p. 112;
   1806, p. 101; *ibid.*, p. 175; 1807, p. 69; *ibid.*, p. 360; 1809, p. 63; *ibid.*,
   p. 107; 1810, p. 229; 1820, p. 184; 1823, p. 279; 1846, p. 439; 1849, p. 671.
   The Yeoman seems to have been paid his sixpence *per diem* only for the
   period from Midsummer, 1674, to Christmas, 1684. (E. 403/1806, p. 200;
   1807, pp. 128 and 369).
3. E. 351/546–9; AO. 1/398/90 to 401/106; E. 351–550/2. Carew petitioned
   the King against Herbert's delays and the matter was referred to the
   Lord Chamberlain, who replied, "In regard therefore the petʳ. hath not
   and cannot conueniently receaue his said Allowances when they are involved and included in the Accompts of the Master of the Reuells," the
   Yeoman's wages should be charged to the Treasurer of the Chamber and
   paid directly to him (SP. 29/75, no. 116).

intended as recompense for his duties at Court I do not
know.

With the exception of the number of days between
the last of October and Ash Wednesday, the Accounts
show only a few insignificant variations, and even run
uninterruptedly through the year of the Plague and Fire.
They are modelled closely on pre-Commonwealth ones,
and cover daily wages, house rent for the Master, Yeoman and Clerk, office rent, book-keeping expenses, and
sundries. I doubt whether they can be taken to prove
anything: certainly the Groom was not — as they claim
— providing rushes for the Revels. They also include
an item for extraordinary attendance during October,
on the authority of a warrant signed by the Lord Chamberlain on 8 March 1666.[1] A transcript of the first account, which covers the season of 1660–61 and amounts
to £266.9.8, will be found in the appendix.[2]

Herbert's accounts stop abruptly with the year 1669–
70. After his death, his son attempted to collect the
balance, amounting to £1448.3.0, which remained due
from the Exchequer, but apparently secured only £120.[3]
It is evident that there were later accounts submitted
by the Master, although they have not survived, for
on 3 December 1675, John Clarke, in his capacity
as Groom, petitioned the Lord Chamberlain against
Thomas Killigrew, "for rec' his ffees & Allowances &
paying nothing."[4] He was enjoined to reply in writing,
but no more is heard of the matter.

1. LC. 5/138, p. 368.
2. See pp. 273–275.
3. E. 403/1786, p. 99, 23 December 1675.
4. LC. 5/190, f. 130.

As I have already mentioned in passing, the Treasurer of the Chamber was also involved in Revels finance. From 1663 on the Yeoman's wages were paid by him,[1] as well as the Theatre-Keeper's £30 *per annum*.[2] His accounts were further charged with £1 a week for the Master's lodgings out of Court, a demand originated by Herbert and carefully continued by the two Killigrews despite the fact that both house and office rent were included in the Revels Accounts.[3]

THE OFFICE OF WORKS

Although the Office of Works was primarily concerned with structural changes and new equipment, which I have already described, it was also responsible for a certain amount of routine work and replacement, and thus comes into a discussion of maintenance. Since, however, the documents are given *in extenso* in an appendix, it will suffice to mention the kinds of work done, without going into details. Repairs at the Cockpit in Court were very slight and of little significance. There was a good deal of mat-mending, and in one entry for it there is an interesting use of the word "closset," apparently meaning the King's box.[4]

When we come to the Hall Theatre, we find certain pieces of work which were done over and over again. Chief among these was laying the floor over the pit when it was wanted for dancing, with the attendant prepara-

1. See p. 79.
2. See Appendix B, pp. 276–277.
3. Chamber Accounts in E. 351 and AO. 1, *passim,*
4. Works 5/2, October, 1661.

tions and subsequent removal.[1] The record of these changes is of value mainly as showing on what dates the theatre was arranged for plays, but we cannot rely on them too completely: the floor over the pit was taken up in December, 1672, although it had not been laid![2]

An even more frequent task, once the practice had been established, was setting up bars or rails to keep off the crowd of people who tried to force their way into the theatre. I have already described the steps by which this system was worked out, and subsequent entries add nothing.[3]

A good deal of small jobbing was done about the theatre from time to time, in the way of mending breakages, making small alterations in the boxes, and so forth. In January, 1666/7, the cracks under the degrees were papered to keep out the wind — an amusing sidelight on the luxury of Charles' Court.[4] An important piece of work was the repairing of the roof in the summer of 1669. So great an undertaking was this that two pounds reward was allowed to William Allingham, Richard Grover, John Harding, William Furbush, and Andrew Osbourne, "for their Extraordinary paines about a difficult peece of Worke in Repaireing the roofe of the Great Hall."[5]

The furnishing of matting was, curiously enough, a prerogative of the Office of Works. Its Accounts include all the matting used for floors, walls, and stairs in the

---

1. See p. 44. Warrants for some of these alterations will be found in Appendix A, as well as the pertinent entries in the Works Accounts. The size of the dancing floor is variously given as 600, 550, 512, and 500 square feet. (See Works 5/9, 5/25, and cf. Works 5/49 in Appendix A.)
2. Works 5/19.   3. See pp. 47–48.
4. Works 5/9.   5. Works 5/13, August, 1669.

royal palaces; all other upholstery was supplied by the Great Wardrobe. There are numerous entries of matting for the Hall Theatre, and quite a few for the Cockpit, but except in the cases already noted, they contribute nothing to our knowledge of those playhouses. I have found only one warrant for this work: it was for the seats in the pit to be newly covered, "they being soe dirty, and vnfitt to place any Person of Quality on for whome they are appoynted."[1]

An important duty of the Office was to supply attendants, when needed, to look after the scenes and lights during performances, but this service is one on which the records are far from clear and cannot be taken to establish dates of performances.[2] A special, and doubtless confidential, order for attendance of a different kind was directed to Wren during the agitation over the Popish Plot. On 18 November 1678, Arlington, then Lord Chamberlain, sent him a warrant,

to cause some discreete honest Person belonging to yor Office of ye Workes to Watch & attend every night vnder the Kings Seate in the Hall, at the tyme His Ma^te shall be at ye Play in ye Theatre in Whitehall, for ye p^rvention of any Danger that may happen to His Ma^tes [*sic*].[3]

At the same time, an order was addressed to the Gentlemen Ushers,

to take Especiall care every night to search vnder his Maties. Seate in ye Theatre in Whitehall & see if there bee anything dangerous for his Maties being there at ye Play, or not.[4]

---

1. LC. 5/147, p. 1; Nicoll, p. 342; 27 October 1685. The order was duly executed at a cost of £2.5.0 (Works 5/39).
2. See Appendix A, pp. 271–272.
3. LC. 5/143, p. 193.   4. *Ibid.*, p. 194.

What a picture of threatened Majesty, seated on top of a "discreete honest Person" from the Works! Charles' life might be in danger, but his pleasures must not be interrupted.

THE GREAT WARDROBE

The Great Wardrobe seems to have been an extraordinarily interesting department of the Royal Household. It was the Army and Navy Stores of its day, and supplied the most miscellaneous wants of the Court, as witness its voluminous records. The series of Annual Accounts are a mine of information on seventeenth-century Latin, full of such delights as "Conservatores ludorum apud Novum Forum," and together with the Bill Books and Original Bills reveal much of the minor economy of the Court stage. Unfortunately, theatre items are not always marked, and the records must often appear more incomplete than they actually are.

I have already referred to some of the upholsterer's work done for the Cockpit in Court.[1] It is rather difficult to tell how many of his tasks there were replacement and how many new equipment. From the reopening of the theatre until the end of the 1663–64 season, curtains were made, seats covered, and new sconces supplied at fairly frequent intervals;[2] but the following

1. See pp. 15–16.
2. Two curtains were made and seats covered on 4 November 1661 (LC. 9/105 and 9/380); the same work was done between Lady Day and Michaelmas, 1662 (ibid.); gilt sconces were supplied in August, 1662 (LC. 5/60, p. 344; LC. 9/105, 9/378); baize was provided "to hang over the Doares" (? on the stage) in November, 1662 (LC. 5/60, p. 385; 5/137, p. 175; Nicoll, p. 341); seats were covered and two curtains made the

year, although the Cockpit was still in use, there are no supplies for it, and one concludes that Charles had already transferred his interest to the projected theatre in the Great Hall.

For this, the Whitehall or Hall Theatre, there are a mass of warrants, bills, and items in the Annual Accounts, many of which I propose to reserve for later discussion. In some cases it is impossible to tell for what use various articles were intended, but I shall group together in a section on staging everything that appears to relate to the stage curtain, baize for the stage, stage lighting, and properties. Suffice it to say here that with the exceptions already noted of certain provisions made by the Office of Works, all these were regularly supplied by the Great Wardrobe. There is, however, a strange letter addressed to Lawrence Hyde, Earl of Rochester, as Lord High Treasurer, by the Lord Chamberlain, and dated 28 November 1685.[1]

My Lord

His Matie haueing Comanded that playes should be Acted at Court every Weeke, there is wanting these perticulers for the necessary vse of ye Comedians (vizt) the stage to be covered with strong course greene cloth, to be done by Munday Night next: two close-stooles, six chamberpotts, six brasse candlesticks, foure paire of Snuffers All wch. I desire yor Lordpp will please to giue Order may be provided Thus with my best respects vnto yor Lopp I rest

Yo^r Lopps most humble Servt

Mulgrave

---

same month (LC. 9/106); seven gilt sconces were provided at a cost of ten guineas in 1663–64 (LC. 5/61, p. 70; 5/138, p. 4; LC. 9/107); and more curtains are implied by an item in the upholsterer's account for the same year, "pro clavic' anulis et tape pro Siperijs" (LC. 9/107).

1. LC. 5/147, p. 24.

There is a postscript, "I desire these things may be delivere [*sic*] to John Clarke Keeper of ye Theatre in Whithall." Why application should have been made to the Treasurer I do not know; the Treasury in turn wrote to Marmaduke Darcy, one of the then Commissioners for the Mastership of the Great Wardrobe, to deliver the items listed and have the stage covered the next day.[1] There is no trace of this in the current Accounts, but oddly enough, without further recorded warrant, the close-stools, chamber-pots, candlesticks, and snuffers all appear in the Wardrobe bills for 1688-89.[2]

After the Restoration, the players seem always to have brought their own costumes to Court (many of which, of course, had been given them by the King, Duke of York, and various noblemen), but it appears that there was once some thought of supplying special ones. Hayward's enquiries regarding his work as Herbert's deputy included one: "whether the vestures belonging to the severall stageplayers, are not to be provided by the Master of the Revells, for that some records . . . in King James his time, doe manifest soemuch."[3] The King had, indeed, gone so far as to appoint as a member of his Household a "Provider in Ordinary to his Matie: of all manner of Tinsells and other Commodityes for the Master of the Revells and other his Maties: Servants performing of any Maskes or Playes before theire Maties:"[4] John Smith had been so sworn on 4 December 1662, and was succeeded at his

---

1. *Calendar of Treasury Books*, under date 29 November 1685.
2. LC. 9/279; 9/123.   3. Adams, *Dram. Records*, p. 128.
4. LC. 3/24, p. 195; 3/25, p. 171.

death by Clement Cullyer, on 30 May 1663,[1] but neither has so much as a single bill in the Wardrobe.

A number of miscellaneous provisions remain to be mentioned. The Indian gowns for the music were not very durable, and as the King seems to have taken a great fancy to them, they had to be renewed, first in January, 1668/9,[2] and again early in 1674.[3] This time there was a good deal of delay, apparently occasioned by some disagreement as to who was to be responsible for them, but eventually they were supplied, with their garlands of flowers and two chests to keep them in.[4]

The furnishings for the King's dais were also replaced in 1673/4. The oft-repeated warrant just referred to included "Twoe Armed Chayres twoe foote, twoe Innches broad of Crimson vellvett for the King, and Queene, Twoe Highestooles of Crimson vellvett for the Duke, and Dutchesse, A Crimson vellvett Cloth to lye before them, And twoe long Cusshions of Crimson vellvett."[5] This is at least an improvement on the red and yellow

1. *Ibid.*   2. LC. 5/62, f. 52ᵛ; 5/63, p. 13; 5/119.

3. The warrant (which includes furnishings for the King's dais and a stage curtain) first appears under date of 24 November 1673 (LC. 5/64, f. 81ᵛ), and specifies delivery to the Master of the Revels. The entry is deleted, and the warrant entered again on 18 February 1673/4, with delivery to Philip Kinnersley, Yeoman of the Removing Wardrobe, (*ibid.*, f. 83, and 5/120 with date 17 February). On 25 March, the warrant was again repeated with delivery to Killigrew, "Notwᵗʰstanding my warrant formerly to the Contrarie" (LC. 5/64, f. 88). The same warrant is entered three times in LC. 5/140: at p. 373, dated 18 December altered from 24 November, and the entry deleted; p. 386, deleted; p. 436, dated 17 February 1673/4.

4. LC. 9/274, pp. 42, 52; 9/111. The taffeta, cherry, blue, and yellow cost £63, the tinsel £9.1.0, the garlands £6, and the making £12. Three trunks for the Indian gowns had been ordered in February, 1670/1 (LC 5/63, p. 237); see also p. 43.

5. Bills for them are in LC. 9/274, pp. 61, 77, 107.

colour-scheme formerly adopted, but one feels for the Duke and Duchess. Stools, however, were popular, for eight cane ones, to be used in the theatre on his Majesty's birthday, were ordered on 28 October 1690.[1]

Among the orders for candlesticks and sconces, it is almost impossible to tell which were for the stage and which for the auditorium. Tin sconces were in use — perhaps only behind the scenes — as well as brass candlesticks.[2] Close-stools and chamber-pots were carefully provided.[3] One of the warrants already mentioned includes "Two Carpettes, Twoe Bumbardes, and Twelue Woodden dishes to drinke in for to be vsed in the Theater in the Whitehall."[4] During the year 1689-90, an expensive cabinet and an "Elme Chest lined" were supplied, and once the Wardrobe, instead of the Works, was called on for a locksmith, to put a lock on a door at the direction of the Theatre-Keeper.[5]

THE LORD STEWARD'S DEPARTMENT

The Lord Steward was nominally in charge of catering for the Household, and his duties embraced the provision of fuel and lighting for the theatre and refreshments

1. LC. 5/69, f. 1ᵛ; 5/150, p. 164; 5/123; LC. 9/124; 9/279. They are described in the Annual Account as "octo quadrat' sedilibus Cannae cum Duobus longurijs caelatis pro singuɫeor'," and cost 48 shillings.
2. LC. 5/62, f. 117; 5/63, p. 90: 6 tin sconces to hang up and 6 to carry about; LC. 5/64, f. 77ᵛ; 5/140, p. 343; 5/120: 6 large brass candlesticks and 12 sconces: LC. 9/123; 6 large brass candlesticks and 4 pairs of snuffers. See also pp. 185-186.
3. LC. 5/138, p. 74; 5/64, f. 77ᵛ; 5/140, p. 343; 5/120; LC. 9/111; 9/123; 9/279. See also pp. 185-186. A warrant for green baize for a play on Princess Anne's birthday ends "as also Six chamberpotts." (LC. 5/69, f. 132ᵛ; 5/151, p. 458.)   4. LC. 5/64, f. 77ᵛ; 5/120; 6 October 1673.
5. LC. 9/279; LC. 5/150, p. 164.

for the actors whenever there were plays at Court. Actually, his work was done by the Board of Green Cloth, and the Lord Chamberlain was responsible for letting them know when supplies would be needed. He repeatedly tried to simplify the task by a standing order, but with little success, to judge from the warrants that have survived. We know from other sources that some seasons there were plays at Whitehall every week, and it is therefore obvious that the extant warrants are far from being a complete series, and that the Lord Steward's records must be woefully defective. However, there was probably little variation in the provisions, and the records we have suffice to give a very good idea of how the actors fared at Court, and are, moreover, of considerable value as fixing the dates of a certain number of performances.

The earliest warrant I have found was addressed to the Green Cloth on 4 September 1662. It is labelled "Necessaryes for ye Comædians acting at Court," and reads as follows:

These are to signifie vnto you his Maties. pleasure that you forthwith prouide and deliuer or cause to bee prouided and deliuered vnto George Iohnson keeper of his Maties: Cockpitt Playhouse at Whitehall these perticulers following for his Maties: Comædians vpon those nights they act at the Cockpitt Playhouse (vizt) Twelue Quarts of Sack twelue Quarts of Clarrett twenty foure Torches sizes[1] three Bunches Eight Gallons of Beere foure Basketts of Coales six dishes of Meate twelue Loaues of white Bread [blank] Loaues of Browne Bread Tallow Candles foure pounds twelue white dishes to drinke in, and two Bumbards to fetch Beere."[2]

---

1. Sizes were half-ounce candles; see LS. 13/171, p. 97. The N. E. D. describes them merely as small round candles.
2. LC. 5/137, p. 353.

The Lord Steward's Accounts, which ought to show how this order was executed, are singularly inadequate. The accounts declared by the Cofferer give no details, the subsidiary books kept in the department are very rough and frequently fail to mention the use to which various supplies were put. In this case, the first reference to the actors is in a Creditor (i. e. an account for extraordinary expenditure) "p Expenss' Diet' Dña Penalva et Comædians" in October and December, 1662, and it is impossible to tell what proportion of the total of £270.19.8½ should be allotted to the players, or how many performances this represents.[1] Another Creditor for the Revels in January, February, and March, 1662/3, records the provision of bread, wine, beer, meat, poultry, butter, pippins, and "Salsar fflor," amounting to £23.4.10½.[2]

The next provisions recorded were for rehearsals, presumably, from the date, of the Queen's ballet or masque which was one of the first performances in the Hall Theatre. In March, 1664/5, candles and torches were supplied,[3] while the following month the Spicery put in a Creditor for wax, £27.5.0; candles, £5.10.6; fine olive

1. LS. 8/5. Dña Penalva is later called Lady Maria of Portugal, Countess of Penalva.
2. LS. 8/6. Presumably to this same period belongs an undated memorandum in one of the Lord Chamberlain's books of the "Allowances for the Comædians those tymes they Act at yᵉ Cockpitt in Sᵗ James Parke." Here the quantities of claret, sack, beer, torches, sizes, and white dishes are given as above; but the bread is to be "White & Cheat Bread 24 Loves," eight bushels of charcoal are substituted for coals, the tallow candles go up to six pounds, and the meat and bumbards are omitted (LC. 5/138, p. 433).
3. LS. 8/6; E. 351/1836 (Cofferer's Declared Acct.). Total £12.15.9.

oil, fine cotton, ordinary oil, pippins, and onions, £3.1.4; total £35.16.10.[1]

After this, there is a long gap in the Accounts, probably almost entirely due to the cessation of acting during the Great Plague. When plays at Court were resumed in the autumn of 1666, the Lord Chamberlain thought it advisable to refresh the memories of the Green Cloth, and repeated his warrant of 1662, substituting "his Ma[ts] Theatre within his Palace of Whitehall" for the Cockpit, and fixing the amount of brown bread at twelve loaves.[2] There is a Creditor covering three plays in October, four in November, and four in December, and the total cost for provisions, which now include bacon and a tart, is £241.5.7.[3] This brings the cost per play to very nearly £22. The next Creditor is for one day in January and one in February, 1666/7, at £38.19.4, but this time there is no bacon or tart.[4] The season closes with a Creditor for plays on 18 April and 2, 9, and 17 May, amounting to £59.11.6.[5] Here the cost per play is only £14.17.8½, so that the average must be taken to range between £14 and £22, depending presumably upon two factors, the season of the year and the number of players.

Exactly what these Creditors are intended to include is not always clear, but apparently they covered the lighting for the whole theatre. In one of the Entry Books of the Board of Green Cloth is the following memorandum:[6]

---

1. *Ibid.*, "Credito[r] in the Office of the Spicery for y[e] practising of the Sceanes in the Hall in Aprill 1665."
2. LC. 5/138, p. 366, 31 October.   3. LS. 8/6; E. 351/1836.
4. *Ibid.*   5. *Ibid.*   6. LS. 13/171, p. 52.

Allowances for yᵉ Players & Dressing roome / Allowances of Bread, Beer, Wine Lightes &c For a Play to begin the 27ᵗʰ. of December 1666, & to Continue till further order for the Comædians /

Cheate Loaves fine & Coarse	xviij Loa'
Sizes	iij bunches
Tallow Candles	iiij ℔
Torches	viij
Charcoales	iiij buzˡˡˢ
Claret	xij bottles
Sack	iiij bottles
Beer	iiij gall

For yᵉ branches { Wᵗ wax Lightes for yᵉ branches xᵈᵈ.℔.
wᵗ. Torchets ij

For yᵉ Guard { Torches jᵈᵈ. vj
Candles ij ℔.

For yᵉ Portʳˢ Candles j ℔.

For yᵉ Chandry { Torches iij
Sizes d' ℔.
Candles j ℔.

The Wayters of yᵉ Hall Torches vj
For yᵉ Scænes yell wax Lights ixᵈᵈ Sizes iij bunches Torches jᵈᵈ Candles viij ℔.
For yᵉ Kings Presence wᵗ. wax Lights ij.
For yᵉ Qˢ. Presence wᵗ. wax Lights ij.

This schedule agrees pretty well with later records.[1]

There must have been frequent preparations for Court plays during the next three years, but if they are

---

[1]. There is another memorandum belonging to 1666 which cannot, I think, be taken as a complete Creditor, but may record a holiday dispensation. It reads:
"The Proporcōn of Beer Bread & wine delivered for the Playʳˢ. Novembʳ. 5ᵗᵒ

Vin' Vascon'	ij pʳ i qrtes
Vin' Dulc'	iij qrtes
Cerviss	vj gall
Cheate bread	xij Loaves " (LS. 13/171, p. 73.)

From other entries, "pʳ" appears to be a gallon measure, and Sir Edmund Chambers suggests the word may be pitcher.

recorded at all, they are indistinguishably combined with other accounts. The next Creditor clearly belonging to the theatre is for an amateur performance, the Queen's masque of February, 1670/1, and bears the delightful heading, "Credito^r. fact' apud Whitehall pro Expenss. magnæ Saltation'. sive Grand Ballad pro iij^{bus}. diebus Menss ffebruary 1670."[1] Bread, beer, wine, two dozen cups, inckle (linen tape), cotton, wax, tallow lights, torch staves, fruit and confections, spices, meat, poultry, butter, and apples provided for these three days cost no less than £165.18.9.

In connection with amateur performances, it may be of interest to note briefly the provision made for Court balls, which, although distinctly not dramatic, seem at this period to have borne some semblance to the masque. The Green Cloth allotted nine dozen yellow wax lights, two and a half dozen torches, two dozen white wax lights, and twelve pounds of tallow candles for a ball in the Hall in November, 1672,[2] and there are numerous other references to balls and dancings.[3]

To return to the players, we find little mention of them in ensuing Creditors, most of which cover all extraordinary expenses within given dates, without specifying the occasions. They, like all other members of the Household, were affected by Charles' attempts at retrenchment, and their reduced fare is set forth in a warrant addressed to the Lord Steward on 14 January 1673/4.[4] According to this, the Theatre-Keeper and

1. LS. 8/7; E. 351/1839.   2. LS. 13/171, p. 289.
3. For balls in the nineties see p. 98.
4. LC. 5/140, p. 407.

Groom of the Revels were to receive for the comedians, each night they acted at Court, six quarts of sack, ten quarts of claret, one dozen torches, three bunches of sizes, four gallons of beer, a quarter of coals, four fine cheat loaves and eight coarse ones, six manchets, and four pounds of tallow candles.

That the Green Cloth kept more careful watch on the delivery of these supplies than their rather haphazard records would indicate is revealed by a petition addressed to them by one Richard Vokins, unhappy Yeoman of the Wax Chandry.[1] He

Humbly Sheweth

That Yo^r. Peticon^r: did in the Month of December last, wayt in the said Office at the request, and onely Accompt of Sr Tho: Monings Barr^t. Serg^t. of the sayd Office, in the Execution of wch. said Dutie or Imployment, hee hath incurr'd the high Displeasure of this Honor^{ble}. Board, by delivering and setting vpp a Certaine quantitie of Wax lights at the practizing for an Opera for his Maj^{tie}. at Whitehall wth.out an imediate Order from some of this honor^{ble}: Board, wch. hee is most heartily Sorry for and most humbly prayeth this hono^{ble} Board to accept of this his Submission, and hee promises for the future never to doe or Committ the like dissorder againe."

He was restored to his waiting, but not until the first of April.

Passing over the provisions for *Calisto*, we find nothing further until May, 1677, when a Creditor was put in "pro le Ball . . . & pro Dñis Parliam^t."[2] This may, of course, have been a real ball, but the date coincides with *Rare-en-Tout*, and I submit that if a masque can be a "Grand Ballad," a French opera with *intermedii* may be a ball.

1. LS. 13/171, p. 298, 18 March 1673/4.   2. LS. 8/13.

On 6 February 1678/9, the Lord Chamberlain saw
fit to jog the elbow of the Green Cloth with a warrant
for candles and "all other vsual allowances of Bread
Beer Wine & Coales" every play-night, to begin "this
Thursday night."[1] The Green Cloth seem to have been
in some doubt as to the proper interpretation of "vsual
allowances," for on the tenth they drew up a new
schedule:[2]

An Estimate of the Charge for one playnight. /

li. s. D.

Manch^{ts}	vj ad ij^d p c̄e	00.01.00
Cheate lo	xvj ad iij^d p c̄e	00.04.00
Beere	vj gal̄l ad iij^d d'q p gal̄l	00.01.06¾
Vin' Vasc̄on iij p^{rs} ad xvij^s vj^d p S^r[3]		00.13.01½
Vin' Dul̄cs p^r		00.08.00

01.07.08¼

White Wax Lights   x dz viij ⎫
White Torchets   ij   ⎬ w^t: xl^{l̄b}   05.06.08.

Yel̄l Wax Lights   xij dz   ⎫
Yell Sizes   iiij bu ⎬ w^t: Cv^{lb} d'   09.15.10
Torches   vj dz xj ⎭
Tallow Candles   xx^{l̄b}   00.10.10.

15.13. 4.

Charcoales   j q^r   00.04. 6.

                    Totall Charge   17.05.06¼

This is very helpful because it gives both quantities and
prices, and serves as a standard of comparison for all the
other entries.

1. LC. 5/143, p. 267.
2. LS. 13/171, p. 402.
3. "S^r," *i. e.* ? Sester or sestern, 4 gallons (N. E. D.). For "p^r" see p. 92
    note 1.

There is a Creditor covering January, February, and March, 1678/9, but it is not very illuminating.[1] After this there are no recognisable entries for several years, and, although allowances must have been made to the players, perhaps there was a tendency to neglect them, for on 15 November 1681 the Lord Chamberlain repeated his warrant, this time addressing it to the Lord Steward himself.[2] But if the actors lacked their bread and beer, they were treated to daintier fare: on the same 15 November, it being the Queen's birthday, they had three dishes of confections at fifteen shillings the dish.[3]

Just a year later, the Lord Chamberlain once more wrote to the Lord Steward for the usual allowances for a play on 15 November and for airing the theatre the day before.[4] Since the warrant is dated the fourteenth, it is evident that, however cumbrous the Household machinery, work could be done at short notice. But perhaps this was a bit too short, for when preparations were made for *Valentinian* the following February, the Lord Chamberlain gave the Lord Steward four days' leeway.[5]

After the accession of James, almost the only information to be drawn from the Creditors concerns lighting. The wax-chandry alone among the offices involved, sometimes indicated the occasions for which it supplied candles, and from it we learn that there was one play in October, 1685, five in November, and one in December; three plays in January, 1685/6, three in February, and

1. I.S. 8/14.   2. LC. 5/144, p. 141.
3. I.S. 8/18.   4. LC. 5/144, p. 304.
5. LC. 5/145, p. 17, 6 February 1683/4; Nicoll, p. 318.

one in April, 1686.[1] Unfortunately the Clerk did not see
fit to mention plays again, except for a vague reference
in January, 1686/7, until April, 1687, when there were
three.[2] He then skips to January, 1687/8, where he
notes one play, and in February four.[3]

1. LS. 8/22.   2. LS. 8/23.
3. LS. 8/24. The first of this group, on 31 January, was, for some unknown
   reason, the occasion of a new memorandum. Space will not permit an
   exact transcript of this, but its contents may be stated as follows:
   For the branches and sconces, 136 white wax lights.
   For the scenes, 120 yellow wax lights, 12 torches, 12 pounds of tallow
       lights.
   For the Gentlemen Ushers Quarter Waiters, 2 torchets.
   For the Yeomen of the Guard, 18 torches, 3 lbs. of tallow lights.
   For Mr Clarke, 1 bunch of sizes, 6 torches, 4 lbs. of tallow lights.
   For the Chandry, 2 torches, 1 lb. of tallow lights.
   For the Grooms of the Chamber, 2 torches.
   For the Porters at the Gate, 1 lb. of tallow lights.
   For the music playing among the scenes, 12 yellow wax lights, 1 lb. of
       tallow lights.
   For the King's Presence and Privy Chambers, 4 white wax lights.
   Total, 140 white wax lights, 132 yellow wax lights, 1 bunch of sizes,
       40 torches, 22 lbs. of tallow lights, and 2 torchets.
   For the Comedians: 6 manchets, 12 loaves, 4 gall. of beer, 2 "prs" of
       Cahors, 1 "pr" of sherry.
   For the Musicians: 6 loaves, 1 "pr" 2 qts. of Cahors.
   For the Gentlemen Ushers: 2 manchets, 2 qts. of Cahors, 1 qt. of
       sherry.
   For the Grooms of the Chamber: 1 manchet, 1 qt. of Cahors, 1 qt. of
       sherry.
   For Mr Howard: 6 manchets, 1 "pr" of Cahors, 2 qts. of sherry.
   For the Yeoman of the Guard: 18 gall. of beer, 18 loaves.
   For the Porters at the Gate: 4 loaves, 2 gall. of beer, 1 "pr" of Cahors
       (LS. 8/25).
The lights in the King's Presence and Privy Chambers had already been
the subject of a special warrant. In this, the Lord Chamberlain informs
the Lord Steward that
   "it will bee fitt & necesarye every night there is a Play or Ball at Court
   To haue two Wax lights for His Ma^tes Presence Chamber & two for y^e
   Privy Chamber more then ye Vsuall allowance on other nights, that
   there may bee lights in these roomes when ye King & Queene returne"
   (LC. 5/147, p. 242).

For the remainder of the century, there are, here as elsewhere, but few notices of the Court theatre. A warrant for allowances for a play that night was signed on 15 November 1689, and there are bills for wax and lamps.[1] The following April, there is a warrant, a bill for wax and one for lamps, all for a play on the thirtieth.[2] Lamps were once more ordered for a play on the King's birthday, 4 November 1690.[3] The Creditors contain no further mention of plays, and balls and "danceings" seem largely to have superseded them in Court favour. No less than seventeen are recorded between November, 1689, and November, 1696, and the cost of the more important ones ranges from £175.0.4 to £582.10.8.[4] The last order for allowances is a warrant from the Lord Chamberlain, announcing a play on Princess Anne's birthday, 6 February 1696/7.[5]

MISCELLANEOUS ORDERS OF THE LORD CHAMBERLAIN

The musicians attached to the Royal Household were, nominally at least, under the Lord Chamberlain, but he seems to have done little more than authorise appoint-

A similar memorandum follows for 6 February, except that it omits the Grooms of the Chamber, and adds four bushels of charcoal for the comedians and a loaf and quart of Cahors for "Mr Little" (LS. 8/25). On the thirteenth, the "Vsual Bills" for a play were signed, and on the same date, five shillings' worth of confectionery was ordered for the players (LS. 8/24). The last play that month, namely on the twenty-seventh, was the occasion of a new warrant from the Lord Chamberlain (LC. 5/148, p. 121).

1. LC. 5/149, p. 321; LS. 8/26, pp. 370–371, 381.
2. LC. 5/150, p. 73; LS. 8/27, pp. 94, 99. The play was *Sir Courtly Nice*.
3. LS. 8/28, f. 24.   4. LS. 8/26 to 34, *passim*.
5. LC. 5/151, p. 458.

ments and order various payments. Although a stout
volume has been compiled from the Lord Chamberlain's records of everything relating to the King's
music,[1] there are remarkably few warrants or orders
which have anything to do with the Court stage. The
provision of costumes for the violins has already been
noted, and payments to Staggins for writing music will
be found elsewhere.[2]

On 4 July 1674, twelve of the violins were ordered to

meete in his Ma^tes Theatre within His Ma^tes Palace of Whitehall
vpon Wednesday morning next by Seaven of ye Clock to practize
after such manner as Monsr. Combert shall enforme them which
things are hereafter to be p^rsented before his Ma^te. at Windsor vpon
Saterday next.[3]

There is no proof that this was for a dramatic performance, but Cambert is said to have produced one or more
of his operas at the English Court.[4] There are so few of
these orders for the musicians either to practise for or
perform at plays that one is forced to conclude they were
issued only when the music had proved refractory or
needed spurring. There is an order for them to attend
"at such tymes as Madam Le Roch & Mr Paisible shall
appoynt" to rehearse for *Rare-en-Tout*,[5] and on 18 February 1678/9, the Lord Chamberlain felt it necessary to
inform Staggins that the twenty-four violins should attend every Court play and that absentees were to be
reported and suspended.[6] Evidently this was no idle

1. H. C. De Lafontaine, *The King's Musick.*
2. See pp. 122, and 222–223, 224.
3. LC. 5/15, p. 15.   4. Lawrence, I, 145.
5. LC. 5/142, p. 38, 22 May 1677; Nicoll, p. 317.
6. LC. 5/143, p. 272.

threat, for on 22 November 1681 the Lord Chamberlain wrote to the Treasurer of the Chamber:

Whereas Jeoffery Ayleworth, Thomas ffarmer, Thomas ffinall & Richard Tomlinson foure of his Ma^{tes} Musitians have neglected theire duty in attending at ye play acted before his Ma^{te} at White-hall on Tuseday night last for which I have suspended them theire places These are therefore to pray & require you to make stop of all ye Wages . . . vntil further notice." ^1

The Lord Chamberlain also issued a number of general regulations for the Hall Theatre and procedure to be followed there on special occasions or in particular circumstances. Some of these will be found in the account of *Calisto*:^2 the following order, issued on 15 November 1689, will serve as an example.

. . . no Persons whatsoever [*are to*] be admitted into the Box in the Theatre in Whitehall, wherein the Forreigne Ministers are appointed to be, before they shall be placed there, nor any Person afterwards to croud the Seats but such as the forreigne Ministers themselves shall admitt.^3

A few days later, Princess Anne was permitted to borrow "the two Christall Branches" from the theatre,^4 and in the summer of 1695, the Yeomen of the Guard had leave to store their trunks there, Francis Aston, one of the Gentlemen Ushers, being instructed to "call to ye Theatre for ye Key."^5 The most surprising of these miscellaneous warrants is the following permit, dated 7 February 1678/9:

1. LC. 5/144, p. 146.
2. See pp. 182–183.
3. LC. 5/149, p. 321.
4. *Ibid.*, p. 329, 20 November 1689.
5. LC. 5/151, p. 416.

I doe hereby giue leaue vnto Anne Capell & her Servants to come into yᵉ Theatre in Whitehall to sell fruite every night that a Play is Acted there And if any other pʳsume to sell fruite there I doe hereby Order His Maᵗⁱᵉˢ Gentlemen Vshers dayly Wayters forthwith to turne them out."¹

I fear Mr Evelyn would have classed this with taking money at the door, as ill befitting a royal entertainment.

Before going on to consider the Lord Chamberlain's relations with the players, I should, by way of completing this survey of his jurisdiction over the Court stage, note that payments for plays were made on his warrant to the Treasurer of the Chamber.²

THE PLAYERS AND THEIR PLAYS

Thus far, I have left the central figures out of my picture, the players themselves, in whom all the activities I have been describing had their beginning and their end. The actors, too, were at least nominally under the jurisdiction of the Lord Chamberlain, but I fear their discipline left much to be desired; at any rate, they did not scruple to keep the King waiting.³ When they were summoned to Court, it was the Lord Chamberlain who sent for them: we have his warrants for *Rule a Wife and Have a Wife* on 15 November 1682, and *Valentinian* on 11 February 1683/4, and in an already quoted order to Charles Killigrew he uses the phrase, "every Night whensoever Playes shall bee by mee Ordered to bee Acted [*at Court*]."⁴ But we may, I think, assume

1. LC. 5/143, p. 267.   2. See pp. 294–299.   3. See p. 74.
4. LC. 5/144, p. 303; Nicoll, p. 318; LC. 5/145, p. 14; LC. 7/1, p. 11; Nicoll, p. 318; see also p. 74.

that the plays were selected by the King himself. Charles certainly knew his own mind in such matters, and in the early days, when Tom Killigrew was always at his elbow, and he had intimate interests in both theatres, there can have been no need for formalities. Later, and particularly when Dorset was Lord Chamberlain, that official may have taken more responsibility for Court programmes, but we know that Mary sometimes ordered her own plays, once with unfortunate results.[1] At times, the choice of plays must have been very largely dependent on what author was in favour at the moment, or was, for various motives, being backed by Rochester, Castlemaine, or other Person of Influence. But never is there any question of leaving the matter to the Master of the Revels.

Whatever the fare provided, a play at Court was an important diplomatic and social event. The performances, in distinction to those in public theatres, were always at night,[2] and afforded excellent opportunity for the display of beautiful clothes, jewels, and faces. They were considered suitable entertainment for distinguished visitors, including foreign ambassadors and ministers, for whom a special box was provided.[3] Charles seems to have been aware of the possibilities of the Court theatre for shaping public sentiment, as well as amusement, for on 31 January 1665/6, Lady Fanshaw wrote to her husband the news from London that

1. *The Spanish Friar* was revived by her command soon after she had accepted her father's crown, and when Dryden was a devout Catholic.
2. This is clear from Pepys' references, but he never names the hour.
3. See p. 100.

the King had a play acted, in which many nations met, and the Frenchman made them all afraid, but the Englishman coming by him as he was vapouring, he gave over and said nothing, but the Englishman, not contented, then withdrew his sword and told him he would make him take notice of him, with which the Frenchman replied that he desired friendship with him and therefore desired him to accept of a present and gave him a purse of gold. This makes much talk and laughter . . . [1]

I think it would be a mistake, however, to lay very much emphasis on this aspect of Court plays: on the whole, they were entertainment for its own sake, and their frequency is to be attributed to the tastes of the King and those he gathered round him. Charles' intimates no doubt considered the Court theatre their special toy, but smaller fry, too, were eager to attend these functions. Another letter to Sir Richard Fanshaw, written in the spring of 1663, informs him that for three months his lodgings at Whitehall had been let to Sir Ralph Freeman, "to accommodate his daughter, who desired to see the Court entertainments, as balls and plays, which have been frequent this last winter."[2]

Indeed, there can, I think, be little doubt that during the winter there were often four or five plays a month, despite the great gaps in the calendar I have compiled.[3] Apart from the Plague Year, 1665–66, many of the breaks can almost certainly be explained by the presence of foreign actors at the Court, whose performances find no place in the Household records, and I question whether the entries in the Lord Chamberlain's books represent all the performances by English companies.

1. Hist. Mss., *Report on Mss. of J. M. Heathcote, Esq.*, p. 231.
2. *Ibid.*, p. 78.
3. See Appendix C.

As early as 6 December 1660, Andrew Newport wrote to Sir R. Leveson that there were plays at Court every week,[1] and for several winters there is documentary evidence that the once-a-week standard was maintained.[2] The season was, however, very short, for there were no plays in Lent and, as a rule, but few during the spring and summer.[3] After the accession of William and Mary, although Dutch housekeeping made for better records, one can count the Court plays on one's fingers, two a year apparently marking the height of William's extravagance, and after the Whitehall fire, none are mentioned, although a stage was built at Kensington.[4]

The patent companies under Killigrew and Davenant were, of course, the only English professionals to appear on the Court stage.[5] One would expect to find that prior to the union of 1682, Killigrew's company, His Majesty's Comedians, enjoyed a marked preference, but this is not borne out by the available records, the two appearing to be very nearly equal in favour. Even more surprising, if we can rely on the little information we have, is the situation following the secession of Betterton and the other leading actors in 1695. Mrs Barry seems to have been a favourite at Court and was probably largely instrumental in securing the warrant by

1. Hist. Mss., V, 158.
2. See pp. 280, 289–290. Describing the theatres in 1666, Chappuzeau referred to "la troupe Royale qui joue tous les jours pour le public et d'ordinaire tous les Jeudys apres soupé à Witthal. . . ." (Chappuzeau, *Europe Vivante*, p. 214.)
3. Hist. Mss., V, 202, and XII, v, 104.
4. See pp. 62–64, and 292–293.
5. Their history has recently been retold by Professor Hotson, and to undertake to add further details here would make the tail wag the dog.

which the actors set up their independence, but there is little trace of the Betterton-Barry company at White-hall: the dedication and prologue of Banks' *Cyrus the Great*, published 1696, indicate a Court performance, which may, of course, antedate the secession, and there is an obscure reference to a play acted by "both companies" on 4 November 1697.[1]

Unfortunately, there is not yet enough material for a very profitable study of what the patent companies acted at Whitehall. If we take twenty performances a year as the average from 1660 to 1688, omitting 1665–66, and allow a score or so for the remainder of the century, we would have some 575 or 600 performances to account for. A great many, perhaps 200, of these could be assigned to foreign players, but of the large remainder, I can identify only some 126 performances, representing 90 or 91 plays. These are not very satisfactory data from which to draw conclusions, and even within these limits a considerable margin for error must be allowed, to cover cases where it is not clear whether a performance known to be before the King was given in the Court or a public theatre. The following analysis is, therefore, offered as purely tentative and the figures must be taken as approximate.

First then, for the revived plays, of which I count thirty-four including adaptations,[2] or thirty-five if *The Beggars*, acted on 1 December 1686, is Brome's *Merry Beggars* instead of *Beggars' Bush*. Beaumont and Fletcher are easily the favourites, with ten unaltered

1. LC. 5/152, pp. 202, 220.
2. But excluding *The Siege of Rhodes*.

plays,[1] two versions of *The Island Princess*, Rochester's
Valentinian and Buckingham's *The Chances*.[2] Shakespeare comes second, albeit "improved," with five plays,
all tragedies;[3] Jonson and Shirley tie on three each;[4]
while Brome, Middleton, Webster, Habington, Suck-
ling, Cowley, Davenant, and Killigrew are each represented by a single play.[5] Two translations, Rutter's
Valiant Cid and Ferdinando Parkhurst's *Ignoramus*
complete the tale.[6]

A study of the plays by which these fourteen dramatists are represented reveals some interesting facts.
Twenty of them were comedies, six tragi-comedies, only
ten tragedies. Yet not one of Shakespeare's comedies
was acted, and *Julius Caesar* is the nearest approach to
history. Most of these plays were acted only once at
Court, but a few proved more popular: *The Humorous
Lieutenant* and *The Scornful Lady* were each revived
four times, *Rule a Wife*, three, while *The Silent Woman*,
Volpone, *Othello*, *Julius Caesar*, *Lear*, and Rochester's
Valentinian (which I hesitate to call a revived play) can
at least claim two performances. This brings the total
up to forty-nine.

1. *The Humorous Lieutenant*, *The Scornful Lady*, *Wit Without Money*, *Rule
   a Wife and Have a Wife*, *The Woman's Prize*, *A King and no King*, *Beggars' Bush*, *The Bloody Brother*, *The Spanish Curate*, and *The Double Mar-
   riage*.   2. An account of all these is given in Sprague.
3. *Macbeth*, *Julius Caesar*, *Othello*, *Hamlet*, and *Lear*. For their treatment
   see Spencer.
4. *The Silent Woman*, *Volpone*, *Bartholomew Fair*; *The Cardinal*, *The Young
   Admiral*, *The School of Compliments*.
5. *The Jovial Crew*, *The Widow*, *The Duchess of Malfi*, *The Queen of Arragon*,
   Aglaura, *The Guardian* (*Cutter of Coleman Street*), *The Wits*, *Claracilla*.
6. For the performance of *Ignoramus*, see an article by B. M. Wagner in
   The Review of English Studies, January, 1929.

Naturally, there were more new plays than old, although not so many as one would expect. I count fifty-seven, but several of these may only have been acted before the King at one of the public theatres. Dryden heads the list of dramatists with ten plays,[1] but despite his laureateship he could not outdo Beaumont and Fletcher. However, he had no close second: Orrery, Crowne, Lee, and Aphra Behn share equal honours with four plays each, and an additional masque for Crowne.[2] A strange couple, Otway and Etherege, come next with three plays apiece;[3] Davenant and Stapylton each boast two;[4] and the single-play dramatists are legion: Porter, Tuke, Settle, Bristol, R. Rhodes, Philips, Sir Robert Howard, the Hon. Edward Howard, Caryl, Shadwell, Ravenscroft, C. Davenant, Leanerd, Roche-Guilhen, Betterton, Banks, D'Urfey, Wycherley, Congreve, and the collaborators Sedley, Buckhurst, and Waller.[5] We

1. *The Wild Gallant, Secret Love or the Maiden Queen, The Indian Emperour, Sir Martin Marr-all, The Conquest of Granada, Tyrannic Love, Aureng-Zebe, All for Love, An Evening's Love, The Spanish Friar.*

2. *The General, Mustapha, Henry V, The Black Prince; The Country Wit, The Destruction of Jerusalem Part I, Sir Courtly Nice, The City Politiques; Sophonisba, Mithridates, The Rival Queens, The Princess of Cleve; Sir Patient Fancy, The Rover, The Feign'd Curtizans, The Emperor of the Moon; Calisto.*

3. *Friendship in Fashion, The Orphan, Caius Marius; The Comical Revenge, She Wou'd if She Could, The Man of Mode.*

4. *The Law Against Lovers, The Siege of Rhodes; The Slighted Maid, The Stepmother.*

5. *The Villain, The Adventures of Five Hours, The Empress of Morocco, Worse and Worse, Flora's Vagaries, Horace, The Committee, The Usurper, Sir Salomon, Epsom Wells, The Citizen Turned Gentleman, Circe, The Country Innocence, Rare-en-Tout, The Amorous Widow, Cyrus the Great, The Fond Husband, The Plain Dealer, The Old Bachelor, Pompey the Great.*

have here twenty-nine dramatists as opposed to fifteen whose plays were revived.[1]

In this second list, comedy still leads, but on account of the craze for heroic drama, her precedence is more effectively disputed. The figures are: twenty-seven comedies, three tragi-comedies, one farce, one masque, three operas, and twenty-one tragedies, thirteen of which are more or less heroic. (Of these, I think several might well be called tragi-comedies, but I follow the accepted classification.) Nevertheless, the most popular plays were comedies. *Secret Love or the Maiden Queen* was acted four times at Court, and so was *The Rover*; *The Adventures of Five Hours* and *Sir Courtly Nice* each attained three representations. *The Villain* was the favourite tragedy, acted three times. *The Wild Gallant, Sir Martin Marr-all, The Committee, She Wou'd if She Could, The Man of Mode or Sir Fopling Flutter, Epsom Wells, The Empress of Morocco* (by amateurs), *Mustapha, The Rival Queens, or The Death of Alexander the Great,* and *The Orphan* were twice put on at Whitehall; while *The Law Against Lovers, The Siege of Rhodes, The Slighted Maid, The Stepmother, The Indian Emperour* (by amateurs), *The Conquest of Granada* (both parts), *Tyrannic Love, Aureng-Zebe, All for Love, The Spanish Friar, An Evening's Love or the Mock Astrologer, Pompey the Great, The General, Henry V, The Black Prince, The Comical Revenge or Love in a Tub, Worse and Worse, Flora's Vagaries, Horace, The Usurper, Sir Salomon, The Citizen Turned Gentleman, Circe, Rare-en-Tout, The Country Wit, The Destruction of Jerusalem Part I, The*

1. It should be noted that Davenant occurs in both lists.

City Politiques, Sophonisba, Mithridates (by amateurs), *The Princess of Cleve, The Country Innocence, Sir Patient Fancy, Friendship in Fashion, Caius Marius, The Amorous Widow or the Wanton Wife, The Feign'd Curtizans, The Emperor of the Moon, Cyrus the Great, The Fond Husband, The Plain Dealer,* and *The Old Bachelor* were acted but once. The total of performances is seventy-nine, and half are of plays that were not repeated.

To count up is easy enough; to evaluate is another matter. How much of Dryden's popularity was due to his official position? How do his ten plays, less than half he wrote, weigh in the balance with Etherege's three and all? Why, in spite of Wycherley's success in the public theatre and Castlemaine's influence, was *The Plain Dealer* the only one of his plays acted at Court, and that nine years after its production? Congreve, of course, came too late for the Court theatre, but where are *The Mulberry Garden, Bellamira, Bury Fair, The Rehearsal?* Why was *The Orphan* acted twice and *Venice Preserved* not at all?

It is useless to multiply these questions, for to answer them is impossible. Were the records far more complete, it would still be a hopeless task to try to say what personal friendships and animosities, what official jealousies, what chance word, what Court intrigue, what indifference, went into the making of this repertory. The whole Restoration drama is in it. Two things alone stand out: the inevitable popularity of the heroic play, the development of which was chiefly due to Charles' tastes and the work of three members of the Court

circle, Orrery, Dryden, and Howard; and a kindly
tolerance of gentlemen-playwrights — if the Matchless
Orinda will allow me to place her in that category. To
comment further on these ninety-one plays would be to
embark on a critique of the whole body of Restoration
drama, and while it may justly be urged that the public
theatre of that day was largely dependent on the patronage of the Court, and that therefore Court taste was a
controlling factor in the development of the drama, such
an undertaking is beyond the scope of this study.

Something further must, however, be said on the subject of opera, and in dealing with opera on the Court
stage we are on somewhat safer ground, for the elaborate scenery and machines which were essential to it
would inevitably appear in the Works Accounts. But
although the evolution of opera constitutes an important chapter in the history of the Restoration stage, and
Charles' French tastes might well be considered an influ-
ential factor therein, it seems to have been almost unknown at Whitehall. The King's attempts to import the
Continental variety met with little success anywhere,[1]
and it was not until late in the century, when the Court
stage was in its decline, that English opera assumed important proportions in the public theatres. I may remark in passing that since Professor Saintsbury calls
Albion and Albanius a masque, it may be equally well
urged that *Calisto* is an opera: the structure is identical,
but there is the fundamental difference that the masque
was designed for amateurs, although they might, if
necessary, be assisted by professionals. For this reason,

1. See pp. 114–115, 126.

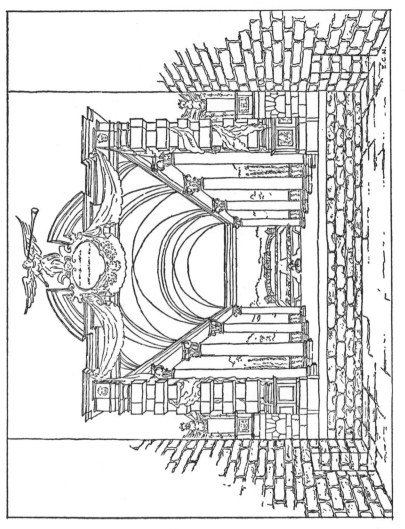

STAGE OF THE HALL THEATRE

I have made what may appear a very arbitrary separation and postponed the masque, while discussing opera along with the other productions of professional actors.

With one possible but somewhat doubtful exception in 1690, *The Siege of Rhodes* appears to be the only English opera sung at Whitehall, a performance of which we learn from an *Epilogue to the King at Whitehall, at the Acting the Siege of Rhodes*, printed, not with the piece itself, but in the 1673 edition of Davenant's works; while the one clear case for French opera is *Rare-en-Tout*. But at this point, I must endeavour to lay a ghost recently raised by Mr W. J. Lawrence. In the *Times Literary Supplement* for 26 September 1929, Mr Lawrence set forth a very ingenious argument to prove that *Ariane*, publicly produced by the Academy of Music at the new Drury Lane Theatre on 30 March 1674, was previously performed at Whitehall. He reminds us that Evelyn saw "an Italian opera in musiq, the first that has been in England of this kind," on 5 January 1673/4; that scenery for the Drury Lane performance was borrowed from the Hall Theatre; and that the frontispiece of the libretto, which is dated 1673/4, shows a stage without an apron, whereas Drury Lane had a very deep one.

When I read Mr Lawrence's article, I was at once struck by the fact that in the fifth act of the opera there is a descending palace, a piece of machinery for which there was no provision in the Hall Theatre. The Works Accounts for January, 1673/4, do, indeed, mention attending the scenes when the "dancing and operas" were practised [1] — a reference I am at a loss to explain

1. See p. 252.

— but there is absolutely no trace of such alterations or equipment as would have been essential for *Ariane*. Since then, my discovery of Webb's design for the proscenium of the Hall Theatre makes further argument unnecessary;[1] obviously, the *Ariane* cut does not depict Charles' private theatre. And as a matter of fact, the pilasters in the *Ariane* frontispiece are very similar to those shown in Wren's plan of Drury Lane,[2] and the curved line of the stage may be a poor attempt at a fore-shortened view of the apron.

It is, of course, still within the bounds of possibility that *Ariane* was produced at Whitehall with simplified staging. I can offer no alternative explanation of Evelyn's remark, except the warning that he may be wrong on the date.[3] As for the scenery, none was made for the Hall Theatre at that time, but it is conceivable that old scenes were borrowed from Whitehall at the last minute because his scene-painters had failed Killigrew.[4]

To return to *Rare-en-Tout*, which was acted in the Hall Theatre on Charles' birthday, 29 May 1677; it was not only a French opera, but was performed by a French company of whom I shall have more to say presently. This production at once raises the question whether other French operas may not have been acted at the English Court by visiting companies. But if they

---

1. See pp. 37–40.
2. Reproduced in Nicoll, *Theatre*, p. 164.
3. He is quite wrong in his dates for *Calisto*, and some other cases are uncertain.
4. The warrants for the loan are in LC. 5/140, pp. 456, 471; Nicoll, pp. 316–317.

had been, it seems reasonable to suppose that the librettos would have been published, and there are none except *Ariane* and *Rare-en-Tout*. The French opera season of February, 1685/6, seems to have been exclusively at the public theatre, and the production of Cambert's *Pomone* is only a tradition.[1]

The other English opera to which I referred is Charles Davenant's *Circe*, which may have been acted at Court in November, 1690. On the seventh of that month, Mrs Barry obtained a warrant for payment of £25 for a performance, but where it took place is not stated.[2] As is well known, *Albion and Albanius* was intended for Whitehall, and Dryden, in the dedication of *King Arthur* tells us it was often practised there, although the belated production eventually took place at Dorset Garden. From the title page of D'Urfey's *Cinthia and Endimion*, we learn that it, too, was "Designed to be Acted at Court before the late Queen," but her death transferred the production to Drury Lane.

On the whole, I think we may safely conclude that the Whitehall stage was not considered suitable for these elaborate productions. The bad acoustics may have had something to do with it, but probably the great expense of operatic settings was the determining factor. At all events, until further evidence is produced, we may consider that Restoration opera belongs essentially to the public stage.

Enough has already been said to make it quite clear that the patent companies were not the only ones to

1. See pp. 127, 99.
2. See p. 246.

tread the boards at Court. Foreign actors were in great favour with Charles and constituted formidable rivals, and sometimes the courtiers themselves stepped over the footlights and provided the entertainment. It is a serious mistake to think of the Court stage, as we are apt, in terms of English companies and good English comedy and tragedy: there are other elements of almost equal importance, and these we must now take into account.

FRENCH AND ITALIAN COMEDIANS

The story of the French and Franco-Italian players who were so popular with Charles II has already been told at some length by Mr W. J. Lawrence,[1] and very briefly by Professor Nicoll, who published a number of new documents relating to them.[2] It is, however, necessary to retell it here in order to fit their visits to Court into the general survey of that stage, and the collation of these two accounts brings out some interesting points that have hitherto escaped notice.

Although not strictly germane to the subject, the King's early attempt to establish Italian opera seems to me to deserve attention. Among the State Papers is the following document which has not, I believe, been printed, although it is mentioned by Professor Nicoll:

Carlo per la Iddio gratia Rè d'Inghilterra Scotia, Francia, et Irlanda Difensore della Fede etc. Douendo Giulio Gentileschi condurre d'Italia in Inghilterra una Compagnia di Musici, per rappre-

---

1. Lawrence, I, 139, *et seq.*
2. Nicoll, pp. 237–241. Some of the conclusions here drawn are scarcely justified by the documents.

sentare nella Città di Londra opere musicali, con machine mutationi di scene et altre apparenze, et à tal' effetto essendogli necessario imporre un teatro confacente à tali opere, per tanto gli concediamo libertà et facoltà di fabbricare d°. teatro, et rappresentare in esso d*. opere musicali, senza essere da alcuno impedito et molestato, anzi gli concediamo particolare Priuilegio che solo il d°. Gentileschi con la sua compagnia, per il spatio di cinque anni uenturi possa fare rappresentare simili opere musicali, et non altri, concedendogli anco il potere sustituire in suo luogo chi gli piacerà, et uorrà con l'istessa facoltà, et autorità à lui concessa, uolendo di più che il d°. Gentileschi, con li suoi seguaci, godino il titolo di nostri serui, et che nel passare il mare, tanto nella loro uenuta, come nel loro ritorno, in tutti li nostri porti gli sia concesso libero passaggio tanto alle persone loro, come alle loro robbe, senza impedimento et molestia alcuna anzi desideriamo gli sia data ogn' assistenza et fauore, che tanto è il nr̄o uolere. Data nel nostro Reale Palazzo d [sic] Whitehall il di 22 Ottobre 1660.[1]

This is interesting not only for the reference to scenery and machines as elements of opera, but in relation to Davenant's project to develop native opera. Possibly he used his influence to get the permit withdrawn; in any case, the enterprise must have proved abortive, for there is no further trace of it.

In the summer of 1661, a French troupe came to London and established itself in the old Cockpit in Drury Lane, the first foreign visitors, I believe, after the Restoration.[2] It was their performance of Le Mariage d'Orphée et d'Eurydice which occasioned the famous pamphlet entitled The Description of the Great Machines of the Descent of Orpheus into Hell, and one wonders that such effects could be staged in that theatre. Mr Lawrence takes this to be the same company that was acting

1. SP. 29/19, no. 16. Endorsed "Grant of Italian Play^rs to his Ma^ty."
2. Lawrence, loc. cit.; Pepys, 30 August 1661.

at Court later in the year, and one wonders still more
how they could adapt their spectacular performance to
the Palladian stage of the Cockpit in Court. But there
is little doubt that they acted there. On 10 December,
a warrant to the Exchequer was issued for payment of
£300 to John Channoveau, "to bee by him distributed
as of his Ma^{ts}: bountie to the ffrench Comedians";[1] and
Evelyn saw a French comedy at Court on the sixteenth.
At that time, the Cockpit was the one place in Whitehall
fitted up for plays.

I can only refer to them in passing, but although
scarcely "Italian players," the puppets must not be
omitted. On 8 October 1662, Pepys relates that the
Earl of Sandwich is "at White Hall with the King, before whom the puppet plays I saw this summer in
Covent-garden are acted this night." Some time that
month a stage was made in the Queen's Guard Chamber,[2] and it may have been for this entertainment.
Charles must have said, "we *are* amused," for the next
month the Lord Chamberlain sent an order to the Jewel
House for a gold chain and medal, worth £25, to be presented to "Signor Bologna alias Pollicinella."[3]

Mr Lawrence quotes from the State Papers a permit
dated 25 August 1663, for a French company to bring
over their scenes and stage decorations,[4] but nothing
further is known of this visit, if, indeed, it took place.
Again, in 1669, a single document reveals the presence
of visiting actors, a permit entered in the Lord Chamberlain's book, which reads:

1. SP. 38/20.   2. See p. 57.   3. LC. 5/107.
4. Lawrence, I, 140, from SP. 29/79, no. 73.

It is his Maties: Pleasure That ye french Comædians haue liberty to Act and Play And that noe Persons p^rsume to molest or disturbe them in theire Acting & playing: Given vnd^r my hand this 26: day of October 1669.
To all whome it may Concerne.[1]

This, of course, refers to acting in public theatres, but I take it to be a safe inference that foreign players under his Majesty's protection would be received at Court.

Another visit made in 1672 by unknown French actors is referred to in Dryden's prologue to *Arviragus and Philicia*, when it was revived in March or April of that year, and still another in his Oxford epilogue of 1673.[2] In the second he says:

> A French troop first swept all things in its way,
> But these hot Monsieurs were too quick to stay,

apparently implying a short visit. But if the French did not stay long, they must have come often, for there is documentary evidence that they were in England between the two visits chronicled by Dryden. In the *Calendar of Treasury Books* are to be found a series of warrants from the Treasurer to the Customs Commissioners instructing them in regard to the luggage of a French company which must have been in England from December, 1672, until May, 1673.[3] The first, dated 17 December, announces that they have arrived, and that their goods, if for their own immediate use, are to be admitted free. On 1 January, Clifford wrote that the goods were to be sent from Portsmouth to the Cus-

1. LC. 5/12, p. 252, with marginal note, "ffrench Comædians to Act"; Nicoll, p. 241.
2. Lawrence, I, 142–143.
3. *Calendar of Treasury Books 1672–75*, pp. 14, 24, 29, 127.

tom House in London, and not opened until they arrived
there, when further order would be given; and finally, on
the ninth, he gave instructions for the examination and
delivery of their "clothes scenes and ornaments." Their
departure early in May is revealed by a warrant dated
on the first, for the Customs Commissioners to inspect
and seal luggage belonging to Sir Leoline Jenkins and
Sir Joseph Williamson, ambassadors to the treaty at
Aix la Chapelle, and also "the goods belonging to the
Company of French comedians at York House, whom
the said Ambassadors are directed by the King to receive into their train."

The great event, however, of the summer of 1673 was
the arrival of Scaramouche and his fellows from the
Palais Royal, who acted at Whitehall from April or May
until September.[1] The Customs Commissioners were
ordered on 21 April to admit their "clothes, vestments,
scenes, ornaments, necessaries and materials" as
"neither contraband nor prohibited" and free of duty.[2]
Evelyn saw them act on 29 May, and then we hear no
more of them until 22 August, when James Vernon
wrote to Sir Joseph Williamson that the company had
desired the King's permission to return to Paris.[3]
Charles was evidently loth to let them go, but on 12 September the free export of their goods on the *Merlin*
yacht was ordered,[4] and at least he did not send them
away unrewarded. The Master of the Jewel House was
instructed on 4 September to deliver "vnto Scara-

1. The real name of the leader was Tiberio Fiorelli.
2. *Cal. of Treas. Books 1672–75*, p. 119.
3. Camden Society: *Letters to Sir Joseph Williamson at Cologne*, I, 179.
4. *Cal. of Treas. Books 1672–75*, p. 392.

mouchi and Harlekin vnto each of them" a chain and medal of gold weighing six and a half ounces, and similar ones were to be made for four others in the troupe.[1] This was followed by another warrant on the twelfth, for twenty ounces of white plate, to be delivered to Scaramouche "as a guift from his Ma^{te} vnto one of his Company"[2] — which one is not difficult to conjecture.

Some time during the summer, a stage had been built for them, possibly at Windsor, for the *Calendar of Treasury Books* contains a warrant for the payment of £52 to Philip Packer, Paymaster of the Works, "to be disbursed in satisfaction for the building of the Italians' stage, as agreed to be paid by His Majesty's order."[3] This can scarcely have been at Whitehall.

Passing over *Ariane*,[4] which, although a French opera, was produced by the Academy of Music, we find the next mention of French comedians in another warrant from the Treasurer to the Customs Commissioners on 1 June 1674,

to permit the export, Custom free, of 52 parcels of goods in coffers or ballots belonging to the French comedians and which now remain in the Custom House among certain goods of the French Plenipotentiaries lately brought over from Cologne.[5]

"Export" is clearly a slip for import, for on the following 19 August, the Customs Commissioners were again ordered to search and permit shipment of the goods of the French comedians then in London.[6] This visit is not

1. LC. 5/140, p. 328; Nicoll, p. 238.
2. *Ibid.*, p. 329; Nicoll, *loc. cit.*
3. *Cal. of Treas. Books 1672–75*, pp. 392, 837.   4. See pp. 111–112.
5. *Cal. of Treas. Books 1672–75*, p. 533.
6. *Ibid.*, p. 571.

mentioned by Mr Lawrence, and Professor Nicoll takes
the documents to refer to the same visit as those quoted
on the preceding page, but I do not think this is possible.
It is, however, surprising that this Gallic invasion should
coincide with the return of Scaramouche.

Fiorelli's second visit seems to have escaped notice,
although it was the occasion of a new stage at Windsor,
specially built for him in St. George's Hall.[1] It was
probably ready for him about the end of July, but no
definite dates can be assigned to his stay. It is curious
that there are no letters to the Customs Commissioners
concerning his arrival and departure, and one wonders
whether his company can be meant in the warrants just
quoted. In every other case, however, careful distinction is made between French and Italian comedians, and
since the Windsor stage was constructed in the very
middle of the Frenchmen's visit, I think we must accept
the documents at face value.

Yet another matter remains to be mentioned before
we leave the summer of 1674. At seven o'clock of a
Wednesday morning early in July, we find twelve of the
King's violins assembled at Whitehall, "to practize
after such manner as Mons[r.] Combert shall enforme
them which things are hereafter to be p[r]sented before
his Ma[te]. at Windsor vpon Saterday next," to wit, on
11 July.[2] The nature of this performance is not known:
the stage in St. George's Hall was not ordered until the
eighth, but there is a tradition that Cambert produced
his *Pomone* at the English Court sometime between the
summer of 1673 and March, 1677.[3]

1. See p. 60.   2. LC. 5/15, p. 16.   3. Lawrence, I, 145.

Scaramouche's next English season is well known, be-ing the famous occasion when Charles permitted him to charge admission, as to a public playhouse, at the door of the Hall Theatre.[1] Here John Evelyn saw him on 29 September 1675, and found the entrance charge "very scandalous" and contrary to all precedent; but he adds, "having seen him act before in Italy, many years past, I was not averse from seeing the most excellent of that kind of folly." Earlier in the summer, Marvell had written to a friend of the doings at White-hall, and stated that a twelve-penny gallery had been built for the convenience of his Majesty's poor subjects.[2] The Works Accounts show no such construction at this time, but probably one of the existing galleries was so used, for a new stairway to it was made in June when other alterations, evidently for the Italians, were under way.[3]

The approximate dates of the Italians' sojourn are set by two Treasury warrants to the Customs Commissioners. The first is dated 20 June, and instructs them "to deliver to Monsieur Brunetts, Custom free, and without opening, several vestments, habits, scenes and other necessaries belonging to the Italian comedians and lately brought from France in the *Portsmouth* and *Ann* yachts."[4] The second is an order of 4 October to allow the free export of their goods in one of the King's

---

1. Not the Banqueting House, as stated by Lawrence and Nicoll.
2. Lawrence, I, 146.
3. See p. 49. This was the first time admission was charged to plays at Whitehall. Pepys' remarks on the expense of going to them do not apply to admission but to coach fare and other incidental charges (see the *Diary* for 23 February 1662/3). But *cf.* p. 173.
4. *Cal. of Treas. Books 1672–75*, p. 757.

yachts.[1] An interesting sidelight on their visit is thrown by two items in a warrant to pay Nicholas Staggins, Master of the King's Music, for his labours in July:

> For the fair writing of a chaccon with severall others that was played at Scaramoucha from the fowle original in score, the foure parts together and the prickers dyes 6.5.
> For drawing the said musick into their severall parts for the band of violins, every man a part to himselfe, and dyes 5.12.[2]

Perhaps even payment at the door proved an inadequate method of recompense, for we hear no more of foreign actors at Court until early in 1677, when Wren was instructed to alter the stage in the Hall Theatre for the French comedians, "in such fashion as it was for Scaramouch's Acting."[3] Although unaware of this warrant, Mr Lawrence deduced the presence of a French troupe at this time from the epilogue to *The French Conjuror*, and suggests that it may have acted in *Rare-en-Tout*, produced at Court on 29 May.[4] In this performance, the King's musicians participated,[5] but that it was acted by Frenchmen is made clear by John Verney's account of it. On 31 May he wrote to a relative:

> On Wednesday his Majesty's birth night, was some gallantry at Whitehall, where was acted a French opera, but most pitifully done, so ill that the king was aweary on't, and some say it was not well contrived to entertain the English gentry, who came that night in

1. *Cal. of Treas. Books 1672–75*, p. 826.
2. De Lafontaine, p. 297. A chaconne is a musical arrangement of variations on a theme. An example will be found in Act II of *Albion and Albanius*.
3. See pp. 49–50.
4. Lawrence, I, 146–147.
5. LC. 5/142, p. 38; Nicoll, p. 317.

honour to their King, with a lamentable ill-acted French play, when our English actors so much surpass; however the dances and voices were pretty well performed.[1]

At the end of the year, a different French company was acting at Whitehall. Henry Saville, writing to Rochester on 17 December, has preserved for us the tradition that they were bound for Nimeguen and cast into an English port by adverse winds.[2] These ill winds that blew Charles so much good also very obligingly blew the actors' luggage into one of the King's yachts: the Customs Commissioners were ordered on 30 November to admit Customs free forty-six coffers and bales, lately arrived in the *Kitchin* yacht now at Greenwich, being the luggage of the French comedians.[3] The favourite in the company was a girl of fifteen, who seems to have set the whole Court by the ears. She has been identified by Mr Lawrence as Mlle Françoise Pitel, later known as Mlle Raisin, the daughter of Henri Pitel, who is said to have remained in England fifteen or eighteen months.[4] A warrant for alterations in the Hall Theatre "after yᵉ same manner as it was for yᵉ Italian Players" gives us 5 December as the date of what I take to be their first performance;[5] and I believe the date of their departure is equally clearly fixed by yet another warrant to the Customs Commissioners as about the middle of April. On the twelfth, they had orders to view at Whitehall *seventy* bales belonging to the French

1. Hist. Mss., VII, 469. Wednesday is an error; 29 May 1677 was a Tuesday.
2. Hist. Mss., *Report on the Mss. of the Marquis of Bath*, II, 161.
3. *Cal. of Treas. Books 1676–79*, p. 803.
4. Lawrence, I, 148–149.   5. See pp. 51, 237.

players and to allow their free export on the *Kitchin* to Dieppe.[1]

The following winter, Charles found some means to get Scaramouche back for a few months. He arrived early in November, with six portmanteaus, two great baskets, and twenty-two trunks, and left about the middle of February on one of the King's yachts.[2] The only other trace of his visit is the setting up of "portholes" on the stage in the Hall Theatre, apparently the "portals" on which he had previously insisted.[3]

Perhaps the state of the King's purse prevented further visits; at any rate, we hear no more of Continental actors for over four years. Then, in April, 1683, Charles instructed his envoy at Paris, Lord Preston, to arrange for the return of Fiorelli's company, and the course of negotiations, diplomatic and financial, can be traced in letters calendared by the Historical Manuscripts Commission.[4] The King desired the comedians to attend him at Windsor during the summer, Louis signified his consent, Scaramouche assured Preston he was ready to obey but —

they could get nothing at Windsor, and therefore they hoped the King would consider them; that there was an hundred pounds of an old arrear due to them which he hoped his Majesty would order to be paid. He also desired that they might have (as they had the last time) some money advanced to them here [*in Paris*], otherwise some of their company could not get away. . . .

---

1. *Cal. of Treas. Books 1676–79*, p. 962. An entry in *Secret Service Accounts*, dated 27 November 1677, "Delivered the said taly to the Etalians . . . 500.0.0," probably refers to the King's Italian musicians.
2. *Cal. of Treas. Books 1676–79*, pp. 1160, 1230.
3. See pp. 50, 52.
4. VII, 285, 286, 288, 331.

These little matters attended to, and a yacht coming to Dieppe for them, they would be ready on ten or twelve days' notice.

Preston sent this news on 21 April (new style), so Charles must have been prepared to meet Fiorelli's demands when, on the twentieth (old style), a warrant was passed for the construction of a new theatre at Windsor.[1] We cannot be sure that this theatre was actually built, although its existence seems to be implied in later documents, nor have we proof positive that the Italians came over. A letter (not mentioned by Mr Lawrence, who thinks they did not come) written from Windsor on 1 May by the Prince of Denmark shows that they were then confidently expected.[2] In it he says:

> God send me a quiet life somewhere, for I shall not be long able to beare this perpetuall motion; all my hopes are in the Italian Players whom we expect heer about ye 20th of this monthe, and having sent soe farr for them, surely wee shall have soe much respect for them as to bee a little constant heer upon theire accounts. . . .

If his prayer was granted, the visit must have been short, for again in August Preston wrote to Sunderland that he had received a letter intimating that the King wished him to treat with the Italians if *divertissements* at the French Court were off for the winter on account of the Queen's death; the comedians, Italians, and opera were all on again, and he desired further instructions.[3] These he presumably did not get, for we hear nothing further of the matter.

1. See p. 60.   2. Hist. Mss., VIII, ii, 458.
3. Hist. Mss., VII, 288.

It was in this same August of 1683 that Betterton went to Paris to try to capture the French opera and caught only the wretched Grabut.[1] The French composer is not known to have produced an entertainment for the Court until *Albion and Albanius* made its belated appearance in June, 1685.[2]

It seems clear that at this juncture nothing further was to be had from Paris, and Charles, who was as ingenious in providing himself with amusement as he was incapable of paying for it, bethought himself to borrow the French players attached to the household of the Prince of Orange. Once more we are indebted to the Customs Commissioners for the information that they were on their way, with sixty-five trunks or packs of old clothes, on 26 May 1684, and apparently intended to go straight to Windsor.[3] They seem to have spent the summer months travelling with the King, for on 29 October £46 was paid "to Francis Duperier for the charge of the French players attending his Majesty at Windsor and Winchester, and returning to London.[4] Their first performance at Whitehall was probably on 29 September, for on that date Wren was ordered to fit the theatre for them "this p'sent night."[5] On the following 11 December their goods were inspected prior to their departure.[6]

James, too, was fond of what Mr Lawrence calls "exotic amusements," and early in 1686 the Court was

---

1. Lawrence, I, 149.
2. Not, of course, at Whitehall, but at Dorset Garden.
3. *Cal. of Treas. Books 1681–85*, p. 1134. Their arrival is also referred to in a letter dated 10 June, Hist. Mss., V, i, 186.
4. *Secret Service Accounts*, p. 93.   5. See pp. 53–54, 238.
6. *Cal. of Treas. Books 1681–85*, p. 1444.

entertained with French opera. To judge from the
letters of Peregrine Bertie to the Countess of Rutland,
much was expected of it, but the performance on 11 February was a little disappointing.[1] Mr Lawrence takes
this opera to have been at Court, but in one of the Lord
Chamberlain's books we find it in a bill of the King's
company as "The King & Queene & a Box for y[e]
Maydes of hono[r] at y[e] French Opera 25 [*li*]," which is a
clear verdict for the public theatre.[2]

There was, however, one more visit of French players
to the English Court before the reign was out. In the
summer of 1688, a troupe was again at Windsor. On
25 July, a warrant was sent to Wren, "to cause ye Playhouse at Windsor to be made ready forthwith & Convenient in every pticuler [*sic*] for ye accommodation of
ye french Comædians as it was heretofore When the
said Comædians was there."[3] One wonders whether this
is to be taken literally; if so, they may have been the
Prince of Orange's servants, or even Fiorelli's company,
although they were usually called, as they were, Italians.
A further warrant, dated 11 August, instructed Wren to
make such alterations as the French comedians should
direct.[4] They had arrived a few days before, the order
for the free import of their goods being dated on the
ninth, and must have spent a short time in London before going to Windsor.[5] On the eleventh, a warrant had
been dispatched by messenger to Thomas Neale, the
Groom Porter, bidding him allow the French comedi-

1. Hist. Mss., XII, v, 102, 104.
2. LC. 5/16, p. 124; Nicoll, p. 312.
3. See p. 61.   4. *Ibid.*
5. *Cal. of Treas. Books 1685–89*, p. 2035.

ans to act "at the Playhouse at Windsor," and provide them with what lodging he could in his own house.[1]
This he furnished for six weeks, from 13 August to
22 September, and in course of time secured a warrant
for £12 in satisfaction thereof, with an extra eighteen
shillings to cover the fees of the office of the Treasurer
of the Chamber.[2] The warrant for the export of their
luggage is dated 29 September,[3] but they must have
lingered a few days, for not until October was £200 paid
to John de Sureis for himself and his fellows, being
twelve in number.[4]

After this, although French dancers and singers were
becoming increasingly popular in the public theatres,
there is no trace of further visits by royal command or
of performances on the Court stage.

Amateur Acting

There is a very persistent tradition that amateur acting was popular at Court in the days of Charles II, but
when one comes to look into the matter, there are traces
of singularly few such performances. Some five or six
plays and a couple of masques are all I can speak of with
certainty, although there may well have been more and
at least there was a survival of earlier Court revels in the
fashionable masquerade.

The Matchless Orinda's *Horace* may have been the
first play acted by Charles' courtiers, although I can

1. LC. 5/17, p. 65; Nicoll, p. 241.
2. LC. 5/148, p. 257.
3. *Cal. of Treas. Books 1685–89*, p. 2082.
4. *Secret Service Accounts*, p. 209.

give no date for their performance. Evelyn says he saw the play at Whitehall on 4 February 1667/8, acted before the King and Queen, with "a masque and antique dance" between each act. This date is certainly wrong, for 4 February that year was Ash Wednesday; and if the play had been done by amateurs, he would surely have said so, especially as professionals would in all probability have been called in for the *intermedii*. But the *Biographia Dramatica* says that *Horace* was acted by persons of quality and that Monmouth spoke the prologue. It may equally well, I think, be argued that amateur would precede or follow professional production, and if it followed, *Horace* must yield first place to *The Indian Emperour*.

Dryden's play was acted at Whitehall on 13 January 1667/8.[1] On the following day, Pepys heard all about it, and wrote in his *Diary*:

> They fell to discourse of last night's work at Court, where the ladies and the Duke of Monmouth and others acted "The Indian Emperour"; wherein they told me these things most remarkable: that not any woman but the Duchess of Monmouth and Mrs. Cornwallis did any thing but like fools and stocks, but that these two did do most extraordinary well: that not any man did any thing well but Captain O'Bryan, who spoke and did well, but, above all things did dance most incomparably.

It is clear that Monmouth, even if he did not cover himself with glory, was a leading spirit in these theatricals, and his Duchess was one of the best dancers until the unfortunate accident on the following 8 May, which left her with a shortened leg.[2] This performance of *The In-*

---

1. It was produced at Drury Lane *c*. April, 1665; Nicoll, p. 359.
2. Pepys, 9 and 15 May 1668, *et al.*

dian Emperour may have been the play referred to in
Margaret Blagge's diary, when that estimable but
exasperating Maid of Honour made herself the precept,
"go not to the Duchess of Monmouth above once a
week, except when we dress to rehearse, and then carry
a book along with me to read when I don't act, and so
come away before supper."[1] Evelyn would not have
agreed with Pepys' report of the play, for he thought
Margaret Blagge acted her part to perfection.

The next Court theatricals I can trace are mentioned
in a newsletter dated 12 April 1670. It states that on
the sixth, ". . . their Majesties were diverted with a
comedy acted at St. James's by the little young ladies
of the Court, who appeared extraordinarily glorious and
covered with jewels."[2] This hitherto unnoticed occasion is doubly interesting, as one of the few references to
plays at St. James',[3] and, if my interpretation is correct,
as the theatrical début of the Princesses Mary and Anne.
Just a year before, Pepys had seen the Duke's eldest
daughter, "a little child in hanging sleeves, dance most
finely, so as almost to ravish me, her ears were so good."[4]
The sisters were to make their most important appearance on the stage in Crowne's masque, but Anne also
acted in legitimate, playing Semandra in Lee's *Mithridates*. Oldys says the play was acted in the Banqueting
House (surely a mistake: it would have been in the Hall
Theatre) by the nobility, and Anne was taught her part

1. Evelyn, *Godolphin*, pp. 15, 64.
2. Hist. Mss., XII, vii, 70.
3. See p. 59.
4. Pepys, 2 April 1669. Mary was taught to dance by a Frenchman who had
   instructed the King.

by Joseph Ashbury,[1] while Cibber claims she was taught by Mrs. Betterton.[2] Lord Fountainhall, however, records that on 15 November 1681, the Queen's birthday was celebrated at Holyrood by "'. . . the acting of a comedy [*sic*] called *Mithridates, King of Pontus,* . . . wheirin Lady Anne, the Duke's daughter, and the ladies of honour were the onlie actors." [3] *Mithridates* was first acted at Drury Lane about March, 1677/8,[4] and published the same spring. In his dedication, Lee says the play has been acted before the Queen, but does not mention the Princess, as he surely would have done had she already taken part in it at Whitehall.

But I am getting ahead of my story, for some years before this there had taken place an important amateur performance at Court, presumably at Whitehall, about which a good deal needs to be said. The play in question was Settle's *Empress of Morocco.* Mr F. C. Brown, in his *Elkanah Settle: His Life and Works,* has argued that this play was acted privately in the winter of 1669/70 and at Dorset Garden in 1671, on the strength of Settle's claim that it was acted less than three years after *Cambyses* and Downes' assertion that *Cambyses* was the first new play acted by the Duke's company after the Great Fire.[5] Professor Nicoll has suggested a variety of reasons for dating *Cambyses* 1670/1,[6] and I am now able to offer proof that the amateur performance of *The Em-*

1. Note in Langbaine, p. 324.
2. Cibber, I, 162.
3. *Historical Observes of Memorable Ocurrents . . . 1680 . . . 1686,* published by the Bannatyne Club in 1840.
4. Nicoll, p. 367.   5. Brown, pp. 12, 9.
6. Nicoll, pp. 107, 371, 386–387.

press of Morocco must have taken place in the winter of 1671/2 at the earliest and may belong to the spring of 1672/3.[1]

Previous commentators seem to have overlooked Settle's definite statement in his dedication to Henry Howard, Earl of Norwich, that he owed the story to the Earl's embassy to Africa. Reference to the *Calendar of State Papers* reveals the fact that Howard (then Baron Howard of Castle Rising) went to Morocco in June, 1669, and returned in October, 1670. Settle could scarcely have had the play ready that season — unless, indeed, he wrote it in a few weeks, in which case, he would certainly have boasted of it — and moreover, since the Court must at that time have been occupied with preparations for the Grand Ballet or Masque danced in February, 1670/1,[2] it would not have been ready for another undertaking of so elaborate a nature.

Settle, of course, had many friends at Whitehall, and it is reasonable to suppose that the play was written expressly for Court presentation. But in that case there would inevitably be new scenery and special preparations made for it, and when we turn to the Works Accounts for 1671/2, we find not so much as a single item for the Hall Theatre. To be sure, this is not conclusive proof that the play was not acted that year: for some unknown reason the work may have been paid for through another channel, or the records may simply be incomplete. On the other hand, in March, 1672/3, there was considerable work on the theatre and some

1. There is no question about the date of the public performance: it was in July, 1673 (Nicoll, p. 310).   2. See pp. 138–139.

new scenery was made, including a back-cloth painted like "rusticke" (*i. e.* rusticated) stonework, and an arch and cross-piece of stone.[1] This at once suggests the prison scene, but alas, there is no mention of the torture chamber, and on the whole, it seems as if Settle's play would have required more new scenery. However, in April, five carpenters were detailed to attend the plays six nights, and there is no record of either patent company at Whitehall that month. While this evidence leaves much room for uncertainty, it seems to me that there is a probability that *The Empress of Morocco* was acted at Court only a few months before the public production, and that, of course, is just what one would expect.

Whenever the Court performance took place, it must have been a brilliant affair. The parts were taken, as Settle put it, "by persons of such Birth and Honour, that they borrowed no Greatness from the Characters they acted." Mulgrave supplied a prologue, and a second performance is indicated by another prologue written by Rochester, both spoken by the Lady Elizabeth Howard.

It is impossible here to go into the further history of the play and Settle's subsequent quarrel with Dryden, Shadwell, and Crowne.[2] One other point, however, I can and must clear up. In the preface to *The Libertine* (published 1676), Shadwell took the opportunity to retaliate for Settle's postscript to *Love and Revenge*, and, *inter alia*, abused him for adding the words "His Majesty's

1. See p. 152.
2. For the facts, see Brown, *op. cit.*, but his conclusions are erroneous.

Servant" to his name on the title-page of his plays.[1] All Settle's plays from *The Empress of Morocco* to *Ibrahim* were so published, and the explanation is to be found in one of the Lord Chamberlain's Registers of the House-hold:[2]

> Sewer in ordinary to His Matie. being one of the poettes in His Ma^{ts} Theatre Royall ffeb. 27: 1671/[2] Elcana Settle   Mr Killigrew.

What Killigrew had to do with it I do not know, but doubtless the place was a sinecure, obtained for Settle by his friends as a means of subsistence while he wrote for the Court.

Early in the eighteenth century, the belief was current that *Sodom*, then accepted as the work of Rochester, had once been acted at Court by members of the nobil-ity, unimpeded by garments. So, at least, Zacharias Conrad von Uffenbach was informed when he visited England in 1710,[3] and recent editors of Rochester seem to agree that such a performance of the piece is likely, although it cannot be verified.[4] I have seen only one manuscript of this play; it is a copy in a professional hand in a volume of poems, and bears no traces of play-house use. But the nature of the stage directions, as well as their form, makes it seem highly improbable that the play was ever acted, even *in camera*. It is regret-table that the prudery which seems to be current among officials and editors makes it reasonable to suspect

---

1. This was the regular practice of the poets laureate.
2. LC. 3/27, p. 94.
3. J. Prinz, *John Wilmot Earl of Rochester*, pp. 170–171.
4. *Ibid.*, and J. Hayward, *Collected Works of John Wilmot Earl of Rochester*, p. xviii. Hayward disclaims Rochester's authorship.

the suppression of any contemporary reference, if such exists, from published calendars and reports on collections of manuscripts.

It is surprising that there are no further references to the amateur acting of plays at Court. Yet if others had been so produced, some, at least, would surely have found mention in the innumerable letters examined by the Commission on Historical Manuscripts. There is always the hope that further sifting of manuscript letters in the British Museum will reveal unsuspected treasure, but meantime we are left with too little information to draw any inferences. I would only point out that Anne's early interest in plays and acting bore no fruit during the last decade of the century.

The subject of Restoration masques is one on which writers on that species of Court entertainment have said about as little as possible. It is indeed difficult ground. *Calisto*, of course, is well known, and is usually said to be the sole exemplar, on the authority of Cibber's statement to that effect.[1] Crowne, too, in his preface, says that he was obliged to write a piece "the nature of which I was wholly a stranger to, having never seen anything of the kind. . . ." It is difficult to tell whether he means this to refer to the whole, or only to the pastoral interludes, but in any case he does not say there had been no masques, merely that he had seen none. As a matter of fact, there had been a Court entertainment four years before which looks singularly like one. Study of the problem is, however, sadly complicated by the contemporary use of the words masque, masquerade,

1. Cibber, II, 209.

ball, and ballet. *Calisto* itself was called by Evelyn first a comedy and then a pastoral, by the Clerk of the Kitchen a ball, and by the tailors a masquerade. But on the whole, a "ball or masque" — the two are frequently so joined — seems to have been either a *bal masqué* or the type of masquerade immortalised by Gramont, in which only a few participated. The words are so interpreted by Reyher, who quotes the prologue to Davenant's *The Man's the Master*:[1]

> No country lady ever yet did ask
> Such shrewd advice before a ball or masque,
> When curious dressing is the court's great task.

On the other hand, masques in plays persist and are so designated. Impossible as it is to arrive at any hard and fast conclusions, I prefer to resort to a brief discussion of the various entertainments in connection with which the name was used.

On 9 February 1662/3, Charles wrote to his sister, the Duchesse d'Orléans:

... ici nous avons eu le projet d'organiser une mascarade et nous en avions assez bien dessiné le plan général, mais il n'y a pas eu moyen d'en venir à bout, n'ayant pas ici un seul homme en état de faire une *entrée* supportable. J'ai fort engagé la reine à suivre l'exemple de la reine mère de France et à se masquer avant le fin du carnaval ... Ma femme a bien debuté dans une affaire de ce genre, car l'autre jour elle a fait exécuter des contre-danses dans sa chambre à coucher par milord Aubigny et par deux autres de ses chapelains.[2]

It is true he speaks of a *mascarade*, but if they were planning *entrées*, they must have been aiming at something

1. Reyher, p. 477.
2. Comte Henri de Baillon, *Henriette Anne d'Angleterre*, p. 109.

very like a masque. There is no trace of such an event at that time, but on 3 July, Evelyn saw a "great masque" at Court, which he unfortunately failed to describe. It was a most unsuitable season for a masque, or indeed, for any Court entertainment.

It is to Evelyn that we are indebted for most of the subsequent references to masques. On 2 February 1664/5, he saw "a masque performed at Court, by six gentlemen and six ladies, surprising his Majesty, it being Candlemas day." This is surely the original masque pure and simple, a remarkable piece of what appears to be deliberate archaism, rather than a survival of the Caroline masque. Later that spring there presumably took place in the new Hall Theatre the "Queen's ballet" which Webb had in mind when he drew the plans for the stage,[1] but I have been unable to learn anything of the performance.

In February, 1666/7, not on Candlemas, but on the eve of Shrove-Tuesday, Evelyn attended "a magnificent ball, or masque, in the theatre at Court, where their Majesties and all the great lords and ladies danced, infinitely gallant, the men in their richly embroidered most becoming vests."[2] These were presumably the Persian costumes then affected by the Court, and not masqueing garments. Again on Shrove-Tuesday,1667/8, there was a "great mask at Court, where the Countess of Castlemaine Apeared in a dress of dimonds & pretious stones."[3]

1. See p. 28.
2. 18 February. The Hall Theatre was, of course, regularly used for balls.
3. Rugge, II, f. 218ᵛ.

These, I believe, were simply Court balls, probably opened by formal dances in which only a chosen few took part. But in February, 1670/1, the Court attempted a more elaborate entertainment, which must, I am convinced, be taken for a genuine masque, although Evelyn perversely calls it a ball, and the Clerk of the Kitchen, "magnæ Saltation' sive Grand Ballad."[1] This was a great occasion, for which the stage was altered and enlarged, and extra accommodation provided for musicians,[2] but the dancing-floor was not laid over the pit, as it would have been for a ball. In the middle of January, Lady Mary Bertie wrote to Katherine Noel:[3]

> The Queen is preparing a ball to bee danced in the greate Hall by herself and the Dutchesse of Buckingham, Richmond, Monmouth, Mrs. Berkeley, and Madame Kerwell the French maid of honor. There are no men of quality but the Duke of Monmouth, all the rest are gentlemen.

On 4 February, she reported the news that "the greate ball" was to be danced the following Monday,[4] that is, the sixth, and it seems probable that Evelyn is mistaken in the date when he says that he saw "the great ball danced by the Queen and distinguished ladies at Whitehall Theatre" on the ninth. Lady Mary, too, may have fallen into error when she included the Duchess of Monmouth, for it seems very doubtful whether she would have been able to dance on account of her lameness.

There were two more performances, on the twentieth

1. See p. 93.   2. See pp. 45–47.
3. Hist. Mss., XII, v, 22.   4. *Ibid.*

and twenty-first, Shrove-Monday and Tuesday.[1] Lady
Mary attended on the twentieth, and sent the following
account of it to her friend:[2]

> I was on Munday at Court to see the grane ballett danced. It
> was so hard to get room that wee were forced to goe by four a clocke,
> though it did not begin till nine or ten. The[y] were very richly
> [*dressed*] and danced very finely, and shifted their clothes three
> times. There was also fine musickes and excellent sing[*ing*] some
> new song made purpose for it. After the ballet was over, several
> others danced, as the King, and Duke of Yorke, and Duke of Somer-
> set, and Duke of Buckingham. And the Dutchesse of Cleveland was
> very fine in a riche petticoat and halfe shirte, and a short man's coat
> very richly laced, a perwig cravatt and a hat: her hat and maske was
> very rich.

It must, indeed, have been a fine spectacle if three
complete sets of costumes were provided. Unfortunately, the details have not survived, but a summary of
the tradesmen's bills is among the State Papers, with a
warrent for payment out of the Receipt of the Exchequer to Lawrence Hyde, then Master of the Robes.[3]
The total comes to £2,316.1.2. Possibly to the same
performance, although it is very late for it, belongs a
bill for a coat and breeches of brocade richly laced, with
hat, stockings, and ribbons, for "Madam Carwell now
Dutchess of Portsmouth," which is dated 24 January 1671/2.[4]

Calisto belongs to the Shrovetide of 1674/5, and then,
some three years later, there was an entertainment at

1. *Ibid.*, vii, 75, where it is called a "ballett"; SP. 44/25, ff. 195/6, called
   a masque; Hist. Mss. XII, v, 22–23.   2. *Ibid.*
3. SP. 44/25, ff. 195ᵛ–196, 14 March 1670/1. In SP. 44/26, f. 98, is a memorandum that this warrant was entered in the "Promiscuous book."
4. Brit. Mus. Add. Ms. 27588.

Whitehall for which five costumes were ordered and provided. The warrant states that the materials are to be chosen and the garments made by one Monsieur Cabin for a play on 8 February 1677/8,[1] but the bills are marked, "For the Mask" and "pro mimo ostenso coram Regem."[2] The quantities of materials are given, but it is impossible to describe the costumes, Cabin's statement of his work, for which he charged £16, being merely "Makeing 5 habbits and Capps with drawers to them and all other materials found by the taylour."[3] It is difficult to imagine a play, masque, or masquerade which would require only five costumes, and if they were to supplement the wardrobe of the French comedians then in London, one would expect them to be mentioned.[4] "For the Mask" cannot, I tnink, be ignored, especially as the *Calisto* bills are also so marked, but the evidence is too slight to come to any conclusion.

The winter of 1685/6 was prolific in masquerades and balls, but, although one of them is once called a masque, I think we may safely conclude that they consisted only of dancing, in some cases by a limited number of people whose costumes were prescribed. Some interesting details of these festivities will be found in the *Twelfth Report of the Commission on Historical Manuscripts.*[5] At as late a date as this, I think we can rely on Cibber: there were no more masques.

1. LC. 5/65, f. 42; 5/143, p. 32; Nicoll, p. 342.
2. LC. 9/115, 9/275.
3. I.e., the lining, stiffening, thread, etc.
4. See p. 123.
5. Appendix v, pp. 99, 101–106, 152.

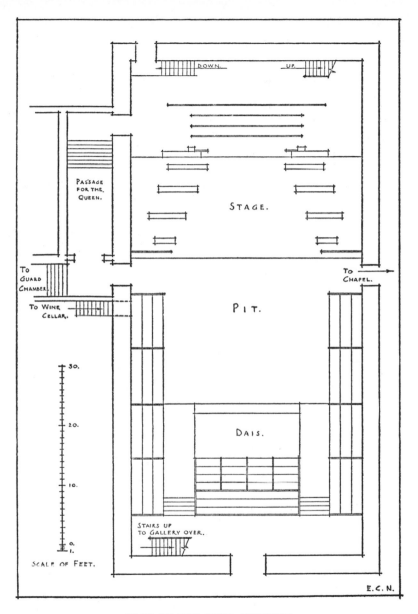

DOWN. UP.

PASSAGE
FOR THE
QUEEN.

STAGE.

TO
GUARD
CHAMBER.

TO WINE
CELLAR.

TO
CHAPEL.

PIT.

30.

20.

DAIS.

10.

STAIRS UP
TO GALLERY OVER.

0.
1.

SCALE OF FEET.

E.C.N.

PLAN OF THE HALL THEATRE

STAGING

On the whole, staging in the Court theatre seems to have been surprisingly simple. The masque stage was, to be sure, chosen for the Hall Theatre, but there is almost no trace of masque spectacle: for this, Charles reversed the order of his father's day, and went to the public theatres. As will be seen, the records reveal very little machinery of any kind for the Whitehall stage, none of an elaborate or complicated nature.

One of the most striking features of the stage in the Hall Theatre is the entire absence of an apron and proscenium doors. Even when the stage was enlarged, the masque tradition was preserved, and the frontispiece taken down and moved forward.[1] This must have had a strange effect on plays written expressly for the public theatre, where much of the business often depended on the use of the proscenium doors and of the apron for unlocalised scenes. One or two concessions were made in the Court theatre to current dramaturgy: balconies were made at the sides of the proscenium,[2] and it seems probable that for visits of the Italian Comedians, temporary "proscenium" doors were set up between the first two pairs of wings.[3] It would be interesting to try to work out how plays written for the public theatres could be adapted to the conditions of the Court stage; it must sometimes have required great ingenuity. At present, however, I can only describe the general features of Court staging without reference to particular productions.

1. Works 5/24, Extraord. Acct.
2. See p. 39.   3. See p. 50.

The Stage Curtain

The Palladian proscenium of the Cockpit in Court did not permit of a stage curtain, but the Hall Theatre seems from the first to have been provided with one. At least, when the playhouse was constructed, the carpenters made "provision to take vp and let downe the Curtain," a phrase which throws but little light on the mechanism employed.[1] Of the curtain itself we hear nothing until the spring of 1673, when Benjamin Shute, linen-draper, put in a bill for 47¾ yards of "broad coloured holland" for "2 trauerse cortaines for the theatre."[2] These may, however, have been properties for a play, for only a few months later the Lord Chamberlain wrote to the Master of the Great Wardrobe for "a Curtaine of blewe, redd, and white in breadths of stuffe of what kind you thinke fitt to fall downe before the Stage."[3] The Master thought fit to provide 168½ yards of "seuerall colored sayes,"[4] and Casbert's bill for making throws some light on how it was done:

For fiue hundred of brass rings for a large trauaise: and for tapes and thread for the said Trauaise: And for making a large Trauaise of three colours in graine being tenn breadths and eleven yards deepe: and done with rowes of rings to pull up and downe for the stage — 04 00 00.[5]

---

1. Works 5/7.
2. LC. 9/273. In the Annual Acct. of the Great Wardrobe (LC. 9/110) this item is followed by 8 ells of very broad Holland "pro mappa."
3. First warrant, cancelled, LC. 5/64, f. 81ᵛ, and 5/140, p. 372, 24 November 1673. For its repetitions see above, p. 87, note 3.
4. LC. 9/274, p. 43; 9/111. Price £13.11.3.
5. LC. 9/274, p. 67; 9/111.

The repetition of "a large Trauaise" leaves little doubt that this was one single curtain. If the say was the standard width of a yard and an eighth, the curtain was, allowing for seams, about 32 feet wide, the proscenium opening 25 feet, so evidently it did not hang in folds. In depth, however, it was very nearly 33 feet, whereas the proscenium opening was only some 23 feet, and this fact coupled with the "rows of rings to pull up and downe" suggests that the curtain was gathered to an effectual depth of 23 feet, and drew up in folds. I do not think the wording of the warrant can be taken to indicate a descending curtain.

A new curtain was ordered for *Calisto*,[1] for apparently everything had to be new for that great occasion, or perhaps His Majesty did not like the way the old one worked. This time it was only 9½ yards deep, but had 16 breadths of stuff, using 152 yards of say.[2] Further order was given for "Lattices to look through to be made in the Curtaine" (a sure sign that it was a single one and not a pair),[3] and for ferret ribbon to hang it on.[4] The upholsterer's bill includes 640 brass rings and 34 leaden plummets, but gives no details of making.[5]

Thereafter the state of the King's finances did not permit of extravagant replacements, and the curtain had much hard wear. In November, 1682, an effort was

1. LC. 5/64, f. 113ᵛ; 5/121; 5/141, p. 77; Nicoll, p. 319.
2. LC. 9/274, p. 272.
3. LC. 5/64, f. 115ᵛ; 5/121; 5/141, p. 77; Nicoll, p. 319.
4. LC. 5/64, f. 117ᵛ; 5/121; 5/141, p. 102; Nicoll, p. 320. The ferret ribbon did not wear well, and in February, 1675/6, was replaced by what is called in one copy of the bill whipcord, in another, strong tape (LC. 5/64, f. 147ᵛ; 5/121; LC. 9/113; 9/275).
5. LC. 9/274, p. 248; 9/112.

made to improve its condition by cleaning, but since the task was allotted to the carpenters, I am doubtful of the results.[1] It is not surprising that when a new one was at last ordered on 30 October 1686, to be like the old one in stuff, colour, and size, the Lord Chamberlain described the curtain then in use as "very old and not fitt to be further made use of where the King and Queenes Ma[ts]: doe intend to come often."[2] At this time the Treasurer seems to have been in some way involved in Wardrobe business. Although this warrant was, as usual, addressed to the Master of the Great Wardrobe, there is in the *Calendar of Treasury Books* a letter to the Wardrobe dated 8 November 1686, ordering various provisions including a stage curtain at £25. This new curtain was the most ample of all, 16 breadths, 10 yards deep, containing 164 yards of serge. It had 600 brass rings, three dozen wooden pullies, and 600 yards of "Laceing line," and the upholsterer's bill concludes with "new casting the lead and adding more lead to them."[3] All this elaborate apparatus surely betokens draped curtains, but the records still read "a large Curtain," "larga Cortina."

The next replacement seems to have been occasioned largely by sentiment, or at least, by what the Lord Chamberlain considered a delicate attention to the new King. His warrant, dated 28 October 1690, called for "a new Curtaine for the Theatre in Whitehall of the Same Stuffe & of the Same Colours as the Old curtaine onely one of the Colours to be Orange the Same to be

1. Works 5/35.   2. LC. 5/68, f. 31ᵛ; 5/147, p. 210.
3. LC. 9/122; 9/278. The serge cost £20.10.0, the making £7.1.6.

made ready to be put vp on the fourth of November next being his Ma[ts]. Birthday and that it be made to draw vp & lett downe as the other."[1] The bill shows that the Wardrobe had the grace to make the substitution for red, and also that the curtain was somewhat more economically contrived, being but 9 yards deep and 11 yards wide.[2]

Yet another curtain was made in the autumn of 1697, only to perish with the theatre in the Whitehall fire.[3] This one was an innovation, too, being made of blue serge, and since it had only sixteen dozen rings "to draw vp the curtain by," it may have worked on a new principle. It was 9 yards deep by 12 wide.[4]

Green Baize on the Stage

It is well known that on the eighteenth-century stage, when a theatrical death was imminent, two stage attendants walked on and solemnly spread a green carpet on which the hero, heroine, or villain, as the case might be, could die in comfort without too much damage to his clothes.[5] But earlier use of a green covering for the stage has occasioned much debate, all hinging on the interpretation of statements made by Monconys, Sorbières, and Misson, in their respective accounts of their visits to England during the second half of the seventeenth century.

1. LC. 5/69, f. 1[v]; 5/123; 5/150, p. 164; Nicoll, p. 319.
2. LC. 9/124; 9/279. The serge cost £14.14.0, the making, £5.6.0.
3. LC. 5/69, f. 148[v]; 5/125; 5/152, p. 32.
4. LC. 9/130; 9/380; LC. 11/5; AO. 3/1141, p. 49. The serge, 112 yards, cost £19.13.9, the making £3.6.0.
5. See W. J. Lawrence, "The Tragic Carpet," in *The Stage*, 30 March 1922.

Describing a visit to Killigrew's theatre on 22 May 1663, Balthasar de Monconys wrote: "Le Theatre est le plus propre & le plus beau que i' aye iamais veu, tout tapissé par le bas de bayette verte ...";[1] and in the same year, Samuel de Sorbières, after speaking of the pit, continued his account: "Le theatre est fort beau, couuert d'vn tapis verd, & la scene y est toute libre, avec beaucoup des chãgemens, & des perspectiues."[2] These two statements are surely clear enough: *theatre* can only mean stage, and the implication is that the green covering was permanent. But a statement made at the very end of the century by another *voyageur*, Henri Misson, has been allowed to confuse the issue.[3] Misson says nothing of the stage, but begins his description of the auditorium, "Le Parterre est en Amphithéatre, & rempli de bancs sans dossiers; garnis & couverts d'une étofe verte."

But all this applies to the public theatre. When we turn to the Court stage, we find that the pit and its benches were covered with bulrush matting,[4] while the stage, from the very beginning, was covered with green baize lined with canvas. Although there is only one case in which I can point to an order for baize for a specific comedy, *The Jovial Crew* on 15 November 1689,[5] it was used for the masque of February, 1670/1,[6] and I think

1. B. de Monconys, *Journal des Voyages*, Pt. II, p. 25 (edition of 1666).
2. S. de Sorbières, *Relation d'vn Voyage en Angleterre*, p. 167 (edition of 1664, Paris).
3. H. Misson, *Memoirs et Observations Faites pas un Voyageur en Angleterre*, pp. 63–64 (edition of 1698).
4. See pp. 40, 245.
5. LC. 5/68, f. 151ᵛ; 5/124; 5/149, p. 318; Nicoll, p. 341.
6. See the table on pp. 300–302.

there is sufficient proof that it served for all productions alike. There is never any mention in either the Works or Wardrobe Accounts of other covering for the stage, whereas the baize supplied (as shown by a table in the Appendix [1]) was ample for all occasions. It is true that at one time the baize was made into a "falce cover" to fasten to the stage with iron buttons, so that it could be removed at will,[2] but this, I think, was only an effort to keep it clean and in good condition by storing it between performances.

I may note in passing that baize was also used to cover the dancing floor laid over the pit for Court balls. That the practice of using it for plays was very widespread is revealed by an item in the 1668–69 Accounts of Trinity College, Cambridge, for £2.18.0. "for sixteen yards of green bays to cover ye stage."[3] This play may have been the comedy *Adelphe*.[4]

Mr W. J. Lawrence has raised the question whether this custom may not hark back to pre-Commonwealth usage, perhaps at Court.[5] The fact that baize for the Cockpit in Court was ordered as early as 24 November 1660 creates at least a strong supposition that it was the revival of an old practice, and Reyher quotes several instances of the use of green carpet for Jacobean masques.[6] It is to be hoped that further search in the Household Accounts will reveal enough evidence to settle the matter.

1. See pp. 300–302.   2. *Ibid.*
3. G. C. Moore Smith, *College Plays*, p. 29.
4. *Ibid.*, p. 71.
5. Lawrence, *loc. cit.*
6. Reyher, p. 358.

Scenery

Very little information about scenery for the Court stage is to be gleaned from contemporary records. The Works Accounts include a few bills for making and painting scenes, but these cannot possibly represent the total equipment, in view of the number of plays acted at Court. The same set was doubtless made to serve a variety of purposes, but it is incredible, for example, that no new scenery was made between the opening of the Hall Theatre and the winter of 1670–71, when the next bill occurs in the Accounts. And as a matter of fact, although scenes are mentioned in the carpenters' and joiners' accounts for the building of the theatre, there is no bill for scene-painting: we learn from other sources that it was submitted separately,[1] and so others may have been.

Such bills as there are, however, suffice to establish some important points. The scenery of the Restoration Court theatre followed closely the masque type of setting made familiar by the Inigo Jones plans for the stage of *Salmacida Spolia*, and Webb's for the *Siege of Rhodes*. This was no doubt in the first instance due to Webb, but it is remarkable, especially in the face of French influence, that the type remained unchanged throughout the next forty years. There is no trace in the Works Accounts of a box set, or of wings placed at an angle to the proscenium. It must be borne in mind, however, that this can be posited only of the Hall Theatre. Of scenery

1. *Cal. of Treas. Books 1669–72*, pp. 1158, 1330, where the bill is referred to but not quoted.

for Windsor, Kensington, or any of the temporary stages we know nothing. There is no mention after the Restoration of scenery for the Cockpit in Court: I am myself convinced that the three designs identified by Mr Keith as for the Cockpit are Caroline,[1] but there is always the possibility of lost bills.

The original scenery for the Hall Theatre was, of course, that designed by Webb for *Mustapha*, which has already been described in some detail by Mr Keith.[2] In the Chatsworth collection are drawings for four scenes, representing Solyman's Pavillion, Buda Beleaguered, the Queen of Hungary's Tent, and Solyman's Tent. There are two more drawings of the same size, which probably belong to the series but are not labelled.

The stage plans are more useful than the sketches in helping us to understand the general scheme of construction. Behind the proscenium are four pairs of wings, arranged in triangular formation, backed by a pair of shutters. This completes an ordinary set for an indoor or street scene. When greater depth is wanted for a vista or "prospect," the shutters can be withdrawn to reveal one or more relieves (three are shown on the plan) placed between them and a back-cloth which marks the full depth of the stage. Corresponding to each section of wings and shutters are upper portions for clouds. The wings are set at intervals of 3 or $3\frac{1}{2}$ feet, the shutters 17 feet from the front of the stage; the first relieve is 2 feet $7\frac{1}{2}$ inches behind the shutters, and the other relieves and back-cloth follow at equal spaces of 1 foot 8 inches. The dimensions of the wings, commencing

1. See p. 14, note 1.   2. Keith, p. 50.

with the pair nearest the frontispiece are given as 3 feet
5 inches by 21 feet 6 inches, 5 feet 3 inches by 18 feet
6 inches, 6 feet 8 inches by 15 feet 6 inches, and 6 feet
6 inches by 13 feet; of the shutters as 15 feet by 12 feet
6 inches. The wings are shown on the plan as rectangles
10½ inches deep, which Professor Nicoll explains as intended "to give depth, for they represent pillars."[1]
Surely they would have been very difficult to paint, and
the rectangles should rather be taken for a block of
wings for the successive changes of scene, similar to
those shown in detail on the *Salmacida Spolia* plan.
The shutters are represented in the same way, but the
clouds are single.[2]

Unfortunately it is impossible to tell how many sets
were then made. There are designs for six at Chatsworth. The joiners made "22 frames and Joyned
formes" which may or may not have been scenes, the
carpenters "severall frames shutting vpon yᵉ said
stage."[3] The execution of them was entrusted to Robert
Streeter, the King's Serjeant Painter, who painted all
the later scenery we know of for the Hall Theatre.
Streeter attained considerable distinction in his day.
Pepys calls him a "history-painter," reports that he is
said to excel Rubens, and describes him as "a very civil
little man, and lame, but lives very handsomely."[4] And
when Evelyn attended the Court performances of *The*

1. Nicoll, *Theatre*, p. 158.
2. Professor Odell, p. 112, and others have interpreted a stage direction in
   Albion and Albanius, "The Change is Total. The Upper Part of the
   House as well as the Side Scenes," as meaning both wings and back scene,
   but surely "The upper Part of the House" is the clouds or heavens.
3. Works 5/7.   4. 1 February 1668/9.

Conquest of Granada on 10 and 11 February 1670/1, he wrote: ". . . there were indeed very glorious scenes and perspectives, the work of Mr. Streeter, who well understands it."

From scattered references in the Works Accounts some details of the mechanism employed can be gathered.[1] All the scenes except the back-cloth and perhaps the ordinary wing clouds were movable. The wings, shutters, and relieves slid in grooves. Permanent clouds were nailed to braces fastened to a grid, described as "a floor over the Stage . . . for ye hanging vp of the workes & frames of ye Sceenes." Ropes were used to draw the scenes, and once, for a special occasion, a floor measuring about 50 square feet was made "at end of ye mooueing [*sic*] shutters for ye draweing of ye same." Oil and soap were applied to make the scenes slide easily, and there are frequent references to brushing and cleaning the grooves. The floor between and behind the scenes was covered with bulrush matting. The scenes themselves were wooden frames covered with canvas. In addition to the usual wings and shutters, we hear of the following pieces: "a paire of back Ceanes" (presumably shutters),[2] "ye Scene," which had a door in it,[3] "the Arch and the cross peece of stone-worke,"[4] "side releises" (perhaps merely a slip for relieves),[5] "ye two rock peices and ye long peices of sky," and "ye two long bourds of sea."[6] It is significant that there is nothing here that can possibly be taken to mean box sets or even transverse

1. See Appendix A.
2. Works 5/15, January, 1670/1.
3. *Ibid.*, February.
4. Works 5/19, March, 1672/3.
5. Works 5/24, Extraord. Acct.
6. Works 5/21, May, 1673.

wings, and still more so that there are no drop scenes or flats for use just behind the proscenium, as all stage historians would have us believe was the practice in Restoration theatres. But I do not wish to attach too much importance to this: it is perfectly clear that in many ways staging at Court differed materially from that of the public theatres.

As I have said, after the building of the Hall Theatre, there are no references to new scenery until December, 1670, when preparations were begun for the Queen's masque danced in the following February. A set of boscage, consisting of four pairs of wings and a pair of shutters was then painted, as were shutters of a garden, and a scene (perhaps shutters) of a mill with a practicable door. There is also mention of work on the clouds, and the figure of Fame in the proscenium was altered and repainted.[1]

In March, 1672/3, frames for shutters were made, but there is no mention of painting them. The back-cloth, which measured 50 square yards, was painted "like rusticke stone worke," and an arch and cross piece to match, containing $17\frac{1}{2}$ yards of canvas.[2] These I cannot connect with any known production unless, perchance, *The Empress of Morocco* belongs at that date. Two months later, extensive scene-painting was undertaken, in preparation for which the carpenters made a pair of shutters and two relieves. The back-cloth was now converted into sky and sea; there were also "long peices of sky," "two rock peices" (perhaps the relieves), "two long bourds of sea," and "two pedistalls like stone."

1. Works, 5/15.   2. Works 5/19.

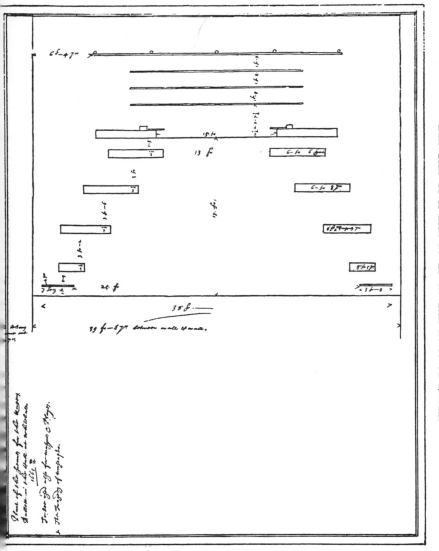

WEBB'S PLAN OF THE STAGE OF THE HALL THEATRE

Again there is no mention of painting shutters, and nothing which can reasonably be taken for them.[1] This scenery may possibly have been for the Italian comedians from Paris, whom Evelyn saw act at Whitehall on 29 May, but as they are known to have brought scenes with them, it does not seem probable.[2]

Except for *Calisto*, no more new scenery is recorded for the Hall Theatre. The Works Accounts include a number of items for repairing the scenes and cleaning them, cleaning the grooves, replacing ropes, etc., including "removing ye Bosketts and Setting vp the Architectures in there places," which I take to be the sets of boscage and stone work.[3] In July, 1687, the younger Streeter, who had succeeded his father in 1679, did 436 yards of distemper in the theatre, but this I think must have been in the auditorium, for the Account states that he also mended the clouds.[4]

For a time, at least, the scenes were in the care of a Scene-Keeper, a servant in the Royal Household, one John Bennett, of whom nothing more is known.[5] The scene-shifting seems as a rule to have been done by workmen detailed by the Office of Works, whose attendance is charged in the Works Accounts.[6] But these apparently do not cover all Court performances, and it is likely that when the changes were but few and simple, they were made by the hirelings of the performing company.

A note on the cost of these scenes may be of interest. The canvas, "ready nailed vp and primed," cost two

1. Works 5/21.   2. See p. 118.
3. Works 5/25. For the repairs, see the documents in Appendix A, *passim*.
4. Works 5/41.   5. See p. 73.   6. See pp. 271–272.

shillings a yard. A pair of shutters cost five or six pounds for painting alone, a set of wings, twenty pounds. Clouds were done by the yard, at two shillings and sixpence. A scene of Denmark House, consisting of a pair of shutters and one pair of wings, cost twelve pounds. Streeter does not seem to have been lucky in collecting his bills. A letter in the *Calendar of Treasury Books* shows that he was not paid for his original work on the Hall Theatre until 1672,[1] and there are several references to money due him, but since they give no details and include work elsewhere, they throw no light on the supply of scenes.

Machines and Properties

It is sometimes difficult to draw any hard and fast line between scenes and machines. In the case of the Hall Theatre, however, the task is simplified by the entire absence of such devices as folding and unfolding clouds, water scenes, etc. The only spectacular effect mentioned in the records is a "glory" for the "Heaven fill'd with Gods and Goddesses" which forms the finale of *Calisto*.[2] I find no reference to the glory either in Miss Campbell's *Scenes and Machines on the English Stage*, or in Miss Welsford's *Court Masque*: Larousse defines *gloire* as "Machine de décoration, suspendue et entourée de nuages, sur laquelle se placent les acteurs qui sont censés descendre du ciel ou y monter." Its English cousin seems to have been rather different, for

1. *Cal. of Treas. Books 1669–72*, p. 1330, under date of 22 October 1672.
2. See p. 211.

it did not descend or ascend, and consisted chiefly in a taffeta covered frame behind which lights were placed, to form an aura for an actor or actors seated in front. The Accounts for it read:

makeing a frame with degrees for lights behind ye glory

ffore ye backe peece for ye glory with a round cutt in it 11 fo^te: ½ by 7 fo^te: ½, ffor a frame for ye taffaty 3 fo^t: & a halfe square

ffor taffaty for ye glory 0.12.0.[1]

The rest of the "Heaven," which, by the way, would be revealed by the simple drawing of shutters, involved nothing more than relieves of clouds and wooden seats for the goddesses. There is no trace of any mechanism or means of motion.

Flying effects, so popular on the Restoration stage, do not seem to have been often attempted at Court. At least, there is only one reference to such devices: in October, 1684, the carpenters fixed "two large balks each 14 fo^t. long to fasten ye flying ropes in the Theatre" and made "two scaffolds there abo^t. 12 fo^t. long a peice and two foote wide."[2]

No details are given of a "Compart seat or Throne for the Queen," made when the theatre was built, but it may have been a machine, for the entry does not relate to her seat on the royal dais. Moreover, preparations for her masque in February, 1670/1, include "Altering the Queens throne & bourding a place for a Chaire to stand on."[3]

1. Works 5/24, Extraord. Acc.
2. Works 5/38.
3. Works 5/7 and 5/15.

One would expect to find traps in the most simply
equipped stage. I infer that there was one in the Cockpit stage, for "v bedmatts to be layd vpon the floore
vnderneath the stage" were provided for that playhouse,[1] and what could they be for if not to soften a
fall? Curiously enough, there were no traps in the Hall
Theatre until March, 1672/3. A hole for one was then
cut, but, although there were several plays in April, the
trap does not seem to have been finished until May.[2]
Alterations in the stage in November, 1674, included
"makeing a new Dore & frame in ye floore of ye said
stage for ye sinkeing vnderneath ye same."[3] This is presumably the trap-door "in the middle of the stage"
which was altered and made good in February, 1678/9.[4]
This is the last mention of traps, but a few years later
there were "seu'all alterations" of an unspecified nature
under the stage.[5]

I have already spoken of the "portalls" and "portholes" set up on the stage in 1675 and 1678.[6] There are
a number of equally mysterious items in the Works
Accounts, which may be properties for particular plays
or, in some cases, equipment for lighting. For example,
in May, 1673, the carpenters set up a table 12 feet long
behind the scenes and made three degrees there — but
whether the degrees were on the table is not clear — a
"wooden horse to stand on the stage" 6 feet high and
6 feet long, and a "flattforme in ye clouds" 5 feet

1. Works 5/2, November, 1661.   2. Works 5/19, 5/21.
3. Works 5/24, Extraord. Acc.
4. Works 5/30.
5. Works 5/35, November, 1682.
6. See pp. 50, 52.

square.[1] The Account for September, 1684, lists "20 fo^t. of Shelves cutting a hole & making a sight in ye doore putting a shelfe vnderneath to slide vp and downe."[2] The last of these strange operations was made in May, 1687, and is described as "enclosing a place within the Scenes for the plays 16 foot long 2 fo^t. ½ high and a flo^r: 3 fo^t: ½ by 3 fo^t. and taking them downe againe."[3]

If the Wardrobe records were kept at all carefully, the Court stage was very scantily furnished. Turkey-work chairs seem to have constituted the staple property. Six had been supplied when the Hall Theatre was built, yet in February, 1666/7, six more, and also a "greate Chayre," all for the stage, were ordered.[4] At the same time, two Spanish tables, six tin candlesticks, six little tin candlesticks for sizes, and two Turkey-work carpets were ordered, and all these I take to be properties, although the candlesticks may have been for a variety of uses behind the scenes.[5] The only other furniture I can find for the stage is a "property Bedd wth a redd Taffata Coverlet & taffata Curtaynes & quilt & one Couch."[6] These, to be sure, are included among supplies for the tiring-room at the Cockpit, but since they were essential for any Restoration repertory, I

1. Works 5/21.   2. Works 5/38.   3. Works 5/41.
4. LC. 5/138, p. 264; Nicoll, p. 342; and see p. 43. Two copies of the bill exist: one describes the half-dozen as 'black Chaires of Turkey worke," the other as "backe chaires," and the great one as a "largc Turkie work chaire Elbowes covered." The six cost £3, the armchair £1.12.0 (LC. 9/271, f. 20; 9/379).
5. The whole order was repeated a year later, on 3 February 1667/8 (LC. 5/62, f. 16; 5/118; 5/139, p. 9; Nicoll, p. 342); and the six Turkey-work chairs appear once more in a warrant of 18 February 1670/1 (LC. 5/63, p. 237).
6. See p. 18.

think they must have been for the stage, and would have been moved to the Hall Theatre when the Cockpit was abandoned. The only property mentioned for a specific play is a large looking-glass borrowed from the Standing Wardrobe at Whitehall for a performance of *Sir Courtly Nice* on 30 April 1690.[1]

Stage Lighting

We still have much to learn about the stage lighting used in Restoration theatres: old prints cannot be relied on to any great extent, and documentary evidence is hard to come by. Happily, the records of the Court stage, while they afford no complete description, still less a technical account of the lighting used, contain a good many scattered details which add materially to our knowledge.

When the Cockpit in Court was rehabilitated, "twenty faire gillt Branches wth three Socketts in each for Candles" were ordered,[2] obviously enough to light both auditorium and stage. But according to the Wardrobe Accounts, the only lights supplied at that time were five pairs of sconces. A little later, however, a more reasonable warrant was issued, for "a Couple of faire brass branches for lights," and these were duly provided, similar ones being rented while the King's were a-making.[3] One is tempted to believe these were for the stage.

In the Hall Theatre, branches seem to have been used only in the auditorium,[4] and indirect lighting for the

1. LC. 5/150, p. 74; Nicoll, p. 319.
2. See p. 15. 3. See p. 16. 4. See p. 46.

stage. Among the numerous sconces and candlesticks ordered for that theatre, it is almost impossible to tell which were for the stage, and the allocation here made is entirely my own interpretation.[1] The Accounts for the building of the theatre make no mention of lights of any sort; the Wardrobe Accounts for that year contain the bi-lingual entry already quoted for black and white plates, wires, lines, Muscovy glass, and pulleys, all apparently for the manufacture of lanterns.[2] I have suggested that these were made with a white plate at the back for a reflector and black ones top and bottom. The pulleys and lines show they were adjustable, and they may have hung in rows behind the proscenium and each of the wings.

Whatever these *"lucernae"* may have been, they were soon abandoned in favour of flat candlesticks backed with tin reflectors. A warrant dated 20 November 1666 calls for "Soe many Tinn plates & after such fashion for the Theater Royall in Whitehall, as M[r] May shall informe you to be necessary for the Sceanes of the s[d] Theater."[3] From the bill we learn that Mr May required one hundred and thirty plates, price £6.10.0, and ten dozen "socketts & panns," price the same.[4] In one of the Tradesmen's Bill Books, for 1667/8, there is a statement of six shillings due for a dozen latten candle-

1. See also pp. 85–86, 88, 157.
2. See p. 43.
3. LC. 5/61, p. 347; 5/138, p. 259. The marginal note gives the name of Hugh May; he had a place in the Office of Works under Denham, and may have been Baptist May's brother. (Wheatley, note on Pepys' entry for 8 June 1665.)
4. LC. 9/375, 9/382. Putting up sockets and plates is mentioned in the Works Accounts for that month (Works 5/9).

sticks "for the Theater att Whitehall on Shroue-tews-day att night."[1] I do not know whether these were for the stage; the occasion was probably the performance of Mrs Phillips' *Horace*, with "a masque and antique dance" between each act.[2]

A new supply of the customary sockets and pans for the masque of February, 1670/1, was supplemented by what I take to be several kinds of sconces, called "yᵉ largest double scollops," "new fashion scollops," and "ball scollops."[3] The N. E. D. knows nothing of scollops in this sense; Professor Richardson suggests a flat candlestick with a shell-shaped reflector. The same Account includes three dozen "Walers." The Clerk of the Works might well consider this a satisfactory rendering of "wallers," if such a word was in use for wall lights, but I think they must have been lamps: the bill includes funnels and there is an accompanying one for oil and "Cotton to fill yᵉ Lamps"; and at this same date, as I shall presently show, footlights, for which lamps were regularly used instead of candles, were instituted in the Hall Theatre.

No less than ninety-six tin sconces and tin plates for reflectors were supplied for the next masque, *Calisto*.[4] These and candlesticks were nailed to the backs of the scenes and set on frames behind them. The description of the work runs:

makeing degrees behind yᵉ backe clouds for yᵉ setting of lights there boarding with slitt deales behind yᵉ vpper sceanes for yᵉ putting vp of sconces & Candlestickes, . . . lineing yᵉ backes of yᵉ shutters for

---

1. LC. 9/271, f. 67.
2. See pp. 128–129.
3. Works 5/17, April, 1671.
4. See pp. 213–214.

ye putting vp of lights, & nayleing ye sconces & Candlestickes to ye backes of ye clouds, makeing a frame with degrees for lights behind ye glory.[1]

Charles' Household did not include a Fire Inspector.

I have already mentioned footlights, and on this important feature of stage lighting the Accounts are fairly satisfactory. In the list of preparations for the masque of 1670/1 is the item: "making a trough at ye foote of the stage for lights to stand in."[2] This may, of course, have been a temporary arrangement for that performance, but although the evidence is slight and inconclusive, I incline to think footlights became forthwith permanent. There is no further mention of them, although they would surely have been essential for *Calisto*, until June, 1675. Then, when the theatre was being overhauled for the Franco-Italian season, "two ledges of bourds" were put up "in ye throughs [*sic*] where the Lamps were sett."[3] The next entry again refers to lamps: a long trough for them was placed at the foot of the stage in February, 1678/9.[4] There seems to be no reason for a new trough at this time, and the making of one may indicate that footlights had been temporarily abandoned. After this, there is no mention of them for a long time, but at this period there were few plays at Court. In September, 1684, the carpenters set up "25 fo^t. of roofing before the Stage to set candles in."[5] Twenty-five feet was the approximate width of the proscenium opening, and roofing appears to be a mere slip for troughing. The entry is of interest as the only

1. Works 5/24, Extraord. Acc.
2. Works 5/15.   3. Works 5/25.
4. Works 5/30.   5. Works 5/38.

instance of candles being used for footlights instead of lamps.

There is one more reference to footlights which, I think, establishes them as a regular piece of stage equipment during the latter part of the century. In November, 1689, the carpenters were engaged in removing the dancing floor and fitting the theatre for a play. The whole entry is obviously a statement of routine work, and it includes "placing the boxes for the Lamps at the end of the Stage next the Pitt."[1] (I doubt whether "boxes" has any special significance: it probably was used to denote a trough made in sections for ease in handling.) At about this time, there are also several items for lamps for the theatre in the Lord Steward's Accounts: although their use is not stated, they were doubtless for footlights.[2]

As I have already said, there are a number of obscure items in the Works Accounts which may or may not have something to do with lighting, and there are other entries too vague to admit of such interpretation. For example, to return once more to the masque of 1670/1, one bit of work is described as "making a place w^{th}: bourds for lights to stand on on both sides."[3] One cannot even be sure that both sides of the stage are meant, still less what kind of "place" was made. Again, "a table behinde ye Ceanes 12 foote long & . . . iij degrees there," and a "wooden horse to stand on y^e stage vj foote high & vj foote long," made in May, 1673,[4] must be placed in the same category, along with 20 feet of

1. Works 5/43.   2. See p. 98.
3. Works 5/15.   4. Works 5/21.

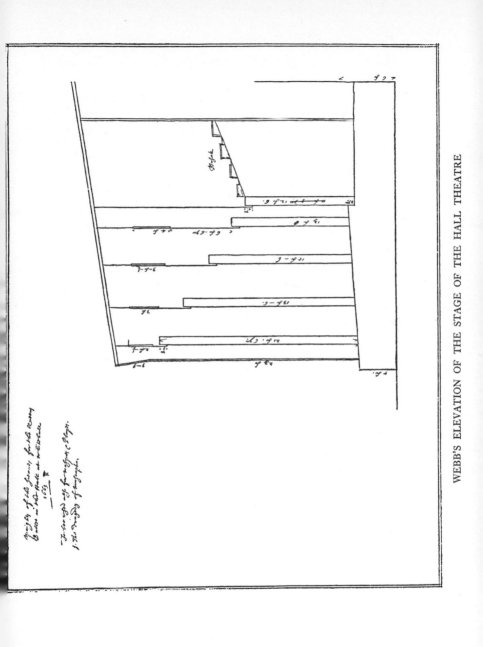

WEBB'S ELEVATION OF THE STAGE OF THE HALL THEATRE

shelves mentioned immediately after the footlights in the Account for September, 1684.[1]

The chandlery supplied for the Hall Theatre has been discussed in my account of the Lord Steward's share in Court production.[2] As a rule, it is difficult to tell how much of the wax supplied was for the stage, but for 1687 there are a couple of detailed statements which specify for the scenes ten dozen of yellow wax lights, a dozen torches, and twelve pounds of tallow lights, with an additional dozen of yellow wax lights and one pound of tallow for the musicians playing among the scenes.[3] The stage lighting was at least sometimes looked after by workmen from the Office of Works, and Glover's bill for oil suggests that he too had some responsibility for it.[4]

Music

The King's Household boasted a large staff of musicians, among whom were to be found many of the best known singers, players, and composers of the day. On the whole, although they regularly provided the music for Court plays, there is very little in contemporary records about their share in productions at Whitehall, and most of the references to them have already been quoted in other connections. Nor can I undertake to discuss Restoration theatre music as a chapter in the

1. Works 5/38.   2. See pp. 91–98.   3. See p. 97, note 3.
4. See pp. 77–78. An interesting bill for special lights for a ball in October or November, 1689, will be found in the Appendix, p. 268. For this occasion, "a place above the Sceens to sett the Lamps on with 3 Steps to it" was made. (Works 5/43.) At this time there were, somewhere in the theatre, "two Christall Branches," which were borrowed by Princess Anne on 20 November (LC. 5/149, p. 329).

history of musical art. But it may be useful to gather into one place what little I have found relating to music as one element in the Court stage.

The music for ordinary plays at Court was furnished by the King's band of twenty-four violinists, headed by a master who was also a composer. This post, after the Restoration, was held successively by Nicholas Lanier, Louis Grabut, Nicholas Staggins, and John Eccles. Unfortunately, we know very little about the musicians' share in a performance apart from the incidental songs, dances, and masques which were conspicuous features of many Restoration plays. Presumably here as in the public theatre there was "curtain music," but inter-act music is more debatable. A few orders for the violins to attend regularly at Court plays and to practise for particular performances have already been quoted,[1] as well as a description of the extraordinary garments in which Charles for some years persisted in clothing them.[2] Apparently they were sometimes called upon to provide special entertainments, if I am right in so interpreting a phrase, "for Mr Abell to represent his Musick," in a warrant for alterations in the theatre, but this may have been a concert pure and simple.[3]

It seems likely that other musicians in the Household sometimes performed at plays. At the very first play at the Cockpit in Court, as Pepys tells us, Charles "did put a great affront upon Singleton's musique, he bidding them stop and bade the French musique play, which, my Lord says, do much outdo all ours."[4] There is no

1. See pp. 99–100.   2. See pp. 41, 87.   3. See p. 53.
4. Pepys, under date of 20 November 1660.

reason to suppose that this attendance of the French musicians was a unique occurrence. The earliest list of them that I know of gives 19 October 1663 as the date on which they were sworn in, and names Ferdinand de Florence, Claude des Granges, Elenor Guigaut,[1] Nicholas Fleuri, Guillaume Sautre, and Jean de la Volee.[2] But they may have been established soon after the Restoration: des Granges, at least, was in England in June, 1660, for he then presented to Charles a most delightful set of very bad verses carefully preserved among the State Papers.

> I'ay sceu, que Vostre Majesté,
> Ouurant les yeux de sa bonté
> Sur mon infortune pressante —;
> À promis presque sur sa foy —
> À Celuy, qui parloit pour moy —
> La premiere place vaccante:
>
> Mais les Muses, comme Apollon
> Sont plus legeres qu'vn ballon,
> Saute parfois de subsistance,
> Et moy, qui les suit pas à pas,
> Je me voy proche du trepas
> A force d'estre en Indigence.
>
> En verite ie n'en puis plus
> Estant de tous membres perclus
> À l'exclusion de ma langue,
> Dont Dieu, prenant pitié de moy,
> Ne m'a pas despourueu, Ie croy,
> Pour vous faire cette harangue.
>
> Grand Roy, Cher fauory de Dieu,
> Qui participez en ce lieu,
> De tous les Dons de la Nature;

---

1. From the writing, it might be Guigant, Gingant, *etc.*
2. LC. 3/26, p. 76.

Faites chercher dans vos tresors
Quelque remede pour mon corps,
Pour en oster la pourriture: —

Ainsy me sortant des abois,
Vous esprouuerez que ma voix
Nous pourra tous deux satisfaire —;
Vous, Sire en m'entendant chanter
Et moy, vous faisant me compter
De ce qu'icy bas fait tout faire: —

Sinon Ie La Supplie au moins,
Pour m'exempter de quelque soins.
Qui font redoubler mon caprice,
Qu'Elle me donne en attendant
Ce qu'Icy l'on nomme vn Warrant
Qui me iustifie en Seruice
                    Desgranges [1]

The band of violins was, of course, supplemented for operas and masques. For example, for the Queen's masque for 1670/1, additional seats were arranged for the Queen's music and the Italian music.[2] One cannot be sure, but the Italians may have been the singers whom Pepys heard on 16 February 1666/7. They had been described to him by Tom Killigrew a few days before, as gathered from several courts of Europe, at a salary of £200 apiece, in place of the four "ridiculous gundilows" presented to Charles by the Doge of Venice. The troupe comprised Signor Vincentio, the master-composer, and six others, including a woman (who was not to be kissed) and two eunuchs.[3] This description is strikingly like "An Establishm[t] of his Ma[ts] Italian Musicke" to be found in a volume of State Papers

1. SP. 29/1, no. 71.   2. See p. 47.
3. Pepys, 12 February 1666/7.

dated 1662 with a query. These two documents, which appear to be rough drafts only, have not, I believe, been printed, and I therefore give them *in extenso*.

La maniera che usa p tutte Le corti si da ordinariamente cinquanta pezza p uno per il Viaggio.
La Donna Costera d'auuantaggio p che si sa le comodità che uogliono.
Per la prouisione non uorranno meno che in germania che sono due cento pezze l'Anno per uno.
La donna uorra trecento pezzè — 300
Il castrato due cento pezze — 200
E se Sᵃ. Mᵃ. uolesse hauere ancora questi accio fosse tutto finito il concerto che se ne potrebbe seruire in Cãmera et in teatro sarebbe bisogno.

Contralto 200
Tenore 200
Basso 200
Il poeta che e' il principale 200

Cher per queste sei persone inportarebbe L'Anno mille e trecento pezze

In quanto a noi sua m . facci come li piace: [1]

yᵉ yearly Saleryes & Entertainmᵗ. of An Establishmᵗ of his Maᵗˢ Italian Musicke.

	li	s.	d.
One Contralto	200.	0.	0.
One Tenore	200.	0.	0.
One Basso	200.	0.	0.
The Poete	200.	0.	0.
The Woman	300.	0.	0.
The Eunuch	200.	0.	0.
Seigʳ. Vincenzo	200.	0.	0.
His Brother	200.	0.	0.
	1700.	0.	0. [2]

1. SP. 29/66, no. 30. Endorsed "Ital. Musicke."
2. *Ibid.*, no. 31. Endorsed "Italian Musicke."

To build this house of cards one story higher, I suggest that Pepys' Vincentio and the Signor Vincenzo here named are the same as one Vencenso Albrigi, who appears in a warrant from the Lord Chamberlain to the Master of the Jewel House, dated 5 May 1668. The King thereby ordered three chains and medals of gold, worth £30 apiece, for "Segnier Vencenso Albrigi Don Bartholomew Albrigi & Leonora Albrigi," three Italian musicians.[1] This was followed on 27 June by a warrant for two medals, value £36, for "The two Italian Musitians," while a gold chain and medal worth £40 was ordered for Matteo Bataglio, Italian musician, as a gift from His Majesty on 8 July 1670.[2]

To return to the Hall Theatre: for masques, professional singers were engaged from the patent theatres, and the Gentlemen of the Chapel Royal were also called upon. The details of their services for *Calisto* will be given later.[3]

One of the most vexed questions in regard to Restoration theatre music is where the musicians were placed. Court practice cannot be taken to prove anything for the public stage, but it is some help to know what was done at Whitehall. Webb's plans for remodelling the Cockpit show a music-room above the central arch of the Palladian façade. In November, 1660, among other works, the carpenters made "two ptitions in the gallery there for the musick and players."[4] This, it seems to me, probably refers to the spectators' gallery, the ends of

1. LC. 5/12, p. 137.
2. *Ibid.*, pp. 138, 160.
3. See pp. 197, 198–199. For payments to Staggins see pp. 122, 222.
4. See p. 14.

which next the stage were converted into the equivalent of proscenium balconies or windows.

In the Hall Theatre there was a bewildering variety of music-seats. One of the *Mustapha* plans shows tiers of seats above the relieves, and these I believe remained in use until the theatre was destroyed, for repairs in November, 1693, included "mending the boards above the Scenes and the floore where the Musick playes."[1] These seats could be concealed by "oval shutters," presumably representing clouds, for they are sometimes called "yᵉ Musick seate in yᵉ Clowds."[2]

I have already spoken of the "room for yᵉ Italian musitions" and the place made at the front of the stage for the Queen's music.[3] The location of the former is not given; the latter was cut out of the stage itself and was, I feel sure, a temporary arrangement. For *Calisto*, the music, or part of it, was established in its modern position in the pit. When the theatre was being restored to its normal shape after a ball in January, 1676/7, the workmen put up "yᵉ Rayle for yᵉ Musicke Cross yᵉ pitt into there places agayne."[4] Thereafter, part of these seats had to be taken down when the dancing floor was laid; mention of them is sometimes made in this connection, but frequently the details of these routine alterations are not given.[5] The seats seem to have been forms, and had desk-boards for the music books, rather like pews.

There was also a place for the music in the gallery,

1. Works 5/46.   2. See p. 40 and Works 5/15.
3. See p. 47 and Works 5/27.
4. See p. 204 and Works 5/27.   5. Works 5/28 and 5/27.

where two rails for them and "2 flapps . . . to keep the
People from the Musickque roome there" were set up
in February, 1678/9.[1] The musicians may have been
moved there when the extension of the King's dais considerably lessened the pit.[2] Boards which were put up
in November, 1673, "to keep people out of the Musick,"
may have been either in the gallery or the pit,[3] but at
least show that the music-seat in the clouds was not the
only one then in use. It is, on the whole, fairly impossible to tell how many of these arrangements were purely
temporary and devised to meet the exigencies of some
particular play or opera. The one indisputable fact is
that the placing of the music in the Court theatre was
a matter of experiment, including adaptations of the
Elizabethan position as well as the modern location.

Some Notes on Finance

A good many references have been made to prices of
various things supplied for the Court stage, but it is
difficult to bring them together into an orderly account
of its finances. This is principally due to the fact that
the items are scattered through so many different sets
of books: as we have seen, the Revels Office had lost
almost all its quondam power, and many departments
of the Royal Household were involved in the maintenance of the Court theatre. Nor was Charles the one to
underline his extravagances by having special accounts
compiled.

1. See p. 261.   2. See p. 51.   3. Works 5/46.

First there are the Accounts of the Office of Works, kept in such a way that the amount spent on the theatres can only be ascertained in the rare cases where there are Extraordinary Accounts. Other expenses are to be found in the detailed Accounts of the Great Wardrobe, the Revels Office, the Lord Steward's Department, and the Treasurer of the Chamber; and for payments for plays and masquing costumes, we must add the Secret Service Accounts and those of the Master of the Robes. Few of these series are complete, and furthermore, it is often impossible to recognise and disentangle the stage items with any certainty. In the face of these difficulties, it has seemed best to give representative prices whenever feasible, without attempting a summary or even collecting a vast and unwieldy mass of details in one place.

A few points, however, can and should be mentioned. The Works Account for the building of the Hall Theatre comes to £737.11.2$\frac{1}{4}$;[1] the items in the Wardrobe Accounts which I take to represent its original equipment total £465.11.8. The alterations made by the Office of Works for *Calisto* are charged at £253.14.2$\frac{1}{4}$.[2] The total expense for this masque cannot be determined, but the extant accounts will be summarized later.[3] The Revels Office probably continued, as it did for the first decade after the Restoration, to draw some £260 a year, and the Yeoman of the Revels and the Theatre-Keeper had their independent fees amounting to some £76 annually, when paid.[4]

---

1. Works 5/7, Extraord. Acct.   2. E. 351/3288.
3. See p. 226.   4. See pp. 81, 273–277.

One important class of payments, namely for the plays themselves, has not yet been mentioned. £20 was the usual "reward" for a play at Court, but once at least the fee was halved, while toward the end of the century, there are several payments of £25 which may be for Court performances. The ordinary procedure was payment by the Treasurer of the Chamber on warrant from the Lord Chamberlain. Many of these warrants cover plays both at Court and before Royalty in the public theatres over long periods of time, but there are also a number of warrants for one or two plays, frequently drawn to one member of the Company as assignee for the rest. Mrs Barry's name appears in most of them, and Professor Nicoll has misinterpreted these as gifts to her.[1] But several of them state definitely that the money has been assigned to her by the rest of the actors, and the explanation seems to be simply that she was *persona grata* to some one at Court who could secure prompt remittance. Even a warrant labelled "Mrs Barry 25^li for playing in ye old Batchell^r" is shown by the corresponding entry in the Accounts of the Treasurer of the Chamber to have been payment for the Company.[2] This surely is also the explanation of another warrant which has mightily perturbed stage historians, one for payment of £20 to John Rhodes for a performance of *Ignoramus*.[3]

I have summarised the warrants and the corresponding items in the Chamber Accounts in an appendix.[4]

1. Nicoll, p. 299.
2. LC. 5/151, p. 352; Nicoll, p. 319. See below.
3. Nicoll, p. 278; Hotson, p. 214. See p. 294.
4. See pp. 294–299.

The list is not complete, for some of the Warrant Books and Accounts are missing, but it is complete enough to show that payment was slow and the book-keeper not infallible. Its implications lend colour to some lines in a *Prologue to "The Sad Shepherd" Spoken by Mr Port-lock:*[1]

> . . . . . they for theyr comeing in
> Did nothing pay, and sure I am the Crew
> Neither of Davenant nor Tom Killegrew
> E're played for nothing, 'less sometymes at Court
> Wether they goe to make the King some sport.

Cibber, too, throws some interesting light on the subject. He says that in Charles' reign,

The King had his Comedians at *Windsor*, but upon a particular Establishment; for tho' they acted in St. *George*'s Hall, within the Royal Palace, yet (as I have been inform'd by an Eye-witness) they were permitted to take Money at the Door of every Spectator; whether this was an Indulgence, in Conscience I cannot say; but it was a common Report among the principal Actors, when I first came into the *Theatre-Royal*, in 1690, that there was then due to the Company from that Court about One Thousand Five Hundred Pounds for Plays commanded, &c. and yet it was the general Complaint, in that Prince's Reign, that he paid too much Ready-money for his Pleasures: But these Assertions I only give as I received them, without being answerable for their Reality.[2]

The only rewards to playwrights recorded by the Lord Chamberlain and the Treasurer of the Chamber were given to John Crowne by James, for *Sir Courtly Nice* in January, 1687/8, and for *Darius King of Persia* in May, 1688.[3]

1. B. M. Sloane Ms. 1009, f. 373.
2. Cibber, II, 210.
3. LC. 5/148, pp. 64, 195; Nicoll, p. 318; AO. 1/406/133.

The musicians presumably were not entitled to special remuneration for plays. There is only one entry of such payment, a warrant for seven of Princess Anne's musicians who were borrowed for a play on the King's birthday.[1] There are, however, a couple of warrants to pay Staggins for writing music for Scaramouche and for *Calisto*, but these were given elsewhere.[2]

Taken collectively, the data presented in the course of this study seem to indicate pretty clearly that the Court stage was at its height during the first fifteen years of the period, — or, at least, that most money was spent on it during those years, — that James ordered plays aplenty but spent little on the theatre or production, and that William spent very little on anything. But so far as Charles' reign is concerned, I doubt whether any official records would reveal the whole truth. There must have been many payments to foreign actors, there must have been more scenery, and there may have been more plays by the Patent Companies. And I do not think the answer is far to seek: after the treaty of Dover in 1670, the King had plenty of French gold, but Bab May and Will Chiffinch were careful to leave no account books to posterity. The money in the Privy Purse was spent as Charles — and his mistresses — pleased, and no one can question the inclusion of the stage among their chief pleasures.

1. LC. 5/152, p. 200; 5/153, p. 97.
2. See pp. 122, 220–221, 222.

PART III

Calisto

III

CALISTO

AFTER discussion of so much detail, there is obvious need to recapitulate, and it seems as if the mass of material here presented can best be brought into focus by describing a single Court play. For this purpose I have chosen the masque *Calisto*, which was performed in the Hall Theatre in 1675, and I propose first to give a general account of the production and then to discuss more fully its various aspects.

But first, I must explain the reasons for my choice. Although *Calisto* is a masque, so called, and all the chief parts were taken by amateurs, it is more typical than appears at a glance. It is not really a masque at all, but a play with an operatic induction and *intermedii*. In structure it closely resembles the Restoration opera, while the interpolated songs and dances point toward the inter-act variety of the sixteen-nineties and at the same time link *Calisto* with the pastorals dear to Henrietta Maria. Then too, these *intermedii* bring singers and dancers from the public stage into the production, so that it represents both amateur and professional talent. Furthermore, so far as I can judge, *Calisto* practically marks the culmination of the Court stage. It was acted when the Hall Theatre was at its best, before plots and enforced economy curbed Charles' taste, and immediately before a period when French and Italian comedians almost monopolised the Court theatre. It is true that for a year or two after the accession of James, there were many plays at Whitehall, and that *Albion and Albanius* and *Cinthia and Endimion* were written expressly for Court performance although they failed to achieve it, but the fact remains that no other play, even among those written, more or less, by command, was produced so magnificently and so successfully.

And finally, with the best will in the world, I could not describe any other performance so fully, for chance has preserved more documents pertaining to *Calisto* than can be assembled for any other play or masque, and while they fail to mention many things which we should like to know, they supply extraordinarily clear and interesting information on almost all phases of production. Nor are they valuable only to the stage historian: there is much to be learned from them of tradesmen and their wares, and the prices of all sorts of commodities; the publication of the text throws some light on the control of the press; the musical antiquary will be interested in the manuscript copies of Staggins' songs and the lists of musicians; and above all, for him who cares to see it, Charles' Court and the Royal Household here live and breathe again, going about their daily tasks and nightly pleasures.

I have already mentioned Charles' interest in masques and his desire to copy the favourite form of divertisement at the Court of Le Roi Soleil, and have ventured the assertion that the "Magna Saltatio" of 1670/1 was a masque.[1] I have found no account of the circum-

1. See pp. 136, 138-139.

stances which led to the decision to put on another in
the winter of 1674–75, but it seems reasonable to suppose that gossip drifting over from Paris was the first if
not the immediate cause, and that the fondness for
dancing and theatricals already displayed by James'
two daughters had a good deal to do with it.[1] At all
events, a masque was decided upon. The next step was
to get it written, and the choice of an author at once
stirred up the literary feud between Dryden and Rochester. Dryden, as poet-laureate, might well expect to have
the writing of Court entertainments, as Jonson and
Davenant had before him, but Rochester was determined to humiliate him and at the same time snub
Settle, who was thinking far too well of himself since
the success of *The Empress of Morocco*.[2] It doubtless
appealed to Rochester's sense of humour to secure the
coveted privilege for a young man who had nothing
to his credit but three bad tragedies, and he apparently
found no difficulty in persuading the Duchess of York
to lay her commands on John Crowne.[3]

This must have happened early in the autumn of
1674, close upon the heels of the production of Crowne's
Andromache at Dorset Garden.[4] With his head full of
the classics, he made a hasty and ill-advised choice of
the myth of Calisto and set to work. The result, despite
some rather clever manipulation of the story, was about

1. See p. 130.
2. For the ramifications of the quarrel, see Dryden's *Works*, I, 152–175.
3. See p. 186.
4. For an account of Crowne and his dramatic works, see A. F. White, *John
   Crowne: His Life and Dramatic Works. A Bibliography of . . . John Crowne*
   was published by G. P. Winship in 1922.

as unsuitable for performance by the little Princesses as can be imagined, but it seems to have been found acceptable, and rehearsals were begun. The principal parts were taken by Princess Mary, Princess Anne, the Countess of Sussex, Lady Henrietta Wentworth, Lady Mary Mordaunt, Margaret Blagge, and Sarah Jennings, the future Duchess of Marlborough. These ladies were, according to tradition, rehearsed by Thomas Betterton, while his wife was called on to teach the Princesses their parts.[1]

Meantime, the autumn had, in some unaccountable manner, come and gone, and it was the end of November before regular rehearsals three times a week were begun.[2] But the production had already assumed such importance that special alterations were being made by Wren in the Hall Theatre, new scenery was being painted by Robert Streeter, and the tailors were reckoning the silks for the costumes by the hundred yards. All this took time. It must soon have become apparent that the production could not be put on before Christmas, and the natural thing to do was to postpone it until Shrovetide, the traditional season for masques.

The exact dates of the performances are difficult to fix, and some of the evidence misleading. Evelyn says he attended a "comedy" at Court on 15 December, and a "repetition of the Pastoral" on 22 December. From the context there can be no doubt that he refers to

---

1. Cibber, II, 336; E. Gosse, *Seventeenth Century Studies*, p. 308. I know of no justification for the statement in Hayward, *op. cit.*, that Rochester "is known to have produced . . . *Calisto*."
2. See p. 205.

Calisto, but he is certainly wrong in the dates.[1] All the bills and the Works Accounts show that the costumes and theatre were not ready until February, and that there was a revival of the piece several months later. Crowne, in his preface, says it was rewritten between the second and third "Representations," and was, in all, "Rehearsed and Acted" twenty or thirty times. Weighing the evidence, I believe the clue to the solution of the problem is to be found in the words "repetition," which certainly means a rehearsal, and "representation" or performance. I suggest that Evelyn attended two rehearsals in December (which were probably frequented by the Court) and made a note of the fact. When he came to write up his diary, perhaps several months later, he confused this memorandum with the account of the real performance, which he also attended, but without recording the date. Crowne's statement is equally confusing, because as it stands in its context it implies that most of the twenty or thirty times came after the revision, but I think this can be explained as indicating a series of performances of the second version.

There must have been performances on Shrove Monday and Tuesday, 15 and 16 February, for on the fifteenth, the Yeoman of the Revels was ordered to receive the costumes from the Great Wardrobe,[2] and William Montague, in a letter written on 4 March, complained that his wife was ill of a cold caught at the

1. The *Introduction* to Bray's edition of the Diary states it was compiled by Evelyn from original memoranda. This readily accounts for the interpolation of later information, the telescoping of two entries on one subject, and so forth.
2. See p. 219, note 2.

Court masque or the Lent Sermons.[1] If there was only one performance later, it must have been in June, for the Creditor (which includes rehearsals) covers April, May, and June;[2] but new costumes were ready for 23 April[3] — further evidence, I think, that there were several public "representations" at that time.

It is not difficult to visualise the Hall Theatre as it appeared on those nights. From the ceiling of sky-blue calico to the matted benches of the pit, it had been swept and garnished. Probably the odour of fresh paint still lingered. The great branches were lit with scores of wax lights, to the babel of voices was added the tuning of violins, before the expectant eyes of the audience hung a new curtain, striped red, white, and blue, gently swaying in the draught which Wren had never succeeded in eliminating. The pit, the degrees around the walls, the galleries, were crowded with the Court in its bravest array and such mere people as contrived to get in. Pepys had once attended a Court ball there, for which with great difficulty he got up into the "loft," and was duly impressed by the "glorious sight" of La Belle Stewart and the other fine ladies,[4] and on such an occasion as this, seats must have been taken hours in advance.[5] The management of the audience had, indeed, given the Lord Chamberlain much food for thought, which finally crystallised in the following regulations:

The Lord Chamberlaynes Orders & directions for the maske
That a Guard be placed on the Guard Chamb[r] stayres to hinder a Crowde of Ordinary People from coming into the Guard Chamber

---

1. Hist. Mss., *Report on Mss. of the Duke of Buccleugh and Queensberry*, I, 321.   2. See p. 207.   3. LC. 9/274, p. 322.
4. 15 November 1666.   5. See p. 139.

That none but the Actors and theire Necessary attendants be permitted to come in at the backe doore according to a list signed by mee with the Musick & officers to attend ye Sceenes Mr Harris hath the list.

That the Privy Gallery doores be stocklocked & other entryes into the House be kept Shutt

That the Barricadoes be sett vp as vsuall

That none but Noblemen & Privy Councellors come into the Pitt on the left hand & ye seats on that side of ye Pitt for Gentlemen of good quality

That ye right hand of ye Pitt be kept for Noble Weomen Privy Councellors wives & on the side for Ladyes of good quality Except the places on ye right hand the Lord Chamberlaynes Box for the attendants on the Dukes Children

That Convenient places be kept in the pitt for Dressers & Maydes of Hono^r

That none but Ladyes of ye Bedchamber doe sitt on the step at the Kings feete

That the keyes of ye Chappell Chamber be deliuered to Mr Vice Chamb^rlayne to bring in Persons of quality that way as he shall see cause

That the Officers of the Guard and Gentlemen Vshers doe attend Mr Vice Chamb^rlaynes Orders & directions

That the Lord Steward & Lord Chamb^rlaynes Old boxes be for Ambassadors & Straungers of Quality

That Mr Vice Chamb^rlayne have the Box next the Lord Chamberlaynes New Box

That the New Box over against the Lord Chamb^rlaynes new one be for ye Lord Steward & in his absence for Mr Treasurer & Mr Comptroller

That the next box to that be for ye Officers of ye Greene cloth

That Mr Vice Chamberlaynes & Lord Newports Old boxes be for Persons of good quality as occasion shalbe

That in the Gallery be placed Gentlemen & Weomen of Lesser quality

A Guard to be placed at ye Back doore And also to hinder Persons from comeing betweene the Sceenes that are not Actors.[1]

---

1. LC. 5/141, p. 549; Nicoll, p. 321.

While the Gentlemen Ushers were struggling to carry out these instructions and preserve some degree of order, far worse confusion reigned behind the scenes. Probably there was not very much happening on the stage itself: the green baize had been laid and the scenes of Somerset House set in place some time before; there were only the candles to be lit and men stationed ready to draw the shutters. But the tiring-rooms were another matter. There were approximately sixty people to be dressed, most of them in costumes that of themselves took up a good deal of space. Moreover, it required four women to dress a princess and two to four for a lady or maid of honour, and what with carpenters, musicians, officers of the Revels, the Works, the Chandry, and the Great Wardrobe, the total number of people to be admitted behind the scenes amounted to one hundred and seventy-nine.[1] One wonders in vain how anyone could move. Yet they contrived to set out the refreshments of bread, beer, and wine provided by the Lord Steward, and Margaret Blagge found a quiet corner to which to retire with a book of devotion.[2]

When the curtain finally rose, John Evelyn was among those who had managed to get in, perhaps even among the "Persons of good quality" who were shown into the Vice-Chamberlain's old box. But his account of the performance is disappointingly brief and vague. He noticed that the ladies were "all covered with jewels," but seems to have been singularly indifferent to the "rich habits" and the glories of a Temple of

1. *Ibid.*, p. 546; Nicoll, *loc. cit.* See p. 199, note 4.
2. Evelyn, *Godolphin*, p. 98.

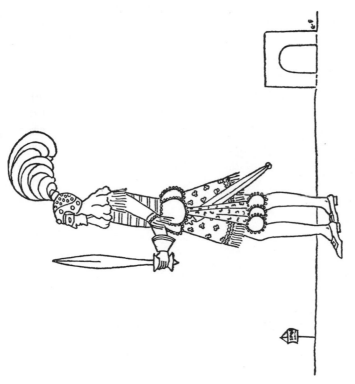

A ROMAN HABIT

Fame which appeared in the clouds. To tell the truth, he had eyes for only one performer, his "excellent creature," Margaret Blagge, who played Diana. To him, hers was the principal part, which she acted to admiration,[1] and she seemed "a Saint in Glory, abstracting her from the Stage."[2] Yet Mrs Knight, whom Evelyn himself had called incomparable, was singing, French dancers performed entry after entry, as Basques, Winds, Satyrs, or Africans, the whole gaudy company filled the stage for the finale, Jupiter offered the Princesses "the small dominion of a star," and then withdrew the gift in order that England might still benefit by their presence.

It was all over, and Mrs Blagge, virtuous and unlucky, had lost a jewel valued at £80, lent to her by the Countess of Suffolk to help make up the "near £20,000 worth" which completed her costume as Diana. The Duke of York, to his credit be it remembered, made good the loss, and Evelyn, to whom we owe the story, philosophically remarked, "The press was so great, it is a wonder she lost no more."[3] The Court withdrew to a magnificent supper,[4] the crowd made its way home as best it could. Nothing remained but to pay the bills and clean the theatre.

The Libretto

Crowne himself tells us a good deal about the libretto, the "cold lean Carkass of the entertainment," as he calls it in his preface. The burden of this and the dedication

---

1. Evelyn's Diary, 15 December 1674.
2. Evelyn, *Godolphin*, p. 97.   3. Diary, 22 December.
4. Evelyn, *Godolphin*, p. 100.

to Princess Mary is that, poor poet as he is, he could have done much better had he had time to mature his conceptions. He had suddenly received a "Powerful Command" to prepare an entertainment — he never calls it a masque, although the word is used on the title-page — which was to be written, rehearsed, and performed in less time than should have been devoted to the writing. And in accordance with his instructions, although the performance was considerably postponed, he finished his part within a month.

The "Powerful Command" was probably laid upon him by Mary of Modena, then Duchess of York, but on this point, authorities differ. Langbaine says that the masque was written at the command of William's Queen when she was Princess; the *Biographia Dramatica* under *Calisto*, at command of the Duchess of York, but under *Crowne*, of Queen Mary.[1] The masque is dedicated to the Princess, but had she herself ordered it, Crowne would surely have said so, and on the whole, it seems likely that the Duchess of York would act on behalf of her small step-daughters.

This command, wherever it originated, brought with it certain restrictions as to the number of characters and the dances or entries,[2] but Crowne's greatest difficulty was of his own making, for he chose the story of Jupiter's love for Calisto, one of Diana's nymphs, whom he ravished and then turned into a bear, and who later escaped death at her son's hands only by being translated to a

1. Langbaine, 1691, p. 92. Later writers have asserted it was Charles' Queen, but this is a misinterpretation; Langbaine says "the present Queen."   2. See pp. 193, 225.

star.[1] Let Crowne describe his problem in his own words:

Next, for my Subject, it was not, I confess, imposed upon me by Command, but it was for want of time to find a better: For I had but some few hours allow'd me to choose one. And as Men who do things in haste, have commonly ill Fortune, as well as ill Conduct; I resolving to choose the first tolerable Story I could meet with, unhappily encountered this, where . . . I involved my self, before I was aware, in a difficulty greater than the invention of the Philosophers Stone, . . . to write a clean, decent, and inoffensive Play, on the Story of a Rape, so that I was engaged in this Dilemma, either wholly to deviate from my Story, and so my Story would be no Story, or by keeping to it, write what would be unfit for Princesses and Ladies to speak, and a Court to hear. That which tempted me into so great a Labyrinth, was the fair and beautiful Image that stood at the Portall, I mean the exact and perfect Character of Chastity, in the person of Calisto. . . . [2]

Needless to say, he chose to alter the story, and thereby evolved a theme not dissimilar to *Comus*, of which he seems to have been totally unaware. In the new version, Jupiter is not only unsuccessful in his attempts on Calisto, but is so moved by her purity that he comes to her rescue when she is accused by Juno, and finally offers her and her sister Nyphe the sovereignty of a star. Substance is lent to this rather tenuous plot by the invention of Psecas, a jealous nymph, and Nyphe, sister to Calisto, and the introduction of Mercury as Psecas' lover, who to please her brings about most of the entanglement, but in the end is responsible for a happy solution. Crowne could have ended his story quite

1. Crowne derives the story from Ovid's *Metamorphoses*, Bk. ii, fables 5 and 6.
2. *Calisto, or the chast Nymph*, 1675, Sig. a1ᵛ.

nicely at this point, but he was instructed to arrange a final entry of Africans. To introduce them, he brings on two women seeking the beauty Phaeton had taken from them; this they find, of course, in Calisto's and Nyphe's cheeks and are content to leave it there. This is ingenious, but overweights the end.

Naturally, compliment to the King and Queen had to be brought in somewhere, but Crowne saved his fable from further encroachment by relegating the adulation to the prologue and epilogue.[1] The former ends with homage to "The God and Goddess . . . of this bless'd Isle," and Jupiter concludes the latter, turning to the King and Queen, with the lines:

> There are the Powers to whom we sacrifice,
> In whose great Presence I may well allow
> To lay aside my useless Godhead now.
> You, Sir, such blessings to the World dispence,
> We scarce perceive the use of Providence.
> And since Your Rule such joy to all procures,
> All should contribute all they can to Yours.
> Wit by Your Smiles a lustre do's maintain,
> And Beauty keeps a long and happy Reign.
> Your right in them is therefore so entire,
> They, above all, Your Pleasure should conspire.

This, I submit, is, in its own way, unsurpassed.

The mention of prologue and epilogue brings me to the question of the form of this masque. In the first place, its length is prodigious, the text with prologue and epilogue running to just over eighty-seven pages. It is, in fact, a play, divided into five acts, with the sing-

---

1. There is an unauthenticated tradition that Dryden wrote an epilogue which was rejected. See his *Works*, I, 162.

ing and dancing confined to the prologue and the "choruses" or *intermedii* between the acts and at the end. The prologue is really an allegorical, operatic induction and is practically a masque in itself. In it, Thames, who is attended by Peace, Plenty, Europe, Asia, Africa, and America, is alarmed by the distress of some of Europe's nymphs, but is reassured by the Genius of England, who has sent two heroes to their aid; they return triumphant, and all are about to make offerings to Fame, when they perceive the King and Queen and do homage to them instead. The *intermedii* are pastoral: Sylvia, Daphne, Corydon, and Strephon present their loves in song, and there are numerous entries. The pastoral scenes and most of the dances have no connection with the myth, and the effect of the whole is decidedly kaleidoscopic, but I think Reyher's "mortellement ennuyeuse" rather severe.[1]

Crowne himself was not pleased with his first effort and, perhaps on his own initiative, perhaps on further command, rewrote a great part of the dialogue, presumably between the winter and summer performances.[2] He says in his preface that it is the second version which is there offered to the public, and that the surviving portions of the original may be distinguished by being in pindaric verse, whereas the later composition is in heroic metre. Examination of the printed text shows that the prologue and *intermedii* are entirely pindaric, the play proper almost all heroic, except the first act where the two are very much mixed. But even in these survivals, as I shall show, he made some slight changes.

1. Reyher, p. 476.   2. See p. 181.

Two days before the first performance, the Lord Chamberlain decided to provide souvenir copies of the masque, and sent a warrant to the Master of the Great Wardrobe to provide:

A Coppie of the Playe for the Queene, A Copie for the Ladie Marie. A Copie for the Ladie Marie, and the Ladie Ann. A Copie to Correct vpon all occasions, A Copie of the Prologue & all the Songs for M[r] Staggins. And Alsoe, . . . soe many Printed Bookes of the Maske, and bound after such manner, as M[r] Crowne, whoe is the Autheur shall give you Accompt shallbee Necessarie. All which Things are to bee delivered vnto M[r] Crowne to bee by him distributed, as hee shall receaue Order from mee.[1]

Apparently the copies for the Queen and Princesses, the regular prompt copy and the special one for Staggins, Master of the Music, were to be manuscript. A bill for £20, covering the entire order, was put in by Crowne himself, and specifies two hundred and four printed books "for the King and Queene and to be distributed amongst the nobility."[2] Now the Queen already had a manuscript text, and taking into account the order in which they are named in both bill and warrant, and the fact that a complete text would be too long for the audience to read, I am very much inclined to think that the printed books contained only the prologue and the *intermedii*. On the other hand, the Lord Chamberlain says definitely, "printed Bookes of the Maske," and I admit this is a serious objection to my hypothesis.

This edition was, of course, privately printed, and there is no mention of it in the Stationers' Register,

1. LC. 5/64, f. 122; 5/121; 5/141, pp. 127, 556; Nicoll, p. 320; 13 February 1674/5.
2. LC. 9/274, p. 254; 9/112.

either in February or later in the year. But the Term
Catalogue for Trinity Term (1675) announces "The
Prologue to *Calistho* with the Chorus between the Acts.
Price 6d."[1] There is a copy of this twenty-four page
quarto in the British Museum,[2] with the following title
page:

THE / PROLOGUE / TO / CALISTHO, / WITH THE / CHO–
RUS'S / BETWEEN THE / ACTS. / [Rule. Device of printers'
ornaments. Rule.] / *LONDON,* / Printed in the Year MDCLXXV.

Not only is this anonymous, but there is no imprimatur
by Lestrange and no imprint. All this looks very much
as if the printer to whom Crowne entrusted the order
for the Court printed a large surplus which he put on the
market after a suitable interval, relying on the Lord
Chamberlain's warrant as a substitute for licensing and
entry in the Stationers' Register. There would be no
reason for Crowne to publish a partial text at that time,
and I do not know of any opera libretto similarly treated.
On the whole, it seems quite possible, and to me probable, that we have here the private edition. In any case,
I shall, for convenience in discussion, refer to it as the
"programme" text.

A few months later, in the Michaelmas Term Catalogue, was announced: "*Calisto,* or the chast Nymph.
The late Masque at Court, as it was frequently presented there by several persons of great Quality: with
the Prologue, and the Songs betwixt the Acts. All

1. Arber's Reprint.
2. Press mark 11626.d.8. Collation: A–C⁴. A1ᵛ and C4ᵛ are blank. No colo-
phon.

written by J. Crowne. In Quarto. Price, sticht, 1s."[1] It is remarkable that this edition should not have been licensed by Lestrange and entered at Stationers' Hall. If the fact that the masque had been written for Court presentation obviated these formalities, further study of title-pages and the Stationers' Register might throw light on the origin of various plays, but this is a subject into which I have not been able to go.

An examination of the prologue and *intermedii* as printed in the full text and in the "programme" reveals few variations, but one or two interesting points. In the complete text, Crowne has added an explanatory note on the dances in the prologue,[2] and one on the lines "Augusta is inclined to fears," which ought to have been sung by the Genius of the Country but were set for Thames. At the end of the prologue, the "programme" prints the words of a "Song to the Minovet," but this, for no apparent reason, was omitted from the later edition. Two of the entries also seem to have been altered. In the first *intermedio*, the "programme" states that the shepherds dance to the song "Kind Lovers, love on"; in the complete text, an entry of Basques precedes the the song and there is no mention of a dance by the shep-

---

1. Arber's Reprint. This is taken *verbatim*, but with variant spellings, from the title-page of the quarto, which adds: "*LONDON*, Printed by *Tho: Newcomb*, for *James Magnes* and *Richard Bentley*, at the *Post-Office* in *Russel-Street* in *Covent-Garden*. 1675." B. M., Press mark 81.d.21(5). Collation: A⁴, a–b⁴, B–F⁴, H–L⁴. G is missing because the copy was divided and given to two compositors; the text is continuous. Magnes and Bentley are well known as publishers of plays and novels. (See Plomer's Dictionaries.) Magnes allowed himself to become involved in one of Tom Killigrew's more questionable financial transactions. (Hotson, pp. 257–258.)   2. See p. 223.

herds. In the second *intermedio*, an entry of Cupids becomes an entry of Winds and Cupids. But these variations, or some of them, may be due to carelessness; the Basques, for example, must always have been in the masque, for their costumes were made for the first production.[1] Finally, the "programme" omits the epilogue. This is indeed a strange oversight, and I can only suggest that it was withheld as a surprise.

THE *Dramatis Personae*

It is not unusual nowadays to hear of a play written expressly for a celebrated actor or actress, but the entire cast for *Calisto* seems to have been settled before Crowne was commanded to write. He tells us that he was limited to seven parts, all to be taken by ladies and only two of them to represent men. This, of course, referred only to the dialogue of the play proper, for many others took part in the prologue and *intermedii*.

The parts of Calisto and Nyphe were taken by the two little Princesses for whom the masque was primarily designed. Mary, eldest daughter of the Duke of York and Anne Hyde, was then not quite thirteen,[2] but she had been an expert dancer for six years; and her sister Anne[3] seems to have had a youthful passion for theatricals.[4] But no one was sufficiently interested in their performance to leave us a criticism of it: we are sadly at a loss for the garrulous Pepys, who would have been

1. See p. 324.
2. She was born on 30 April 1662. Biographical details not otherwise attributed are taken from the D. N. B. and G. E. C.'s *Complete Peerage*.
3. Born on 6 February 1665.   4. See pp. 130–131.

sure to tell us whether the future queens distinguished themselves.

Lady Anne Fitzroy, eldest daughter of Charles by Castlemaine, was, perhaps a little maliciously, given the part of Juno. She was nearly fourteen and already married to Thomas, Lord Dacre and Earl of Sussex. Her "ruler of gods and men" was Henrietta Wentworth,[1] daughter of Thomas, fifth Baron Wentworth, to whose dignities she had succeeded at the age of five. Her love affair with Monmouth, which may possibly have begun about the time of *Calisto* and was to end only with their tragic deaths, seems to have been one of the few real romances of the Restoration period.[2]

For the part of Diana, Margaret Blagge (not to be confused with the sister immortalised by Gramont) was called back to Court.[3] She had been Maid of Honour to the first Duchess of York, and after her death, to the Queen, but had recently retired from Court, according to Evelyn to devote herself more completely to religious study and contemplation. The diarist, who for many years was her guide, philosopher, and friend, and who later wrote her life, tells us that to play this part was to her "a Mortification . . . that cost her not only great reluctancy, but many tears," and that she finally submitted only on the direct commands of both the King and his brother. She was much older than most of the performers, having been born on 2 August 1652, the daughter of Col. Thomas Blagge of Suffolk. On 16 May,

1. Born 11 August 1660.
2. See A. Fea: *The Loyal Wentworths.*
3. In the records, she is repeatedly called Mrs Blake.

between the two productions of *Calisto*, she was secretly married to Sidney Godolphin, then a Groom of the Bed Chamber and later Lord Godolphin,[1] so that her reluctance to take part in *Calisto* may not have been altogether due to such lofty principles as Evelyn ascribed it to.

It must have been a delicate matter to ask Lady Mary Mordaunt to play Psecas, the haughty and envious nymph who makes all the trouble and has not one redeeming trait. She was the daughter and heir of Henry, second Earl of Peterborough,[2] and later married Henry Howard, seventh Duke of Norfolk, who divorced her in 1700. Thereupon she married her lover, Sir John Germaine, for the century and the fashion had changed. In the play, she was wooed by Mercury, who aided and abetted her iniquities. The sprightly Sarah Jennings probably enjoyed the rôle of the mischief-maker. She had begun her spectacular career by being born on the day Charles returned to a repentant London, and was to end it as the first Duchess of Marlborough and the power behind Anne's throne.

This completed the speaking parts for the play, but other members of the Court participated as dancers and attendant nymphs. According to the *dramatis personae* printed in the complete text, the nymphs danced in the prologue and in several entries in the play, and were the Countess of Derby, the Countess of Pembroke, Lady Katherine Herbert, Mrs Fitzgerald and Mrs Frazier. But in the Lord Chamberlain's order for admitting

1. Evelyn, *Godolphin*, pp. 93–100.
2. She was born in 1659.

people behind the scenes, which belongs to the February performance, Mrs Fitzgerald is omitted and a Lady Dacy is named, which I take to be an error for Lady Dacre, Countess of Sussex.[1] The Countess of Derby was Elizabeth, daughter of Thomas Butler, Earl of Ossory, sister of the second Duke of Ormonde, and wife of William, ninth Earl of Derby, who was far from a model husband. The Countess of Pembroke was Henriette Mauricette de Queroualle, whom her more famous sister had married to Philip Herbert, the seventh Earl. Lady Katherine Herbert was her sister-in-law. Mrs Fitzgerald was probably another Katherine, daughter of John Fitzgerald of Dromana, who later married Edward Villiers, son of Viscount Grandison.[2] Mrs Frazier was Carey Fraser or Fraizer, daughter of Sir Alexander, head physician to the King.[3] She was a Maid of Honour and married Charles Mordaunt, who eventually became third Earl of Peterborough.

Calisto was the Princesses' masque, and all the principal parts were to be taken by ladies, but the Duke of Monmouth could not be altogether excluded. He and his attendant gentlemen therefore danced a totally irrelevant minuet in the prologue, and he apparently reappeared very shortly thereafter as a hero "Crown'd with a Mural Crown," attended by warriors dressed as "Roman combatants."[4] The companion part, played

1. LC. 5/141, p. 546; Nicoll, p. 320.
2. Evelyn, *Godolphin*, p. 255.
3. A. Fea, *Beauties of the Seventeenth Century*, pp. 286–289.
4. There is in the British Museum a collection of memoranda of tailors' and mercers' bills for *Calisto*, and in a bill for caps (Add. Ms. 27588, f.35) is the following item:

by a Mr Harpe, was called the Hero of the Sea, so I think we may call him Hero of the Land. Mr Harpe appears in the list of gentlemen dancers, and I think there can be no doubt that these two parts were taken by amateurs, although the rest of the prologue was sung by professionals.

The eldest of the royal bastards, born at Rotterdam on 9 April 1649, had for many years now been one of the brightest stars in the Whitehall galaxy, and delighted in dancing and acting.[1] In the minuet he was accompanied by Peregrine, Viscount Dunblaine, the third son of Thomas Osborne, Earl of Danby, whom he was to succeed as second Duke of Leeds; Robert Leake, Lord Deincourt, son of the second Earl of Scarsdale; John Trevor, son of the late Secretary of State; and a Mr Lane whom I cannot identify. Perhaps to this list should be added two equally unknown gentlemen, Mr Leonard and Mr Franshaw, included in the Lord Chamberlain's list already mentioned.

So much for the amateurs. The professional singers were drawn from the public theatres, the Chapel Royal, and the King's Private Music, and on them devolved the important function of opening the performance. Thames became a nymph for the nonce, personated by Moll Davis, who, of course, was not strictly speaking a

"feb[r] y[e] 7th 74/5 ffor a Combatants Capp fo[r] the Duke Monmouth
01:05:00"
Moreover, that year's Account of the Master of the Robes (AO. 1/2052/25) includes
"A Roman habitt being a shape for the Body w[th]: scollups & furniture for the same w[th]: a black Velvett Capp & white Plume of ffeathers" price £18.4.6.

1. See pp. 129, 138, and Fea, *King Monmouth.*

professional, since, as the King's mistress, she had left the stage and settled comfortably in Suffolk Street some six years before. Pepys is full of comments on her dancing, for she surpassed even Nell in a jig,[1] and the story of her singing her way to "the bed royal" is too well known to bear repetition.[2]

Thames was attended by Peace and Plenty in the persons of two other actresses, Mary Knight and Charlotte Butler. The former seems to have been almost equally famous for her swearing and her singing. Evelyn praised her voice as incomparable, and we are indebted to him for the information that shortly before *Calisto*, she had been in Italy and had thereby greatly improved her singing.[3] She, too, was one of Charles' mistresses, and Nell's neighbour in Pall Mall. Among the warrants to the Great Wardrobe, is one dated 10 December 1675, to provide her with "Crymson Dammaske for a Bed and furniture for a roome not exceeding the value of one hundred pounds."[4] Her companion, Charlotte Butler, Cibber describes as the daughter of a decayed knight, and recommended to the stage by no less an authority than Charles himself. He admits, perhaps a little grudgingly, that she "was allow'd in those Days to sing and dance to great Perfection."[5] Thames was also waited on by the four quarters of the world, each of whom had four attendants. Mr Hart was Europe, Mr Richardson Asia, Mr Marsh (Jr) Africa, and, appropriately enough, Mr Ford America. The first three were Gentlemen of

1. Pepys, 7 March 1666/7.   2. Downes, *Roscius Anglicanus*.
3. Evelyn, 2 December 1674.
4. LC. 5/141, p. 305.   5. Cibber, I, 163–165.

the Chapel Royal, as was Mr Turner, who represented the Genius of England.[1]

Mrs Davis and Mrs Knight, Mr Hart and Mr Turner reappear in the pastoral scenes as Sylvia, Daphne, Strephon, and Corydon respectively. Mrs Butler doubled Plenty and an African woman, and her companion in the second rôle was a Mrs Hunt for whom there was also a shepherdess' costume,[2] but who is not mentioned elsewhere. The third African woman who appears with them in the last scene is a mystery: the tailors and mercers persist in calling her Mrs Blake, but obviously Margaret Blagge could not take the part. A Mrs Masters and a Mrs Peirce were also costumed as shepherdesses, and one of them may have doubled for it.[3] This completes the list of actors and actresses who had speaking parts. In addition, there were, of course, professional dancers, whom I shall discuss later, and there were shepherds and shepherdesses for the chorus, and some "heavenly" and "airy" spirits summoned by Jupiter to remove his wife, but it is impossible to say who took these parts.[4]

1. Delafontaine *passim*.
2. See p. 327.
3. *Ibid.*
4. There is, however, a complete list of those to be admitted behind the scenes at the February performances, which it seems worth while to print (LC. 5/141, pp. 546–548; given in part by Nicoll, pp. 320–321):

"Ladyes in the Maske. 1674.

Attendants

Lady Mary ⎰ Mrs Walsingham
            ⎨ Mrs Langford
            ⎩ Mrs Leigh
              Mrs Trelawney

ALTERATIONS IN THE THEATRE AND VARIOUS
PREPARATIONS

The importance attached to *Calisto* is nowhere more
evident than in the work done on the Hall Theatre. It
was completely renovated, and apparently no pains or

Lady Anne	Mrs ffasden Mrs Jones Mrs Walmestey Mrs Bush
Pages of the Backstairs	Mr Leigh Mr Langston
Lady Pembrooke	Mrs May Mrs Cousin Mr Soursin Mr D'alma
Lady Henrietta Wentworth	Mrs ffaningam Mrs Avenij Mr [*blank*] a ffrench
Lady Mary Mordant	Mrs ffisher Mrs Warsup
Lady Derby	Mrs Pomery Mrs Maccarty
Lady Dacy	Mrs Lister [*blank*]
Lady Herbert	Mrs Mabb Mrs ffleete
Mrs Blake	Mrs Seagraue Mrs Grim
Mrs ffrasier	Mrs Harrell Mrs Betty Mrs Lombard
Mrs Jenings	[*blank*]
Lords and Gentlemen	Attendants
Duke of Monmouth	Mr St Gill Mr Jambe [*blank*] barber two footemen

expense was spared to provide a brilliant setting for the performance. When the Surveyor General was ready to begin work in mid-November, many details were not

Lord Deincourt
Lord Donblayne
Mr Orpe*

Mr Lane

Mr Trevor
Mr Leonard
M^r ffranshaw

Mr Hardy
Alexander
{ Luke
{ George

{ Dumon
{ Ferrin

Will
Mr Masden
Mr Morrell

Singers

Mrs Davies
Mrs Knight
Mrs Butler
Mrs Blunt†
Mrs Masters
Mrs Peirce
Mr Hart
Mr Turner
Mr Richardson
Mr Marsh
M^r fford
Mr Robert
Mr Degrang
Mr Shepheard

Mrs Shepheard
Mrs Dorcase
Mrs Benson

Mr Maxfield
Mr Preston
Mr Letelier
Mr Bopins
Mr Bury
M^r [blank]
M^r [blank]

Boys { Jack
{ Waters
{ Coninsby
{ Smyth

Harpsicalls 2	Theorboes 2	Bass Violls 3
Mr Corneille	Mr Marsh	Mr Coleman
Mr Bartleme	Mr Lylly	Mr Stephkins
		Mr Bates

Recorders 4	Gittars 4	Trumpetters 4
Mr Paisible	M^r ffrasico Corbett	Mr Bounty
Mr Bootell	Mr Outom	Mr Thompson
M^r De Breame	Mr Deloney	Mr Ragway
Mr Giton	Mr Delloney	Mr Christmas

Mr Van Bright, Kettle Drumer

* Mr Harpe   † Mrs Hunt

yet decided upon, and the Vice-Chamberlain merely issued a warrant to Wren "to make such Alteracõns in the Sceenes in His Ma^{tes} Theatre in Whitehall from tyme to tyme as you haue or shall receive directions

Violins	Violins	Violins
Mr Nicholas Staggins	Mr Theo: ffitz	Mr Dorney
Mr Singleton	Mr Greetinge	Mr Spicer
Mr Clayton	Mr Ashton	Mr Price
Mr Tho: ffitz	Mr Gamble	Mr Pagitt
Mr Hewson	M^r ffashions	Mr Duffill
Mr Myres	M^r fflower	Mr Kidwell
Mr Tho: ffarmer	Mr Isaack Staggins	M^r Jo: ffarmer
Mr Aleworth	Mr John Strong	Mr Basrier
M^r Jo: Bannister	M^c finell	Mr Viblett
Mr Ledgier	Mr Browne	Mr Hall
Mr Harris	Mr Brookwell	Mr Eagles

Dancers

Mr St Andre
Mr Isaacke
Mr Delisle
Mr Herriette
Mr Dyer
Mr Smyth
Mr Motley
Mr Berto
Mr Letang
Mr Muraile
M^r Le Roy
M^r Le Duke

Officers of ye Revells

Master
    Comptroller
Clarke
Groome
Sceenekeepers
Hallkeeper

Officers of ye Workes

Mr Surveyor
Serjeant Paynter

Carpenters

Mr Little
Mr Allingham
    Rowland
    Fourbush
    Webster
    Trevers

Chaundrey

Mr Bartlett

Greate Wardrobe

These are the Names of such as are admitted to come in at ye Dore behind ye Sceenes and none other
                                        Arlington
To Mr Harris yeoman of ye Revells."

from mee."¹ Then, on 25 January, when much of the
work must already have been completed, the Lord
Chamberlain signed another warrant stating in detail
what was required.² From this and the Works Accounts,
we can form a fairly accurate idea of the changes made.

There is no need to pause over the mending of holes
in the walls, setting bars in the windows and similar repairs, and I have already described the construction of
two new galleries.³ One of the most important changes
was the enlarging of the stage by extending it one yard
into the pit.⁴ The stage floor was relaid, with a new
"Dore & frame" in it "for yᵉ sinkeing vnderneath yᵉ
same," despite the fact that the libretto reveals no occasion for a trap. The frontispiece was moved forward to
preserve the picture-frame arrangement intact, and although there is no mention of carpenters' or joiners'
work on it, it must have been altered, for Streeter's bill
includes "paynting yᵉ addition in yᵉ top of yᵉ frontispeece & mending seuerall partes about it 5.0.0." This
stands first in his account, while the last item reads,
"ffor paynting [yᵉ peacocke, yᵉ Eagle] the Vine, the
flory banke . . . ." The vine and flowery bank seem to
be pieces of scenery, but since the peacock and eagle are
deleted, they must be already covered in the bill, and I
suggest that they are the additions to the proscenium.

There were a few alterations and repairs in the tiring-
rooms, and various changes in the auditorium. The

1. LC. 5/141, p. 64, 16 November 1674.
2. LC. 5/141, p. 551; Nicoll, pp. 43, 321. See p. 236.
3. See p. 48.
4. This and the following details are drawn from the warrant last quoted
and Works 5/24, Extraordinary Account. See pp. 252–255.

small pit was considerably diminished by the extension of the stage, and was still further encroached upon by the music, some of which was placed in its modern position. The warrant instructs Wren "To enclose the front of the pitt next the stage for the musick the whole breadth of yᵉ house." There is no corresponding entry in the Accounts, but the work must have been done, for there is a later entry for "putting vp yᵉ Rayle for yᵉ Musicke Cross yᵉ pitt into there places agayne."[1] There is, however, another item for the musicians in the *Calisto* Account: "takeing downe yᵉ Musicke seats & layeing two large floores & rayseing another floore with seuerall degrees for yᵉ Musicke." This I take to refer to a re-modelling of the old music-seat in the clouds. A large orchestra was used, and it would almost certainly be divided.[2]

To return to the auditorium, some of the space lost by extending the stage and placing music in the pit was retrieved by shortening the King's dais,[3] and a number of minor alterations follow: two boxes "on each-side the degrees next unto yᵉ pitt," a seat for the Master of the Revels, changes in the Lord Chamberlain's and Lord

1. Works 5/27, January, 1676/7. There is no reference to it in the interval.
2. See p. 221.
3. The general intention here is clear enough, but the details decidedly confused. The warrant reads, "to bring back the Kings Platforme, to alter the Wings on each side the Kings Platforme & to make Boxes there." There is no other reference to these wings, and I do not know what they can be. The Account describes the work as "Cutting yᵉ Throne three footᵗ shorter to Enlarge yᵉ pitt & bourding vp yᵉ foreside agayne next yᵉ pitt, Remooveing yᵉ pitt into Itts former place agayne & Makeing benches there & Cutting yᵉ Kings seate shorter." In this, throne clearly means dais, and the "Kings seate" may be the footpace on the dais (see p. 30), but further explanation I cannot offer.

Newport's boxes and a new one for the Surveyor General. A partition was set up in the passage between the theatre and Whitehall Bridge and taken down again, I suppose immediately after the February performances. A good deal of new matting, 600 yards of distemper on the walls, boxes, and galleries, and the theatre must have been quite fresh and tidy.

This completes the work on the theatre with the exception of the scenery, but before I discuss that, it may be well to note various preparations which went on there during the winter. A new curtain was included in the warrant to the Surveyor General but was not properly his job, and he very wisely ignored it. As a matter of fact, one had been ordered from the Great Wardrobe on 3 November, "of Blew Red and White in Breadths of stuff," and duly supplied.[1] For at least two months, the theatre had to be heated and lighted for rehearsals. On 28 November, the Lord Chamberlain sent a warrant to the Lord Steward, to

giue Order for lights to be sett vp in the Theatre at Whitehall for the practising of a Maske and such a quantity of Charcoale as will make fires in the Vper attireing roome where the Maskers are to attire themselues and also fires in Panns betweene the Sceenes and in y[e] Pitt by reason the Duke of Yorkes Children wilbe there The practiseing wilbe on saterday Nights Tuseday Nights & Thursday Nights and if at any other tymes, Notice shalbe giuen by a Gentleman Vsher.[2]

In December, the Groom Porter (whose prerogative it was to supply such articles) was instructed to provide

1. See p. 143. The curtain and various other supplies for *Calisto* were to be delivered to Philip Kinnersley, Yeoman of the Removing Wardrobe, instead of to the Yeoman of the Revels or the Theatre-Keeper.
2. LC. 5/141, pp. 74, 551; Nicoll, p. 319.

fire shovels, tongs, fire-dogs (creepers), and a Spanish table;[1] and there is a tradesman's bill for candlesticks.[2] When it came to the actual performances, a good deal more warmth was found necessary for the aristocratic cast, and "Tenn Brasiers to hold Coales in to warme the Actor[rs]. att their Attyreing" were ordered on 9 February.[3]

Apparently refreshments were provided at the rehearsals, but the warrant for them was not signed until 28 January, when one was sent to the Lord Steward and Board of Green Cloth, in accordance with His Majesty's own instructions, to deliver to the Theatre-Keeper "a reasonable Proporcõn of wine Beere & bread for those that Act & practize in ye Maske at such tymes as they shall Act or Practice there."[4] The Creditor is headed "pro diu'sarum Expensaru' per mandat' Dni Regis pro le Ball et pro diu'ss practisings m̃ Octob[rs] &c Martij 1674/5."[5] The only items dated March are almonds, China oranges, and olives for the Queen, and I do not think they betoken a March performance; either the bill

---

1. LC. 5/141, p. 82; Nicoll, p. 319; 15 December. There is no bill; presumably they were included in the Groom Porter's Annual Account. There is also a memorandum, dated 15 February, for ten Spanish tables for the masque (LC. 5/190, f. 185). I do not know what these were.
2. For 3 doz. large tin hanging candlesticks, £1.16s.; 2 doz. the next size hanging candlesticks, 16s.; 3 doz. flat candlesticks, 12s.; and a basket, 1s. Supplied by John Baldwin (LC. 9/274, p. 223).
3. LC. 5/64, f. 121; 5/121; 5/141, p. 554; Nicoll, p. 321. Warrant to the Great Wardrobe to deliver to the Yeoman of the Revels. The bill is for 2 firegrates at 8s. apiece, 2 at 12s., and 6 with 28 bars each at 18s. 6d. (LC. 9/274, p. 253). Supplied by Richard Cawarden. There is also a February bill for 6 large brass candlesticks at 5s. apiece (ibid., p. 241).
4. LC. 5/141, p. 555; Nicoll, p. 321.
5. LS. 8/11, ff. 82–85.

came in late, or they do not belong to *Calisto*. The charges are briefly as follows:[1]

	£.	s.	d.
Bread	1.	5.	$2\frac{3}{4}$
Beer		13.	$6\frac{1}{2}$
French wine	6.	18.	0.
Canary	1.	14.	6.
Wax lights and torch-staves	107.	10.	$3\frac{1}{4}$
Oil	4.	10.	0.
Almonds olives & oranges	3.	13.	6.
Tallow candles	9.	3.	1.
Clerks' fees	2.	10.	0.
Mutton		6.	5.
Charcoal	2.	7.	3.
Wood and coals	2.	4.	9.

| Total | 142. | 16. | $6\frac{1}{2}$ |

There is another Creditor for the later performances, headed as before, and covering April, May, and June; but unfortunately one leaf is missing from the book in which it was entered.[2] The only interesting item in what has survived is one for "Venice lights" at £23.4.8. The end of the Creditor is lost, but from the Declared Accounts we learn that the total was £148.12.0$\frac{3}{4}$,[3] so there must have been many rehearsals and probably several performances.

1. This is not a transcript.
2. LS. 8/12, ff. 1–2. Fol. 3 is missing.
3. E. 351/1843. Some time during the year, Richard Pigg supplied 12 maple dishes and 2 large "Bumbard Iacks" — presumably for the beer (LC. 9/274, p. 245; 9/112). They cost £1.17.0.

SCENERY, MACHINES, STAGE PROPERTIES, AND LIGHTING

Calisto was probably the most elaborate production staged at Whitehall during the entire Restoration period. Special scenery was required, and to meet the situation, Streeter [1] attempted more spectacular settings than had yet been used in the Hall Theatre. It would be interesting to know how much of the technique of these scenes and the lighting of them was due to Streeter's own initiative, and how much Wren, as Surveyor General of the Works, concerned himself therein. The Works Accounts tell us exactly what was done, but of course reveal nothing of the inventor.

When the great red, white, and blue curtains were drawn, they revealed the enlarged stage set for the Prologue: a "Prosspect of Somersett house & yᵉ Thames," topped by clouds. This, and indeed all the new scenery, had been built by Richard Rider, the King's Master Carpenter and one-time tenant of the ground on which the first Theatre Royal in Drury Lane was erected.[2] Somerset House consisted of a pair of shutters 15 feet wide and 14 feet 9 inches high, and two side frames 4 feet by 14 feet 9 inches.[3] Over these billowed a complete set of clouds, the shutters of which were pulled off at the appropriate moment to reveal a Temple of Fame.

---

1. See pp. 150–151.   2. Hotson, p. 243.
3. The warrant calls for "a New paire [*of shutters*] & releiues" (LC. 5/141, p. 551; Nicoll, pp. 43, 321); the bill is for a pair of shutters and a pair of side frames. Streeter charged £12 for painting them. These and the following details are from Works 5/24, Extraord. Acct.

This must have looked a little odd, perched atop Somerset House, which the actors would have had to scale had they carried out their announced intention to proceed to the Temple. Fortunately, they were deterred by catching sight of the King and Queen. And the Temple, *per se*, was one of the triumphs of the production, made of silk-covered frames [1] behind which lights were set.[2]

At the end of the prologue, perhaps actually during the last entry,[3] the cloud shutters were run in again, and Somerset House withdrawn to disclose the "boscage" already in place behind it. This was the woodland set for the play proper, for which were supplied a new pair of shutters and a pair of wings.[4] In connection with this set must be taken another item in Streeter's bill, "ffor clenseing all ye wall betweene the wings of ye sceanes & twice colouring it & afterwards paynting there & boscage on it 3.0.0." If only one pair of wings was used, the side walls of the theatre would undoubtedly show and have to be painted to match, but the new scenery may have been supplemented by stock wings.[5] Certainly some old scenes were used, for the Account for November — the month in which the work was begun — includes "Take-

1. Rider charged "ffor a frame . . . 11fo^t: & a halfe by 7 fo^{te}: & a halfe, ffor 2 side frames 11 fo^{te}: & a halfe by 3 fo^{te}: each being open in ye middle & boarded round about." The dimensions show that the side frames were wings. The varnishing cost £5. There is no item for silk, but *cf*. pp. 212–213.
2. The warrant reads: "a Temple in the Cloudes with sceenes of Varnished silke & places for lights for ye same."
3. See p. 224.
4. Shutters 13 by 15 feet, wings 13 by 4 feet. The painting cost £10. The wings are called "side releises" in Streeter's bill, but this I think is only a slip for relieves: tree-wings would, of course, be cut-outs.
5. The warrant calls only for a pair of shutters. For old boscage pieces, see p. 152.

ing downe yᵉ said scenes¹ & cutting them less & Makeing yᵉ groues shorter, & rayseing yᵉ back shutters."²
Perhaps also for this set were two small pieces, a vine
and a "flory banke," both made with cut edges.³

The woodland scenes should, according to the libretto,
change before the second *intermedio* to a "Scene near the
Vale, whither the Winds carryed Calisto," but there are
no scenes answering this description.⁴ It is, of course,
quite possible that an old set was used, but it does not
seem very likely in a production for which so much was
new that old scenery should be put on for the greater
part of the play. It seems more probable to me that the
second woodland set was made later, and that Streeter
submitted a separate bill for it.

There remain the clouds. Some old ones were used,
heightened and supplemented,⁵ but a good many were
specially made for the occasion. A pair of shutters 13
by 15 feet and two side frames to match, 13 by 4 feet,
were made; and Rider charged for three more pairs of

1. They had not been mentioned.
2. This may, however, refer to clouds; see below.
3. They were cut by the carpenters and painted by Streeter.
4. On the contrary, there are items for an "Arbour" which has no place in
   the text as it stands. I suggest this was made for the first version of the
   masque and discarded in the revision. It is, however, of interest. It
   consisted of a "backe part" 14 feet 9 inches by 15 feet, two side frames
   14 feet 9 inches by 4 feet, and a front 14 by 15 feet, "being open and
   boarded round." This would seem to be a curious attempt to substitute
   a series of flat frames for a built-up piece, presumably to facilitate the
   change of scene.
5. Wren was instructed to enlarge the stage by drawing back and shortening
   the scenes, "To alter all the Cloudes aboue suiteable to the same by
   heightheninge[*sic*] and ading to them, To make an openinge for a Heaven
   aboue with all the sceenes of Cloudes & shutter of Cloudes Necessary, . . .
   To make seates for yᵉ Goddesses & diverse Releiues proper for that repʳ-
   sentacōn . . ."

wings which are listed after the frames for the temple
of fame, but which I think must have been clouds.[1]
Streeter's bill is made out simply for 139 yards of
clouds.[2] The bulk of these were set up in the usual formation of a truncated triangle, and the wings remained
in place throughout the play; but after the Temple of
Fame was removed, relieves were put up behind the
shutters for the "open Heaven" which appeared in the
last scene. Among them were placed circular seats for
the gods and goddesses. Apparently these were only the
four deities who had figured in the story, but they would
doubtless be attended by the "airy spirits," the "boys
in the clouds," and various musicians, and considerable
splendour was added by the use of a glory.[3] This con-
sisted of a "backe peece" $11\frac{1}{2}$ by $7\frac{1}{2}$ feet, with a round
hole in it over which taffeta was stretched on a frame
$3\frac{1}{2}$ feet square, and behind which lights were set on a
"frame with degrees."

Rider's work on all this scenery totalled $235\frac{2}{3}$ yards,
and cost £27.9.10½. In Streeter's bills are included 267
yards of primed cloth costing £26.15.4, and 600 yards of
distemper in the auditorium at £15, bringing his charges
to £97.14.10 in all. There was also a certain amount of
work done on the scenes by the carpenters, for which no
specific charge can be given.[4]

1. The dimensions given are $11\frac{1}{2}$ by 3 feet, 13 by 4 feet, and 13 by 4 feet.
2. The carpenters' account mentions fastening up "Circular clouds" and
   cutting out edges of clouds.
3. See pp. 154–155.
4. They made a new flight of eight steps going up into the clouds and a
   "floore Joysted & boarded at end of y⁰ mooueing shutters for y⁰ draweing
   of y⁰ same cont.' about 50 fo^te:."

According to the stage directions, Jupiter descends from the heaven to speak the epilogue, but there is no trace of machinery for this in the Works Accounts. On the other hand, they refer to a trapdoor for which the stage directions reveal no use. However gorgeous the Temple of Fame, however impressive the vista of clouds terminating in the glory, there was no attempt at mechanical wonders; from that point of view, the setting was exceedingly simple. And there were no adjuncts to the scenery in the shape of stage properties except a "great umbrella," which I take to be the canopy under which Calisto and Nyphe enter in the last scene, since there is no other place in the masque where anything remotely resembling an umbrella could be used. Jay Devoe, who provided the "hand props," put into his bill six shillings for "An Arbor to practise in stead of the umbrella," £20 for "the great umbrella," and 1ˢ 2ᵈ for "a rope to drawe the umbrella out of the way."[1] The rope is, I think, explained by the fact that the Africans who supported the canopy were to take part in the last entry, and the canopy, no longer needed, had to be quietly pulled back into the flies.

Twenty pounds would seem to be quite enough to include materials, but others were supplied which I can account for only by supposing them to be for this canopy. On 19 January, a warrant was issued to the Wardrobe to deliver to Henry Harris

Sixty yards of cherrie colored avinion thirty yards of white avinion: one and thirty yards of aurania Avinion: thirty yards of greene avinion: one yard of skey colored avinion: Eighty four yards

1. LC. 9/274, pp. 271–272.

of Silver gawes six yards of gold gawes and four peices of tinsey ribboning.[1]

At the end of Fownes' bill for materials for the costumes stand the following items:[2]

60 yds.	cherry	avinnion		10.10.0.
30 "	green	"		4.10.0.
30 "	white	"		4.10.0.
31 "	gold	"		4.13.0.
1 "	sky	"		3.0.
94 "	broad silver gauze			9. 8.0.
6 "	"	gold	"	12.0.
6 pcs.	gold tinsey ribbon			4. 4.0.
2 "	silver "	"		1. 4.0.

Their use is not designated, but clearly, despite discrepancies in the amounts, they were supplied on this warrant and have nothing to do with costumes; and in a memorandum of some of the *Calisto* bills preserved at the British Museum, these same items are marked "Mr Devoes pacell stage."[3] The umbrella is the only thing Devoe provided for which these materials could be, and if the silk and gauze were tightly gathered or ruched, I suppose so many yards could be used.[4]

Doubtless much of the effectiveness of the setting was due to the lighting, achieved by a sublime disregard of safety. The Creditor for the masque shows no less than £107.10.3¼ for wax and torch staves, and £4.10.0. for oil (for the footlights),[5] but when we read the carpenters'

1. LC. 5/64, f. 119ᵛ; 5/141, pp. 109, 556; Nicoll, p. 321.
2. From LC. 9/274, p. 269. This is not a transcript.
3. Add. Ms. 27588. "pacell" seems to be a slip for parcel, but may represent parasol.
4. It is, however, possible that some of them were for the Temple of Fame (see p. 209), which Devoe may have worked on.
5. See p. 161.

accounts, these huge sums cease to be incredible. Their labours included

makeing degrees behind yᵉ backe clouds for yᵉ setting of lights there boarding with slitt deales behind yᵉ vpper sceanes for yᵉ putting vp of sconces & Candlestickes, . . . lineing yᵉ backes of yᵉ shutters for yᵉ putting vp of lights, & nayleing yᵉ sconces & Candlestickes to yᵉ backes of yᵉ clouds.[1]

It will be recalled, too, that the Lord Chamberlain's orders called for lights behind the varnished silk of the Temple of Fame, and I have also mentioned the lights of the glory. The receptacles for the candles were supplied by the Great Wardrobe: there are warrants for eight dozen of tin wall sconces, eight dozen white tin plates to put over them, six dozen of plain tin sconces, four extinguishers, two hand candlesticks, and six dozen of black tin plates (reflectors).[2] There is no mention of footlights, but they had already been employed in the Hall Theatre,[3] and I see no reason to doubt that they were used for this performance.

THE COSTUMES

The costumes were undeniably the greatest glory of *Calisto*. Moreover, most of them were supplied by the Great Wardrobe, and the detailed accounts have survived. This special and — so far as I am aware — unique dispensation of providence would alone be suffi-

1. Works 5/24, Extraord. Acct.
2. LC. 5/64, f. 115ᵛ; 5/121; 5/141, p. 77; Nicoll, p. 319; LC. 5/64, f. 117ᵛ; 5/121; 5/141, p. 102; Nicoll, p. 320; LC. 5/64, f. 121ᵛ. There is also a memorandum to put up sconces in the theatre, dated 8 February, 1674/5 (LC. 5/190, f. 185).
3. See p. 161.

cient justification for going into the matter at some length, but the costumes and the descriptions are delightful in themselves. A few accounts and memoranda of them were, indeed, published in *Notes and Queries* many years ago,[1] but the information now available reduces these to comparatively little interest.[2] There are also some manuscript memoranda in the British Museum, chiefly of materials delivered to the tailors by a mercer named Fownes.[3] But among the Wardrobe Accounts in the Public Record Office are bills for the materials and making of forty-six designs for the February performance, and four more for April. Many of these were made in sets for the dancers and musicians, so that the total number of costumes comes to one hundred and sixty-one, and to this we can add one charged to the Master of the Robes.[4] Yet only one of the amateurs was clothed by the Wardrobe: Margaret Blagge presumably could not afford the required magnificence and nearly £300 was spent to array her suitably as the chaste Diana. The inference is that the other ladies spent at least as much, but the only bill for them is one for properties.

The costume bills, as passed in the Annual Account of the Great Wardrobe, come to £2328.9.9,[5] but this figure does not represent the actual cost. In one or two cases,

1. A writer who signed himself J. D. C. printed, from an unnamed source, a bill for haberdashery, a list of costumes, estimates of materials for several, and summaries of the tailors' bills. (Second Series, 1858, pp. 341 *et seq.*)
2. They do, however, establish Cabbin's identity as a tailor; see p. 140.
3. Add. Ms. 27588.
4. See p. 196, note 4.
5. The amount given in LC. 9/112 less several bills which are for the masque but not costumes.

advances had been made, perhaps in order to secure de-livery of the goods,[1] and some bills were "allowed in gross" at several pounds less than the sum of the items.[2] If we allow £300 apiece for the amateurs who supplied their own costumes, the total cost must have been over £5000.[3]

In reading the Accounts, one is immediately struck by the elaborateness and sheer bulk of the garments.[4] Diana's costume *begins* with 24 yards of gold brocade, and a Cupid is clad in 6 yards of white satin lined with fustian. The masque was first given in February, and no doubt Wolsey's Great Hall was cold enough, but this does not seem an adequate explanation: Inigo Jones did not design his costumes on the principle of protection from influenza. I incline to think the new style was pure ostentation, display rather than beauty or appropriate-ness being its aim, and, like most fashions in dress, was imported from across the Channel. Louis and the ladies and gentlemen who danced his masques were gorgeously attired;[5] the English courtiers, too, would see how many yards of silk and how many pounds of gold and silver lace could be carried without collapse.

There was nothing subtle about this magnificence, for the erudite symbolism of the Jacobean masque was a lost art. But there is one rather remarkable instance of classical learning: the satyrs' costumes for the second

1. *E.g.*, LC. 9/274, pp. 258, 269.
2. *Ibid.*, pp. 252, 291.
3. £275.16.9 for costumes was charged on the Account of the Master of the Robes (AO. 1/2052/25).
4. See Appendix F.
5. Bapst, *passim*, and H. Prunières, *Le Ballet de Cour en France, passim*.

A SATYR

production are obviously modelled on the traditional make-up of early Athenian comedy. I do not know who was responsible for this. There is no clue to the designer of any of the costumes; the warrant for the greater part of them states that directions will be given to the appointed tailor, and that is all.[1] But I think Tate, in the preface to the 1693 edition of *A Duke and No Duke*, indicates the source of information pretty clearly, although, since he is writing twenty years later, I may be mistaken.[2] He says:

> Next to Tragedy came Satyr, which was but a Species of the former, as appears by the *Cyclops* of *Euripides*. This sort of *Dramma*, (though less practised as the World grew more civilized) had also it's peculiar *Personae* or χηματισμοῦς, [sic] made of Goat Skins and Hides, and other Beasts, which are described by *Dyonisius*, *Pollux* and *Causabon*.

The costumes were made of pink taffeta, "the bodyes stiffned with bone and Buckerome and Canvas with a halfe Belly made out with Cotton and Callicoe," the breeches were covered with "sad-colloured worsted ffringe," and the whole was "garnished with greene vine leeves made of Parchment: with bunches of grapes annexed thereunto."[3]

There are also a number of costumes in which one can dimly trace tradition, but a tradition altered almost past recognition. The Roman combatants afford an excel-

---

1. LC. 5/64, f. 116; 5/141, pp. 83, 552; Nicoll, pp. 319–320. Other warrants for costumes will be found in LC. 5/64, ff. 113, 120, 121ᵛ; 5/141, pp. 74, 550, 553, 555, 556; Nicoll, pp. 319–321. They do not cover all the costumes supplied.
2. The only other source would be vase-paintings, and I doubt if they were known in Charles' Court.   3. See p. 339.

lent example. They were in silken armour of gold and silver, plentifully decorated with gold fringe, "gold purle rosets," jewels, spangles, and feathers.[1] The Emperor of America, too, with a costume covered with six thousand coloured swan's feathers, was no doubt fondly supposed to resemble an Inca.[2] But many of the costumes seem to have differed but little from the ordinary dress of the day. So far as we can tell, Diana was distinguishable only by her bow and arrow from a Court lady with a taste for gold and silver lace; only the ordinary full-skirted Restoration gown and overskirt could use up the materials allotted to her.[3] The shepherds and shepherdesses were far more appropriately dressed for the galleries of Whitehall than for the smoothest pastures,[4] and except for his wings of red and white "estridge feathers," Cupid was a perfect Restoration gentleman.[5] And lastly, there were certain costumes which were purely imaginative. The Winds, for example, had embroidered bodies and short skirts (baces) of silver tabby trimmed with cherry and silver fringe, with sleeves of cherry satin, and hanging sections of gold tabby lined with cherry. They wore hats trimmed with garlands.[6]

On the whole, the costumes may be described as either contemporary or fanciful.[7] One notices the predominance of red, green, gold, and silver,[8] the eighteenth century passion for feathers is already virulent, and

1. See pp. 321–322.
2. See pp. 315–316.
3. See pp. 323–324.
4. See pp. 324–329.
5. See p. 332.
6. See pp. 330–331.
7. Many of the latter suggest costumes worn in Tudor masques. (See A. Feuillerat, *Documents Relating to the Revels, etc., passim.*)
8. *Cf.* Reyher, p. 413.

white taffeta drawers seem to be as universally satisfactory a termination as ληκύθιον ἀπώλεσεν.

All these costumes were decidedly too expensive to be
discarded or neglected, and now that a beginning had
been made, Charles doubtless hoped that masques would
be frequent. Considerable care was accordingly taken
to preserve them,[1] but so far as I can discover, they were
never worn again. The Yeoman of the Revels was responsible for their custody, "to keepe them safe for his
Ma[tes] further service," and if he carried out his instructions, they must have perished in the Whitehall fire.[2]

THE MUSIC AND DANCING

At the conclusion of his remarks to the reader, Crowne
tells us that the music, both vocal and instrumental,
was composed by Mr Staggins, whom he compliments
highly. Nicholas Staggins was sworn Master of the
King's Music and leader of the Band of Violins on
29 January 1674/5, only a couple of weeks before the

1. Wren was ordered to make two presses to keep the habits in (LC. 5/141,
   p. 553; Nicoll, p. 321), but there is no mention of them in the Works Accounts. The Wardrobe provided "Thirtie Seaven Cases of Flannell" —
   called "twilights," i. e. toilets, in the bill — and 35 wooden boxes for the
   hats and feathers (LC. 5/64, f. 121; 5/121; 5/141, p. 554; Nicoll, p. 321).
   The tailors charged sixpence apiece for making the toilets, and used
   131 yds. of flannel (LC. 9/274, pp. 269, 291). The bill for the boxes is very
   strange: forty-two were made, of fifteen different shapes and sizes, each
   of which is fully described (LC. 9/274, p. 251). Further storage was provided in the shape of four large trunks covered with Russia leather
   (LC. 9/274, p. 329).
2. The Yeoman was to receive the costumes from the Wardrobe, to deliver
   them to the actors, and to collect them again after the masque (LC. 5/141,
   p. 555; Nicoll, p. 321; 15 February 1674/5).

performance, but in all probability he had then officiated in that capacity several months.[1] Very little of his music seems to be known, but several of his songs are to be found in a manuscript music-book in the British Museum, and among them I have identified seven airs from *Calisto*.

This book is a slim folio, on the first page of which is written "Charles Campelman his book — Iune ye 9. 1681–."[2] Below this is added in another hand "God giue him grace 1682/." On folio 18 and its *verso* are written a group of songs from the masque, without any title or heading, but with "Mr Stagings" added at the end. They are written continuously, only the musical symbols showing where one ends and the next begins, and the airs and words are given without accompaniment.[3] Most of them show only slight verbal variations from the printed text, but the manuscript adds as the words of a second stanza to "Joy Shepheards Joy" the last four lines of Sylvia's concluding song after Act V.

Staggins' position in the Household seems to have been considered ample compensation for composing, but he did manage to get paid for the mechanical part of his labours, and I am not sure what is meant by the last item in the following bill:

1. LC. 3/24.   2. B. M. Add. Ms. 19759.
3. The passages set are those beginning as follows:
    "Augusta is inclined to fears" (Prologue)
    "Poor Corydon, thy flame remove" (First *Intermedio*)
    "Kind Lovers, Love on" (First *Intermedio*)
    "Alas poor Shepherd" (Second *Intermedio*)
    "No Longer complain" (Third *Intermedio*)
    "Joy Shepheards Joy!" (Fourth *Intermedio*)
    "Since all our grief" (Fourth *Intermedio*)

For the faire writing of the Aires composed for the Maske from the fowle original, on score, dyes included £13.10.

For fire, candle, chamber rent, ruled paper, ink and penns 3.5.

For drawing the said musick for the voyces, with the instrumentall musick composed at the same time 10.0.[1]

The instrumental music probably consisted chiefly in dances and accompaniments for the songs, although there may have been "symphonies" during the prologue and before each act. It was performed by thirty-three violins, two "harpsicalls," two theorboes, four "Kittars," three bass viols, four recorders, four trumpets, and a kettle-drum.[2] Costumes of bright coloured taffeta and avinnion were provided for twenty of the violins, the guitars, two of the recorders or "Hoa Boyes," the trumpets and drum,[3] who evidently were visible to the audience and were, in all probability the section of the orchestra for whom space was railed off between the pit and the stage.[4] The rest may have been concealed behind the scenes, where the carpenters had raised a "floor with seuerall degrees for yᵉ Musicke."[5]

The vocal music was strictly limited to the prologue and *intermedii*, in other words, to professional singers. I have already mentioned the more important of these; the complete list runs: Mrs Davis, Mrs Knight, Mrs Butler, Mrs Blunt (an error for Hunt), Mrs Masters, Mrs Peirce, Mr Hart, Mr Turner, Mr Richardson, Mr Marsh (Jr), Mr Ford, Mr Robert, Mr Degrang(es),

1. De Lafontaine, p. 298.
2. According to LC. 5/141, p. 547. See pp. 201–202, and *cf.* the list given below from LC. 5/141, p. 197.
3. See pp. 304–306.   4. See p. 204.
5. *Ibid.*

Mr Shepheard, Mr Maxfield, Mr Preston, Mr Letelier, Mr Bopins, Mr Bury, two other men whose names are not given, and four boys, Jack, Waters, Coningsby, and Smyth.[1]

There is a warrant, dated 27 May 1675, to pay Staggins £221 for himself and those named below, "for theire service & attendance in ye Maske at Whitehall."[2] There is, however, no sum entered for Staggins, and the entire amount is assigned, as follows:

Vocal Musick	li	Harpsicall & Lute Extra-ord^ry Attendance	
Mr Turner Ext' attendance	10	Mr Marsh Sen'	10
Mr Hart Ext' attendance	10	Mr Bartholomew	10
Mr Marsh Jun'	5	Violins	
M^r fford	5	Hall	5
Mr Maxsine	5	Eagles	5
Frenchmen		Ledger	5
Bury	3	Ashton	5
Beaupins	5	Pagett	3
Robert	5	Duffill	5
Le Tillier	3	Kidwell	5
Panine	3	John Farmer	3
French Violins and Hoboyes		Price	5
Paisable ⎫	5	Dancers	
de Bresmes ⎬ Hoboyes	5	Mr Isaack Ext' attendance	10
Guiton ⎪	5	Mr Dyer	5
Boutet ⎭	3	Mr Smyth	5
Bejard	3	Mr Mottley	5
Cornelius	5	French Dancers	
Violett	5	De Lisle	5

1. LC. 5/141, pp. 546–547.
2. LC. 5/141, p. 197. The *Calendar of Treasury Books* shows that a royal sign manual and money warrant for this amount passed on 7 February 1675/6.

French Dancers		Harriette	5
Le Duc	5	Le Roy	5
Lestant	5	Mr Clarke	5
Dunnraille	5		
Berteau	5		——
For writeing & pricking the tunes in the Maske & for paper pens & Inke &c	10		106
	——		
	115	Arlington	

Obviously this is not an inclusive bill for all the music; almost all the important singers are omitted, as are the twenty-four regular violins, but it is the only payment to musicians that I have found.

Like the singing, the dancing in *Calisto* is to be found only in the prologue and *intermedii*, and almost all of it is done by professionals. Reyher's complaint that this is a masque without masquers [1] is, strictly speaking, true enough, but we must not overlook a note which Crowne interpolated in the prologue when the complete text was published. The "programme" edition reads: "*Enter Nymphs, who Dance, and go off.*"[2] For this has been substituted the following:

> An Entry of Shepherds and Nymphs, Dancing round the *Thames*, &c. as they stood in their Figure.
>> Here the Princesses and the other Ladies danced several Sarabands with Castanets. A Minouet was also danced by his Grace the Duke of *Monmouth*; which ended, *Thames* proceeds.[3]

Turning back to the "programme," we find at the end of the prologue the words of "*The Song to the Minovet,*

1. Reyher, p. 476.   2. Sig. A3.   3. Sig. A4^v.

Danced in the Prologue, to be sung by Shepherds."[1] I do not know why this should have been omitted in the larger edition.

The sarabands would have been danced by Princess Mary, Princess Anne, the Countess of Derby, the Countess of Pembroke, Lady Katherine Herbert, Mrs Fitzgerald, and Mrs Frazier. The Duke must have been attended by Viscount Dunblaine, Lord Deincourt, Mr Trevor, and Mr Lane, as shepherds. The printed *dramatis personae* adds Mr Harpe, who enters only a few lines later as the Hero of the Sea. The *dramatis personae* also states that the ladies danced several entries in the play, but there is no trace of them.

By far the greater part of the dancing was done by professionals, both in the prologue and in the *intermedii*. Most of the entries, particularly those in the prologue, are led up to in the dialogue, but some of them seem rather incongruous. There are ten in all, in addition to the sarabands and minuet. In the prologue there are four: Sea Gods and Tritons, Warriors, Rural Gods and Nymphs, and Carpenters.[2] The entry of carpenters who are "to make ready the stage" is the one really clever thing in the masque. In the first *intermedio* there is an entry of Basques;[3] in the second, one of Cupids and Winds;[4] in the third, an entry of Gypsies,[5] and one of Satyrs;[6] in the fourth, of Bacchuses;[7] and in the last,

1. Sig. B1v.
2. There are costumes for four Sea Gods, but none for Tritons; for six Roman combatants; none for Rural Gods and Nymphs; twelve for Carpenters.
3. Costumes for seven.
4. Costumes for two Cupids and eight Winds.   5. No costumes.
6. Costumes for eight for the first version, and four for the second.
7. Costumes for four Bacchants for the second version.

Africans.[1] Crowne was enjoined to make his last entry Africans, and considering the difficulties, I do not think he did too badly to have African women find the beauty of which Phaeton had deprived them in the cheeks of the Princesses.

The dancers were twelve in number, most of them French and perhaps the same ones over whom Tom Killigrew and Grabut had trouble at Drury Lane.[2] In an order of the Lord Chamberlain's, their names are given as St. Andre, Isaacke, Delisle, Herriette, Dyer, Smyth, Motley, Berto, Letang, Muraile, Le Roy, and Le Duke.[3] The dances were presumably originated by Joseph Priest, who, with Luke Channell, arranged the dances for the gaudy Dorset Garden production of *Macbeth*.[4] I infer his share in *Calisto* from an entry in the *Calendar of Treasury Books*, under date of 15 September 1675, of a royal sign manual for £100 to "John (Joseph) Preist" for his services in the late ballet.[5]

FURTHER NOTES ON FINANCE

Calisto was a magnificent extravagance. It cannot, indeed, rival the *Masque of Queens*, which Reyher estimates at £6000.[6] But Sir Edmund Chambers ventures

1. Costumes for six African slaves and for four African kings, but perhaps all of them did not dance.   2. Nicoll, p. 317.
3. LC. 5/141, p. 546; Nicoll, pp. 320–321. *Cf.* the list given on p. 281. On 5 March 1674/5, the Lord Chamberlain issued a warrant to apprehend Le Roy, Le Duke, De Lisle, Berteau, and Hurriet, "to answer such things as shall be objected against them," but they were released the next day (LC. 4/190, ff. 118–118ᵛ).
4. Lawrence, I, 214.
5. It was paid by the Exchequer on 12 October (E. 403/1786, p. 22).
6. Reyher, p. 72.

£2000 as the average cost of a royal masque in Jacobean days,[1] and the late Caroline ones seem to have been limited to £1400.[2] The extant bills for *Calisto* come to no less than £3526.19.11¾, comprising

	£	s.	d.
Office of Works (Extraordinary Account)[3]	253.	14.	2½
Great Wardrobe[4]	2460.	4.	5
Great Wardrobe[5]	11.	11.	0
Master of the Robes[6]	275.	16.	9
Lord Steward's Department[7]	290.	18.	7¼
Musicians and Dancers[8]	234.	5.	0

The Wardrobe bills, as I have shown, include only one costume for an amateur, Diana's, and there seem to be a number missing for the professionals. Margaret Blagge can scarcely be supposed to have outshone the other principals, and I believe a conservative estimate of their costumes and two more sets for the dancers would push the total well over £5000. And even that does not include jewels.

The amateurs doubtless supplied their own costumes, and some of the others, Moll Davis' for example, may have been paid for out of the Privy Purse. But it is clear from the accounts that the greater part of the expenditure was charged in the regular way to the various departments of the Household. An imprest of £1000

1. Chambers, I, 211.
2. LC. 5/134, pp. 34, 215, 225, 359.
3. E. 351/3288.
4. LC. 9/112.
5. LC. 9/274, bills not included among those for the masque in LC. 9/112.
6. AO. 1/2052/25.
7. E. 351/1843.
8. LC. 5/141, p. 197; De Lafontaine, p. 298.

payable to Richard Coling, "to be employed towards
the Expences of Masques to be hereafter p^{r}sented before his Matie: from tyme to tyme," was ordered on
9 November;[1] but for the rest of their money, the
tradesmen had to wait their turn in the slow process of
paying Household Accounts which were chronically in
arrears. It is not surprising that Charles abandoned
the masque in favour of the masquerade.

1. LC. 5/141, pp. 50, 550.

Conclusion

THE boundaries of what at the beginning seemed to be a very limited field have receded at every step until I now find myself in the middle of an open common, with paths running in all directions. It is difficult to write a conclusion to a study which at almost every point calls for further investigation. But my aim was primarily to bring together new materials, and I hope the data here presented for the first time will serve as a fresh starting-point for research. The Windsor theatre, plays at St. James', the history of the French and Italian actors who visited England and their possible repertories — these are only a few of the subjects which one might pursue with profit and delight, and an exhaustive account of *Calisto* would run to twice as many pages as I have devoted to it.

But I doubt whether further research would controvert one fact which seems to emerge quite clearly. Before the Civil Wars, the Court stage was an important contributing factor in the development of theatrical art and the drama, but it was not a controlling factor: the stage was essentially a national institution. By the end of the seventeenth century, the Court stage had ceased to matter: it is true that in the eighteenth century, summer companies played at Richmond Palace, and I suspect the Windsor theatre too may have been used occasionally; but the increasing popularity of opera and the logical development of the patent houses brought the Court more and more to the public theatres. But for thirty years or so the theatre in Whitehall occupied a very considerable part of the energies of both players and dramatists. Companies which had to act at Court two or three times a month, and occasionally more than once a week, had to plan accordingly.

So far as the technique of production was concerned, this influence was not constructive. The development of what Webb called "the scenicall art," which had indeed originated at Whitehall in the Caroline masques, passed at the Restoration to the public theatres. The Court theatre, presumably because of its owner's lack of funds, had no resources to compete with those of Dorset Garden or even Drury Lane, and its picture-frame stage was probably — and perhaps rightly — regarded as a limitation by the best producers of the day. If a play was likely to be commanded for White-hall, a good many settings and a good deal of business must either be ruled out or so arranged that they could be adapted to the physical conditions of the Hall Theatre.

This must have had far-reaching effects. A considerable number of Restoration dramatists were protegés if not actual members of the Court circle, and doubtless it was every playwright's ambition to be put on at Whitehall. Then, too, the very number and variety of plays acted there indicates that the dramatist wrote always with the possibility of Court performance in mind, and, of course, not a few plays were written specifically to be produced there before they were given to the public. In other words, Court taste must have determined the style, subject matter, and technique of a very great many of the four hundred and odd plays written between 1660 and 1700. Furthermore, the Court sponsored frequent visits by continental companies, and their performances must have affected both the drama and the technique of acting.

The Court stage, therefore, from the point of view of dramatist, producer, and actor alike, may have been regarded as a mixed blessing, but it could not be ignored. And all this, I think, was largely due to Charles, as witness the frequency with which he has appeared in these pages. James, too, often attended the public theatres, began his reign with a play at Whitehall every week, and brought French actors to Windsor. He might have become a second Charles had he had time. But William was too preoccupied, and perhaps too indifferent, his wife too eager to have the past forgotten, to maintain the traditions of the Hall Theatre. When one thinks of the Court stage, one thinks of Charles, and both are inseparably bound up with the history and significance of the Restoration stage in general.

APPENDICES

APPENDIX A

WARRANTS AND ACCOUNTS FOR WORK ON THE COCKPIT IN COURT AND THE HALL THEATRE

THERE are very few warrants for work on the Court theatres, and many of these give no details of what is to be done. The important ones are quoted in full (except for the formal beginnings and endings), but I have summarised those which merely state that the theatre is to be prepared for a play. All of them are addressed to the Surveyor General by the Lord Chamberlain.

The accounts are taken from the ledger books in which the clerk recorded, month by month, the work done at each of the King's houses by the Office of Works. For example, all the work done by carpenters at Whitehall in any given month is recited in one long paragraph, with the exception of "extraordinary" work, that is, new construction, not part of the routine work of the office, and therefore requiring special authorisation. The items relating to the theatres have, accordingly, had to be extracted from the rest, and consequently are never complete in form, although they are complete transcripts of all that pertains to the theatre. Each extraordinary account is entered separately at the back of the book. In a few instances, to avoid much repetition, or where the entry has little significance, I have given a summary instead of a transcript, and I have omitted entries for sweeping up after the workmen and other unskilled labour.

WARRANTS

Warrant "to cause to be forthwith made a box of Seaven foot long in ye Gallery in ye Theatre in ye Hall the breadth of two seates in the Middle of ye Gallery And to put a lock & key vpon it." 4 November 1668. — LC. 5/12, p. 210.

Warrant "to make a Box in the Theatre in the Great Hall for the Lord Newport vnder the Box where now the officers of the Guard are to make a passage to come out that way." 24 September 1673.
LC. 5/140, p. 334.

Warrant[1] "to make such Alteracõns in the Sceenes in His Ma^tes Theatre in Whitehall from tyme to tyme as you haue or shall receiue directions from mee." 16 November 1674. — LC. 5/141, p. 64.

Warrant "to cause these alteracõns followinge to be made in the Theatre at Whitehall for the rep^rsentacõn of a Maske (vizt) that you make two Galleryes on each side ranginge with the Gallery at ye End & to bring forward the stage into ye Pitt, to bring back the Kings Platforme, to alter the Wings on each side the Kings Platforme & to make Boxes there To enclose the front of the pitt next the stage for the musick the whole breadth of ye house, To make Such other changes of Boxes as I shall direct vpon view, To widen the whole stage by drawing Back the side sceenes & altering the frames & Groves accordingly, To alter all the Cloudes aboue suiteable to the same by heightheninge [sic] them and ading to them, To make an openinge for a Heaven aboue with all the sceenes of Cloudes & shutter of Cloudes necessary, To make a new paire of shutters of Boscage, To make a new paire & releiues rep^rsentinge ye Prosspect of Somersett House & ye Thames, To make a Temple in the Cloudes with sceenes of Varnished silke & places for lights for ye same, To make Seates for ye Goddesses & diverse Releiues proper for that rep^rsentacõn, To fix a new Curtaine To make severall new Partitions in ye Tireing roomes, to mend ye staires goeing to ye Tireing roomes To new matt all ye Benches & staires, To paint new in distemper all ye Walls & Galleryes to new Glaze all ye Windowes & paint them And such other things as shalbe found necessary for that service." 25 January 1674/5. — Ibid., p. 551; Nicoll, pp. 43, 321.

Warrant "to Alter the stage in the Theatre in ye Whitehall by covering all the Pitt very Plaine to be fitt for Danceing at a Ball on ye nyne & twentieth of May instant." 26 May 1675. — Ibid., p. 196.

Warrant "to take the floore of ye Pitt in ye Theatre in Whitehall & leaue only such a stage as formerly for acting of Playes there." 31 May. 1675. — Ibid., p. 201.

---

1. Signed by the Vice-Chamberlain.

Warrant "to make a New Ceelinge in the Theatre in Whitehall that ye Voyces may ye Better be heard, & alsoe to make the roome Warmer." 13 October 1675. — *Ibid.*, p. 267.

Warrant "to cover ye pitt & soe alter ye stage in ye Theatre at Whitehall that it may be fitt for danceing on Munday next." 12 No^{e}vember 1675. — *Ibid.*, p. 288.

Warrant to cover the pit and alter the stage for dancing on the Queen's birthday (15 November). 4 November 1676.—*Ibid.*, p. 471.

Warrant "to alter the stage in the Hall, from being a stage to dance as it is now, into a stage to act vpon." 17 January 1676/7.

Ibid., p. 520.

Warrant "to cause ye stage in ye Theatre in Whitehall to be altered and made in such fashion as it was for Scaramouch's Acting And his Ma^{tes} seate to be placed & made as then it was, And that ye doore be opened as the Acto^{rs} then went in at . . . you are also to make such boxes & partitions as the ffrench Comœdians shall desire you for theire Accomodation." 5 February 1676/7.

Ibid., p. 528; Nicoll, p. 342.

Warrant "to p^{r}pare & fitt the Theatre in Whitehall for a Play to be acted before his Matie on Tuseday next & that you make ye Place where his Ma^{te} vsually sitts convenient for ye Chayres to be placed as formerly." 28 May 1677. — LC. 5/142, p. 40.

Warrant "to alter ye Theatre in Whitehall, & to make it for ye ffrench Players to Act there: And to be made after ye same manner as it was for ye Italian Players, & ye seate for ye King to be made as at that tyme, & ye Coming in for ye Company to be as it was then: this to be made ready by Wednesday night if it may be done." 4 December 1677. — *Ibid.*, p. 160; Nicoll, p. 342.

Warrant "to p^{r}pare & fitt the Theatre in Whitehall for a Play to be Acted before His Matie: on Tuseday next being the Queenes Maties Birthday, and that you make the place where His Ma^{te} Vsually Sitts Convenient for ye Chaires to be placed as formerly." 11 November 1681. — LC. 5/144, p. 140.

Warrant to floor the pit for dancing "vpon Saterday next." 13 February 1682/3. — *Ibid.*, p. 360.

Warrant "to cause the Passage into the Theatre in Whitehall coming vp from ye Cellar doore to be opened, for Mr Abell to represent his Musick And if he shall desire any Small Alteracõns to be made in ye Seates that you cause it to be done without prejudice to ye place." 27 November 1683. — *Ibid.*, p. 510.

Warrant to make the theatre ready for a play on 11 February. 6 February 1683/4. — LC. 5/145, p. 14.

Warrant "to fitt and p^{r}pare the Theatre in Whitehall for his Ma^{tes} Service for ye french players this p^{r}sent night." 29 September 1684.
Ibid., p. 90.

Warrant to make the theatre ready for dancing on the Queen's birthday.   10 November 1684. — *Ibid.*, p. 107.

Warrant "to cause the Kings seat in the Theatre in Whitehall to bee made after the same manner as it was when the french Comœdians acted there, some yeares since And this to bee done tomorrow." 1 January 1684/5. — *Ibid.*, p. 135.

Warrant "to rayle in two benches betweene ye Lord Stewards box and ye Scenes in ye Theatre for ye Ambassadors & foreigne Ministers, the two Benches to bee the two next ye Wall on ye left hand the Kings Seate."   14 October 1685.
LC. 5/17, p. 20; 5/146, p. 27; Nicoll, p. 342.

Warrant to prepare the theatre for a ball on the King's birthday (4 November).   14 October 1689. — LC. 5/148, p. 267.

Warrant to have men take care of the lights within the scenes at the ball on 4 November. 30 October 1689. — *Ibid.*, p. 293.

Warrant to prepare the theatre for a play on Wednesday, 30 April, being the Queen's birthday. 28 April 1690. — LC. 5/150, p. 72.

Warrant to prepare the theatre for a play on 4 November.   18 October 1690. — *Ibid.*, p. 156.

Warrant to make a new floor for a ball on 4 November. 22 October 1694. — LC. 5/151, p. 388.

Warrant to prepare the theatre for a ball on 4 November. 28 October 1697. — LC. 5/152, p. 36.

ACCOUNTS

THE COCKPIT IN COURT

November, 1660.

Carpenters: "Makeing of v large boxes wth seuerall degrees in them at ye cockpitt and doores in them, taking vp the floore of ye stage and pitt and laying againe the floore of the stage & pitt pendant, making of seuerall seats round and in ye pitt making of two ptitions in the gallery there for the Musick and players setting vp a rayle & ballisters vpon the stage making two other seats for ye gentlemen Vshers a [sic] Mr Killigrew cutting out a way and making a paire of Stayres cont. [blank] stepps to goe into ye Gallery ouer the stage & incloseing the said stayres wth a doore in it Cont. about one square, making of two new doores goeing vnder the degrees and bourding vp one doore vppon the degrees, setting vp xj squares of ptitioning vnder the degrees wth vj doores in them." — Works 5/1.

To John Davenport: "for money laid out by him to ye workmen at ye Cockpit for their extraordinary paines. x^s." — *Ibid.*

Matlayers: "new matting some of the seats of ye degrees in ye Cockpit and the seats & floore where his Matie: sitts there, . . . new [matting] seuerall other seats and the flatt belowe the stage of the cockpit." — *Ibid.*

December, 1660.

Matlayers: "new matting y^e degrees in one of y^e boxes at y^e Cockpit." — *Ibid.*

January, 1660/1.

Carpenters: "Setting vp one ptition for m^r Johnson at y^e Cockpit Cont. j square D$\bar{\imath}$: wth a doore in it." — *Ibid.*

February, 1660/1.

Matlayers: "mending y^e matts at y^e Cockpit wth new bull rush matts." — *Ibid.*

August, 1661.

Plasterers: "Lathing and plaistering part of a wall on both sides at the cockpitt playhouse." — Works 5/2.

October, 1661.

Plasterers: "poynting the glass in three windowes at the cockpit playe house." — *Ibid.*

Matlayers: "mending the matts at ye Cockpit playhouse in the Kings closset there." — *Ibid.*

November, 1661.

To John Anstree, Matlayer, for "v bedmatts to be layd vpon the floore vnderneath the stage at the Cockpit playhouse" at 12^d a piece. — *Ibid.*

January, 1661/2.

Carpenters: "making a new doore at the Cockpit playhowse bourding vp 2 windowes there & putting vp a raile of pinns 30 fo^t. long there alsoe, Incloseing the Top of a paire of staires leading vp from a roome behind the Kings Closset into ye leads, & putting vp 2 shelues in the sade roome there." — *Ibid.*

April, 1662.

Joiners: "making shutting windowes for ye Cockpit playhowse 4 fo^t. 3 iñ: wide & 4 fo^t. 10 iñ: high in 4 leaues." — Works 5/3.

September, 1662.

Carpenters: "putting vp 24 battins in the boxes at the Cockpit playhowse." — *Ibid.*

Matlayers: "mending the matts vnder the state at the Cockpit playhowse." — *Ibid.*

November, 1662.

Carpenters: "mending a floore & making a new gutter at the cockpit play howse." — *Ibid.*

Bricklayers: "Cuttinge way for 2 Chimneys & building them vp at the Cockpit playhouse & mending tileing there." — *Ibid.*

December, 1662.

Matlayers: "mending the matts in the Cockpit playhowse." — *Ibid.*

January, 1662/3.

Plumbers: "making & putting vp a Cistern at ye Cockpit playhowse." — *Ibid.*

October, 1663.

Carpenters: "making a paire of staires of 12 stepps goeing vp from the vpper tiering roome into ye leads at the Cockpit playhowse, Incloseing the said staires wth: whole deale & slitt deale, wth a new doore at ye foote of them, making a portall in the same roome wth a doore in it." — Works 5/4.

Matlayers: "mending the matts at the Cockpit Play howse wth: old matt." — *Ibid.*

March, 1670/1.

The Cockpit lodgings were partly rebuilt; the "vpper gallery & boxes lookeing downe into ye Cockpit playhowse" were turned into "guardrobes"; there is also mention of "a lower roome next vnto the pitt." — Works 5/17.

November, 1671.

Plumbers: "Cutting vp p^t. of the old lead over the Cockpitt playhouse and laying 7 Cants there with new sheet lead in ye top of A Chimney over the greate Buttery, and doeing divers other needfull workes there." — *Ibid.*

April, 1672.

Plumbers: laying new lead "on the lanthorn at the cockpit, playhouse." — Works 5/19.

May, 1672.

Plumbers: mending the leads over the Cockpit playhouse. — *Ibid.*

The Hall Theatre

August, 1660.

Masons: "Takeing vp some paueing in the great hall and makeing two holes in the wall there for the putting in of two peices of timber to fasten the roapes for the Dancers to dance thereon and makeing the same holes vp agayne and Layeing the paueing againe."

Works 5/1.

Carpenters: "Joysting and boarding about vij square in the great hall for the Daunceing on the roapes and setting iiij square of ptitioning there [*and*] lx^{tie}. foote of ledging for hangings there."

Ibid.

December, 1662.

"To John Angier Carpenter for his taske of Carpenters worke done in ye hall he finding onely nailes & workmanship vizt:

ffor xviij squares iij q^{r}ters & x foote of vpright worke & flooreing on the stage at x^s the square	09:08:06
ffor xxxix square & iij q^{r}ters in the degrees & staires at xij^s ye square	23:17:00
ffor setting vp xij fo^t. Di': of railes & ballisters on ye said staires at vj^d ye foote	00:06:03
ffor xxvij foote of raile & termes on ye stage at vj^d ye foote	00:13:06
ffor making one broad stepp ladder x foote long & ij foote wide	00:02:06
ffor lvj foote of Elme Board at ij^d ye foote	00:09:04

34:17:01."
Works 5/3.

Matlayers: "new matting part of the degrees in the hall wth bull-rush matt." — *Ibid.*

January, 1662/3.

Carpenters: putting up 182 ft. of ledges for hangings in the great hall, "Enlarging the degrees for ye musick there Encloseing the state with slitt deale Cont.' j square & one quarter." — *Ibid.*

February, 1662/3.

Carpenters: "takeing downe the throne in ye hall and makeing good the raile & termes on the stage there, & bourding vp part of the fore-side of the stage wth slitt deale, making a foot pace at ye vpper end of the hall Cont' j square & 40 foote, bourding vp ye window at ye vpper End of the hall Cont': 160 foote, putting vp 5 peeces at 5 of ye windowes there, for ye hangings, fitting & laying bourds on part of ye floore there Cont'. 3 square & 60 foote." — *Ibid.*

February, 1662/3.

Matlayers: "takeing vp ye matts wch lay on ye throne in ye hall & laying them on ye other throne there, & matting 9 foormes ther alsoe." — *Ibid.*

March, 1662/3.

Matlayers: "new matting seuerall ffoormes in the hall, matting the passage goeing into the hall from the wineseller." — *Ibid.*

February, 1664/5 to April 1665.

Extraordinary Account.

"Workes & Reparacõns don in the Gr^t: Hall at Whitehall in ye Moneths of February March & Aprill 1664/5.

Masons Employed in working and putting in a Truss of Kentish stone to beare a peece of timber and the hearth of a Chimney in one of the tiring rooms working and putting in 2 trusses of free Stone in the outside of the wall at the north end of the hall to beare ye Chimneys of the tiring roomes there. Cutting 2 door wayes through the stone wall, one at the head the other at the foot of the Staires of ye new passage into ye hall, and working vp the Splayes thereof wth stone worke, & pinning in Two door Cases there. Joynting and laying 40 foot of new purbeck paving at ye foot of ye s^d Staires. Cutting a hole through a stone buttress there for ye laying a Trough of lead to carry ye wat^r off the Roofe of ye said passage, & cutting holes in ye wall for the Cieling joysts of the s^d passage. Cutting way through ye said wall & working vp the splayes thereof wth stone worke, and raysing ye outside of the said door way and wall 2 foot high & pinning in a doorcase and laying ye lintells higher, Cutting seuerall holes in ye walls of ye said hall to lay in timb^r & making room to draw back the staires.^{1} . . . (£9.15.1.)

Carpenters Employed in taking downe all the old degrees in the hall & raysing the old Stage there higher & cutting it shorter, making & putting vp 12 boxes and severall degrees round ye said stage, boarded underneath with slitt deale, making a gallery at ye south end of ye hall 40 foot long 7 foot wide wth degrees and severall boxes in it, and a paire of staires leading vp to it, making a foot pace vpon the stage for the K & Queen wth a rayle about it, making a pendant floor in ye pitt wth degrees at each end wth 16 seates in it, making a Stage for the Sceens 39 foot long 33 foot wide and v foot high, making a frontispeece and boarding over it to ye roofe of the hall, and making severall

---

1. There follows a list of workmen employed, with the number of days each worked and the wages due to him; I shall give only the total cost of the labour, enclosed in parentheses, and so throughout the account.

frames shutting vpon ye said stage, making a large seat wth severall degrees in it for ye musick, making a floor over the Stage 43 foot long 39 foot wide for ye hanging vp of the workes & frames of ye Sceenes making enclosing & flooring 4 roomes at ye north end of the hall for tiring Roomes for ye Actors and Musick, & making 4 pair of staires leading vp to ye great Stage and ye said Tiring Rooms boarding vp all the windows round ye hall, making 2 large doorcases & doores wth 4 stepps of staires goeing downe to ye stage where ye footpace was made for ye K & Queen to sitt in and making seuerall scaffolds for ye painting of ye frontispeece & Sceens and taking y^m down againe, making provision to draw ye Ovall Shutt^{rs} before ye musicke and to take vp and let downe the Curtain: Setting vp seuerall benches in the Tiring Rooms and making seuerall benches in ye tiring rooms, making seu^{r}all Tables tressells & formes for y^m: enclosing seuerall rooms under the great Stage for severall necessary vses and Keeping of Provisions in. . . . (£196.1.2.)

Bricklayers Employed in taking downe ye Jammis and breast of the great Chimney in the Hall and new working it vp againe, Cutting way through the stone wall at the north end of the hall and making two Chimneys there for the tiring Roomes, and laying 2 hearths and foot paces wth brick in the said Chimneys, taking downe a particõn wall at the foote of the staires going vp to the K^s Guardchamber to make way for a passage into ye Hall and pinning vp Lintells and working a bricke wall 9 inches thick to face between 2 walls there, pinning a doore case at the bottom of the said passage, working vp a brick wall wth rubbd bricks 18 foot high 12 foot wide to enclose the said passage from ye great Court, Cutting rubbing and setting a streight Arch over a window there and cutting bricks for ye Copeing and making tables of the said wall lathing and tyling wth pantyles the Roofe of the said passage, making good the tyling wch was broken wth making of scaffolds to ye aforesaid Chymneys. . . . . (£13.14.4.)

Joyners Employed in making a moddell for the Sceenes making 22 frames and Joyned formes making a Compart seat or Throne for the Queen, making a framed table wth turned feet 3 foot di long and 2 foot and a halfe broad. . . . (£13.17.6.)

Plaisterers Employed in lathing and plaistering in the new passage to ye Hall and rendering the walls there, Plaistering the walls where the 2 new Chimneys were made for ye tiring rooms and also the backs and Jammes of the said Chimneys. . . . (£0.6.6.)

Matlayers Employed in new matting the back and seats of all the boxes in the hall and ye degrees in the gatt at the south end of the hall and the seats below. matting the Stepps of 6 pair of staires and ye walls thereof, and ye seates and walls for the musick room, new matting ye walls and benches in the tyring roomes and ye floores between the Relieves and ye walls and floores in ye passage behinde the relievs, the walls and floore between ye said sceens and all the Degrees and seats in the Pitt. All don wth bullrush matt. . . . (£3.8.4.) To Robt. Little, Carpenter, for his Extraordinary paines early and late in hastening the Carpent^rs worke. Allowed in reward for this whole worke v^li.

To Iohn Angier, Carpenter for two Oaken doorcases Posts 7 and 9 inches scantling 8 foot and 4 foot di wide wrought wth an Architrave molding 7 inches broad wth 2 glewd lined and battind doors at lv^s the door Case and door in the passage for the Queen to goe into ye Sceenes — vli. x^s. for 2 window lights there at 4^s the light . . . for one large door Case Posts 7 and 9 inches scantling 8 fot: high 6 foot wide working wth. an Architraue molding 7 inches broad with one pair of glewd leynd and battind doors at the south of the hall for a passage for the King into ye hall –iij^li.viij^s. — xiij^li.ij^s." [1]

Works 5/7.

October, 1666.
Carpenters: "making 4 scaffolds in the hall for ye putting vp wyers for the hanging of branches thereon, Joysting & boarding a floore ouer the pitt there Cont': about 6 square, mending & fitting the Ceanes." — Works 5/9.

Matlayers: "new matting the Kings throne in ye hall, & new matting 6 foormes there w^th: bull rush matts, & mending the matts in the passage there also." — *Ibid.*

November, 1666.
Carpenters: "Joysting & bourding the floore ouer the pitt in ye hall, taking it vp againe & plaineing ye bourds putting vp socketts, & plates for ye lights in ye scheanes." — *Ibid.*

---

1. There follow bills for building materials, etc., and for the work of sawyers and labourers, and the services of a Clerk of the Works; then a summary of the whole, amounting to £737.11.2¼.

December, 1666.

Carpenters: "bridging the floore ouer the pitt in yᵉ hall & new laying the bourds againe, Cont': about 5 square Dĩ:" — *Ibid.*

January, 1666/7.

Carpenters: "Quartering vp 7 windowes in yᵉ hall Cont': 6 square ½ & 24 foᵗ. putting vp two peeces at yᵉ vpper end of yᵉ hall, 20 foᵗ: long a peece for yᵉ Curtaine there, & putting vp pullies & weights of lead for yᵉ same." — *Ibid.*

Plasterers: "Lathing & plaistering 5 windowes in yᵉ hall, papering the cracks of two more there, papering ouer yᵉ Cracks vnderneath all yᵉ degrees, to keepe out yᵉ wind, lathing & plaistering vppon yᵉ bourds in yᵉ Greate dooreway next yᵉ winesellar, lathing & plaistering on yᵉ bourds at yᵉ outer doore, vnderneath yᵉ stage, lathing & plaistering part of yᵉ outside of yᵉ great window at vpper End of yᵉ hall." — *Ibid.*

Matlayers: "mending the matts in yᵉ hall." — *Ibid.*

Plumbers: "Casting weights for a Curtaine in yᵉ hall." — *Ibid.*

"To Phillip Lasenby for 73 yards of fine blue Canvas at
xvijᵈ yᵉ yard for a curtaine for the Hall Window	5:03:5
ffor 6 doz: of thred line at xvjᵈ yᵉ doz:	0: 8:0
ffor 40 large brass rings	0: 2:0
ffor thred to make yᵉ Curtaine	0: 1:8
ffor 5 dayes worke to make the Curtaine & the rings	0:15:0
ffor 20 yards of yᵉ best blue tape for yᵉ rings	0: 1:6"

Ibid.

February, 1666/7.

Carpenters: "laying downe the Joysts & bourding the floore in yᵉ hall for Danceing Cont': 5 square & 12 foᵗ: quartering vp 2 windowes there Cont': 2 square ½ & 2 foᵗ:, making seates for the musick there, Cutting out a dooreway & hanging a doore to Sʳ John Dinhams box." — *Ibid.*

Plasterers: "lathing a little seeling betweene yᵉ Joysts vnder ye Stage in the hall . . . lathing & plaistering a little partition vnder Sʳ John Dinhams box in yᵉ hall . . . lathing & plaistering vp 2 windowes in yᵉ hall." — *Ibid.*

May, 1667.

Carpenters: "making & hanging a doore in yᵉ hall." — Works 5/10.

September, 1667.

To Phillip Lasenby: "for 10 peeces of blue fferrett ribbin for the Curtayne in the Theatre at 4ˢ a peece cont' 36 yards in a peece 2.0.0." — *Ibid.*

February, 1667/8.

Carpenters: "making two boxes in yᵉ hall one for yᵉ Lords Comision^{rs}. of the Treasury The other for the Vicechamberlaine." —*Ibid.*

Plasterers: pointing the glass in the lantern over the hall. — *Ibid.*

Matlayers: "new matting a paire of staires in yᵉ hall & a half pace below it, new matting 3 degrees in yᵉ Gallery there, & another half pace there." — *Ibid.*

May, 1668.

Plasterers: mending and whiting the passage from the great Hall to the Water staires. — Works 5/11.

November, 1668.

Carpenters: "Giuing attendance in the hall seuerall nights when the Playes were there."[1]

Joiners: "putting vp a bourd to raise the Duke of Munmouths seate in the Hall." — *Ibid.*

December, 1668.

Carpenters: "quartering up a windowe in the Hall Cont about iiij squares . . . waiteing seu' nights in yᵉ Hall on the playes."
                                                            Ibid.

Plasterers: "lathing & plaistering the inside of a great window in the Hall." — *Ibid.*

January, 1668/9.

Carpenters: "waiting seuerall nights in the Hall on the playes."
                                                            Ibid.

February, 1668/9.

Carpenters: "Giuing attendance on the Playes in the Hall seuerall nights." — *Ibid.*

---

1. For details of these and later attendances, see pp. 271–272.

May, 1669.

Masons and carpenters repaired the roof of the Great Hall, and there
was more carpenters' work on it in June, and carpenters' and plumbers' in July. In August, £2 reward was allowed to Wm. Allingham,
Richard Grover, John Harding, Wm. Furbush and Andrew Osbourne, "for their Extraordinary paines about a difficult peece of
Worke in Repaireing the roofe of the Great Hall." — Works 5/13.

October, 1670.

To Sir George Waterman, Kt. and Alderman of London, for 1 piece
of whipcord at 1ˢ. "for yᵉ scenes in yᵉ hall." — Works 5/15.

November, 1670.

Carpenters: "making a scaffold in yᵉ hall for Cords to be putt cross
to hold vp a ceiling of Cloth, 50 foᵗ: long & 40 foᵗ: broad making a
nother scaffold there aboue the Cloth Ceiling to Goe rownd to hang
vp yᵉ branches, Cutting out a dore way & hanging a dore to Come
out of yᵉ Clouds on the said scaffold, making & hanging a dore to yᵉ
Surveyʳ: of yᵉ works his box." — *Ibid.*

Plasterers: pointing the windows in the hall and "pasting paper on
yᵉ Joynts of yᵉ bourd vndʳ the boxes there."

Matlayers: "new Matting one part of yᵉ staires in yᵉ hall, new Matting 6 foormes & mending yᵉ matts in seuerall places there." — *Ibid.*

Mazerscourers: "sweeping the Inside of yᵉ roofe of yᵉ Hall, & the
Ceans & yᵉ walls there." — *Ibid.*

December, 1670.

Carpenters: "taking downe the Great Scaffold in yᵉ hall, & making
two scaffolds to goe rownd aboue the Ceiling, making a ladder there
26 foᵗ: long, making a paire of large shutters in yᵉ Ceans there."

Ibid.

Plasterers: "Poynting yᵉ Glass of yᵉ lanthorn ouer yᵉ hall, pasting
paper on yᵉ Joynts of yᵉ bourds about yᵉ pitt." — *Ibid.*

Matlayers: "new Matting two paire of staires, in yᵉ hall, new
matting a bench belowe & two benches in yᵉ Gallery, straining yᵉ
matts in yᵉ passage & mending yᵉ matts in seuerall places there."

Ibid.

Mazerscourers: "fetching the shutters for ye Ceans in ye hall from longacre." [1] — *Ibid*.

January, 1670/1.
Carpenters: "making a paire of back Ceanes in ye theater in white-hall, Joysting & bourding a staige ouer ye pitt Cont': About 3 squares, & bourding vp one side wth: slit deale Cont'; 90 foote, wth: a little dore there alsoe." — *Ibid*.

To Samuell Wells: "by him payd to seuerall taylers, for sewing the Cloth for the Ceiling in the Theater in whitehall and making knotts & other workes donne there by them in ye months of nouember and december last 3:16:2." — *Ibid*.

"To Robert Streeter Serjant Painter ffor painting done in the Theater vizt.

ffor painting 4 paire of wings of boscage at v^{li} the paire one wth: ye other	20: 0:0
ffor painting a paire of shutters	05: 0:0
ffor the Cloth for ye shutters Cont': 19 yards at ij^s ye yard ready prim'd	1:18:0
ffor new painting the figure of fame and Altering the posture	1: 0:0
ffor Colouring the Cord in ye Ceiling	0:10:0
Payd by him to ye Joyner for new putting together the figure of fame & Cutting all ye bourds & naileing them on ye 4 p of wings	0:10:0
	28:18:0"

Ibid.

January, 1670/1.
"To Phillip Lasenby for 15 peeces of fine skey Coloured Callico being 17 yards long & i yard & half quarter brode at xxiiij^s the peece being for a false Ceileing in ye Theater

	18: 0:0
ffor 6 peeces of ye best skye coloured Cotten Ribbon at 6^s The pecce	1:16:0
ffor 24 ounces of Skye Coloured thred there	0: 8:0
ffor 3 large Hand baskets There	0: 2:0
ffor Carr': at twice	0: 3:0
	20: 9:0"

Ibid.

---

1. Streeter lived in Longacre (Pepys).

February, 1670/1.

Carpenters: "putting vp 8 degrees in ye hall 14 fo^t: long a peece, wth: two foote paces to them, taking downe two boxes there, & Enlarging 8 benches, 4 fo^t: long a peece, wth: foot steps to them, Enlarging the stage wth: new Joysts & bourds, about one square, Cutting out part of the stage & fitting a place there for ye Queens musick, wth: railes about it & bourded, putting vp 54 foote of double q^{r}ters for the hangings to hang on, putting vp 4 bourds behind the hangings to fasten sconces to, laying Joysts for a Cloth Ceiling in ye Queens roome Cont': one square & ½ Bourding wth: slitt deale about ye Musick seate in ye Clowds Cont': about one square, Incloseing a roome for ye Italian musitions Cont': one square ½, making a trough at ye foote of the stage for lights to stand in, Altering the Queens throne & bourding a place for a Chaire to stand on, making a place wth: bourds for lights to stand on on both sides, taking downe all ye boxes in ye Gallery there alsoe, putting vp railes wth: flapps & bourded vp, in the Queens presence, Kings Guardchamber & on the guardchamber staires, Cont': about 2 squares." — *Ibid.*

Plasterer: stopping and whiting two chimneys in the hall. — *Ibid.*

Matlayers: new matting a step in the hall and mending several places there. — *Ibid.*

Mazerscourers: "attending in the Hall when ye Dancing was there."
Ibid.

To Robert Streeter, Serjeant Painter.
"For painteing a paire of Shutters of a garden in y^e
 Theater at Whitehall   6: 0:0
For 20 y^{r}ds of Cloath for ye said Shutters ready nailed vp
 and primed at 2^s p y^{r}d   2: 0:0
For paynting ye Scene of ye Mill there   4: 0:0
For ye Joyners worke to make ye dooe [*sic*] there in y^e
 said Scene and for stuffe to doe it withall   0: 5:0
For painting ye Clouds and seu'all Works done aboute
 them   4:16:0
                                                                         ————————
                                                                         17:01:0"
                                                                         Ibid.

April, 1671.

To John Wells, Tinman, "for wares made & deli^{ed}, for his Maties. seruice in the Theater in Whitehall in ffeb: last vizt, ffor xxxvj socketts and Panns xxxv^s: for xij large Walers xvj^s for xxiiij large Walers xxxij^s: for ij of ye largest double scollops xiiij^s: for ij new fashion scollops xij^s: for ij ball scollops ix^s: for iij large and j small Extinguisher x^d: for ij funnells ix^d for a paire of Snuffers xviij^d: for a hand Candlestick xviij^d — vj^{li}: ij^s: vij^d:" — Works 5/17.

June, 1671.
"To Henry Glouer by him laid out for the theator in Whitehall vizt. for iij quarts of oyle at xviij^d: ye quart iiij^s: vj^d: ffor Cotton to fill ye Lamps viij^d: for iij pints of oyle more ij^s: iij^d: for thredd: ij^s: vij^s: vij^d:" — *Ibid.*

December, 1672.
Carpenters: "taking downe the staige ouer ye pitt in the theater putting vp two barrs at the Kings guardchamber, & taking them downe againe, setting 5 locks on ye boxes there." — Works 5/19.
Matlayer: "mending the Matts of ye degrees in the theater & the matts behind ye Cenes & other places there." — *Ibid.*

January, 1672/3.
Bricklayers: "mending ye slatting ouer the Theater." — *Ibid.*

March, 1672/3.
Carpenters: "making frames for shutters in ye Theater, making a bench with a back to it in the pitt there, putting vp two railes in the Musick seates, & making a broad stepp ladder 7 fo^t: long, Cutting out a way in the stage for a trapp dore, there alsoe, setting vp two Railes at the Guardchamber dores wth: barrs and taking them downe again." — *Ibid.*

To Robert Streeter:
"ffor paynting like rusticke stone worke the greate backe cloath for
the sceanes in the theater cont' 50 yards at 10^d ℗ yard   02:01:8
ffor 17 yards and a halfe of cloath for the Arch and the
cross peece of stoneworke at 2^s ℗ yard   01:15:0
ffor paynting the stone worke on the Arch and cross peece 02:15:0"
Ibid.

May, 1673.
Carpenters: "makeing a paire of Shutters for the ceanes in ye Theater, makeing two releiues there seting vp a table behinde ye Ceanes 12 foote long & makeing iij degrees there, cuting way on ye stage for a trapdoare & making & hanging ye dore & makeing a

wooden horse to stand on ye stage vj foote high & vj foote long making a flattforme in ye clouds v foote square there alsoe, seting vp ij railes in ye Kings guardchamber to keepe people of & takeing them downe againe." — Works 5/21.

Wm. Beach, Smith: "for . . . ij new large plate spring boults for a trapp doare on ye Stage in ye Theater v^s." — Ibid.

Robert Streeter:
"For viij yards and a ½ of new cloath for ye two rock peices and ye long peices of sky at ij^s p y^rd. ready nailed vp and primord [sic] xvij^s for painting the ij peices of rocks xxx^s for colouring ouer the great cloath to put out ye stone worke that was painted on it cont' liiij yards at ij^d ye yard ix^s. ffor painteing ye great back cloath with sky & Sea and ye two long bourds of sea cont' all lvij y^rds and a halfe at ij^s ij^d yard v^li. xiiij^s for painting and mending ye rest of ye screane [sic] & painteing two pedistalls like stone iiij^s — viij^li: xiiij^s Charles Streeter." — Ibid.

June, 1673.
Carpenters: "takeing upp ye old flattforme ouer ye Porch by ye Theatrye, new Joysting And boarding it againe cont' two squares xxiiij foote." — Ibid.

Plumber: work on the same, covering it with sheet lead. — Ibid.

December, 1673.
Matlayer: "mending the matts of the staires & degrees in the Theater." — Ibid.

January, 1673/4.
Carpenters: "setting vpp the railes in the Kings Guardchamber and the passage leading thence to the Kings Chappell to keepe people from thronging at the doore goeing into the Theater and takeing them downe againe mending ye railes aboute the Throne there, and doeing divers other necessary workes there, giveing attendance seu'all nights when the Danceing and Operas were practissed."

                                                                    Ibid.

November, 1674 to February, 1674/5.
Extraordinary Account.
"Charges about Altering the Theatre at Whitehall in the Monthe of Nouember 1674
Mason Imployed in stopping seuerall holes in ye stone Wall & letting in & yoteing with lead six Iron barrs into ye stone Window at ye Westend of ye Theatree   Henry: Gray–one Daye–o:2:6.

Carpenters Imployed in makeing a scaffold to take downe ye frontispeece for ye Enlarging ye stage, takeing vp ye floore of the stage &
playning & shooteing ye boads [sic], & layeing them agayne, & Enlarging ye said staige one yard broad into ye pitt & bourding y^e
fore parte thereof next ye pitt, makeing a new Dore & frame in y^e
floore of ye said stage for ye sinkeing vnderneath ye same takeing
downe ye said scenes & Cutting them less & Makeing ye groues
shorter, & rayseing ye backs shutters, takeing downe ye Cloudes
agayne, & bourding vp behind ye said Clouds agayne takeing downe
ye Musicke seats & laying two large floores & rayseing another floore
with seuerall degrees for ye Musicke, Cutting ye Throne three foo^t
shorter to Enlarge ye pitt & bourding vp ye foreside agayne next y^e
pitt, Remooveing ye pitt into Itts former place agayne & Makeing
benches there & Cutting ye Kings seate shorter playning & listing of
bourds & setting on locks. . . . (£28.8.0.) [1]

More Worke done in the Theatre at Whitehall in the Month of December, 1674.
Mason Imployed in cutting severall holes in ye stone walls of y^e
Theatre for ye fastening of ye trusses of [sic] to supporte ye new galleryes there. . . . (£0.4.8.)
Carpenters Imployed in makeing two boxes on eachside the degrees
next unto ye pitt, takeing downe ye staires goeing vp into ye tireing
roome & makeing a new p [sic] of staires instead thereof cont' tenn
stepps, makeing a boarded p^rtition [sic] in ye tireing roome, with a
dore & case in it, makeing a new paire of staires goeing vp into y^e
clouds cont' about 8 stepps makeing a floore Joysted & boarded at
end of ye mooueing shutters for ye draweing of ye same cont' about
50 fo^te: fastening vp ye Circular clouds & putting vp one paire of
shutters for clouds & makeing new groues for them to slide in frame-
ing & putting vp 8 trusses of timber for ye supporteing ye galleries on
each side ye pitt & makeing ye said galleries each 36 fo^te: long 4 fo^te:
& a halfe wide & boarding vp ye foresides thereof & vnderneath
ye degrees, makeing two degrees for seates in ye said galleryes at y^e
whole length of ye galleries takeing downe ye boarding of three windowes behind ye galleries for ye fastening of ye timber worke of y^e
said trusses and putting in 5 peeces of timber into y^e Iambs of y^e
said windowes for y^e takeing downe of y^e trusses & boarding vp y^e

---

1. Cost of labour. *Cf.* p. 243. For supplies, see below.

windowes agayne & takeing vp y^e cloath before y^e said windowes. . . .
(£30.16.6$\frac{3}{4}$.)

Matlayers Imployed in takeing vp y^e old matts vppon y^e staires &
y^e halfepace goeing out of y^e lodg: to y^e Theatre & new matting them
agayne takeing vp y^e old matts of y^e throne & new matting it agayne
new matting all y^e benches in y^e pitt & seuerall formes & benches in
other places, matting with old matts ye staires goeing vp to ye tireing
roome & mending ye matts of another paire of staires; . . . (£1.17.6.)

More Worke done at ye Theatre in Whitehall in Ianuary & ffebruary 1674
Carpenters and other workmen Imployed in altering ye Lord Cham-
berlains & ye Lord Nuportes boxes & makeing a box for ye Survey' of
ye workes & makeing bracketts for ye Candlestickes, cutting ye rayle
behind ye Kings seate & hanging it in two partes & putting vp two
side barrs there, cutting a hole in ye vpper dore & battening ye hole
with a flapp to it, makeing degrees behind ye backe clouds for y^e
setting of lights there boarding with slitt deales behind ye vpper
sceanes for ye putting vp of sconces & Candlestickes, makeing of
grooues aboue & below for sceanes of Denmarke howse & ye arbour
& putting vp ye said sceanes lineing ye backes of ye shutters for y^e
putting vp of lights, & nayleing ye sconces & Candlestickes to y^e
backes of ye clouds, makeing a frame with degrees for lights behind
ye glory cutting ye edges of ye arbour & ye flory banke and ye edges
of seueral clouds makeing seuerall circular seates for ye Goddesses to
sett in ye clouds makeing a frame 4 foote high to sett ye Kettledrum
on setting vp seuerall releiues in ye clouds, takeing downe the p^{r}ti-
tions [sic] in that which was ye Lord Chamberlaines box & new boarding ye floore of it 10 fo^{te}: long & 3 fo^{te}: broad & makeing one degree
there 15 fo^{te}: long & boarding vp ye doreway goeing into ye said box
putting vp a rayle & a flapp at one end of ye new gallery for a box
for ye Countess of Suffolke, & putting vp a rayle & a post for a seate
for ye Master of ye Reuells, makeing & setting vp 26 foote of ptitiõ
in the passage betwixt the Theatre and Whitehall bridg giueing
attendance by night to drawe the sceanes & shutters & doeing other
necessary workes there. . . . (£15.7.11.)

Matlayer employed in new matting the staires goeing vp to the
stage And the bourded floore at the staire head and the floore where
the Kings Chaire is sett. . . . (£0.7.6.)

To Richard Rider Mr Carpenter ffor one paire of sceanes of y^e boscage 13 foote by 15 fo^{te}: ffor 2 side frames for y^e same each 13 fo^t: by 4 fo^t: ffor y^e backe peece for y^e glory with a round cutt in it 11 fo^{te}: $\frac{1}{2}$ by 7 fo^{te}: $\frac{1}{2}$, ffor a frame for y^e taffaty 3 fo^t: & a halfe square, ffor a frame for y^e temple of fame 11 fo^t: & a halfe by 7 fo^{te}: & a halfe, ffor 2 side frames 11 fo^{te}: & a halfe by 3 fo^{te}: each being open in y^e middle & boarded round about, ffor 2 side frames 11 fo^{te}: $\frac{1}{2}$ by 3 fo^{te}: each, ffor 2 side frames 13 fo^{te}: by 4 fo^{te}, ffor 2 side frames more 13 fo^{te}: by 4 fo^{te}: each, ffor one paire of shutters for cloudes 15 foote by 13 fo^{te}: ffor 2 side frames for them 13 fo^{te}: by 4 fo^{te}: each, ffor y^e frames for y^e sceanes of Denmarke 15 foote by 14 fo^{te}: 9 inches, ffor 2 side frames for it 14 fo^{te}: 9 inches by 4 fo^{te}: each for ye backe part of y^e Arbour 15 fo^{te}: by 14 fo^{te}: 9 inches, ffor 2 side frames for it 14 fo^{te}: 9 inches by 4 fo^{te}: each, for the front of y^e Arbour 15 fo^{te}: by 14 fo^{te}: being open & boarded round in all 235 y^{r}ds and two thirds of a y^{r}d at ij^s: iiij^d p y^{r}d. . . . (£27.09.10$\frac{1}{2}$.)

To Robert Streeter ffor paynting y^e addition in y^e top of y^e frontispeece & mending seuerall partes about it   5: 0: 0

ffor paynting y^e sceane of boscage being a paire of shutters & a paire of side Releises   10: 0: 0

ffor clenseing all y^e wall betweene the wings of y^e sceanes & twice colouring it & afterwards paynting there & boscage on it   3: 0: 0

ffor paynting ye temple of fame in ye clouds   5: 0: 0

ffor paynting ye sceane of Denmarkehowse   12: 0: 0

ffor paynting 139 yards of cloudes at ij^s:vj^d p yard   17: 7: 6

ffor taffaty for ye glory   0:12: 0

ffor 267 yards 6 fo^{te}: of cloath ready nayled vp & primed to paynt on at ij^s p yard   26:15: 4

ffor paynting 3 times in distemper & nayleing vp ye cloath about ye walls of the Theatre & paynting all ye boxes & galleries cont' 600 yards at vj^d p yard   15: 0: 0

ffor paynting [y^e peacocke, y^e Eagle] the Vine, the flory banke, [& y^e clouds before] y^e seates in y^e clouds   3: 0: 0"

(£97:14:10.)[1]

                                    Works 5/24.

---

1. There are bills for building materials and supplies amounting to £52.15.9$\frac{3}{4}$.

December, 1674 (Ordinary Account).

Plasterers: "poynting the glasse of 18 window lights in y^e theatree, plaistering with lime and haire y^e slitt Deale lineing behind y^e degrees in y^e new gallery made in y^e theater, lathing and plaistering seuerall broken places in y^e windowes behind ye sceanes and ye tireing roome." — Works 5/24.

February, 1674/5.

Carpenters: "taking downe seuerall Boxes in the theater, taking downe the partitions in ye passage Leading to ye waterside, by the theater." — *Ibid.*

April, 1675.

Carpenters: "putting up a boarded fence in ye passage to Whitehall bridge before ye Theater dore 25 foo^t in length, putting up railes with flapps to them att ye Staire head going to ye Kings Guard Chamber & in ye guard Chamber & att ye Theatree dore next ye guard Chamber to keepe ye people from Crowding into ye Theatre, . . . makeing a Box in ye Theatree 8 foote long with a dore & lock to it." — *Ibid.*

May, 1675.

Carpenters: "fitting & laying a floore Ioysted bridged & bourded over ye pitt att ye Theater in Whitehall Cont' about 5 squares, Cutting fitting & setting seuerall formes vppon ye stage & makeing 4 new formes to be vsed there Carryeing & recarryeing 4 musick formes from ye Queenes p^{r}sence to & from ye said Theater, putting vp ye Railes in the Kings guard Chamber & the staires head there to prevent ye Crouding of ye people into ye Theater." — *Ibid.*

June, 1675.

Carpenters: "takeing away the foote pace & the raile that encompassed ye Kings seat in ye Theater & making 3 boxes there with 4 benches in each box cutting way through ye Degrees on one side of ye Theater & makeing a paire of staires of 8 stepps to goe into the Theater with an hand Raile on each side the staires and bourding up ye End of ye degrees on each side ye staires Enclosing ye fore side of ye degrees on each side ye pitt & takeing downe ye Surveyours Box there Setting up ye 2 portalls vpon ye Stage removing ye Bosketts and Setting up the Architectures in there places, putting up two ledges of bourds in ye throughs [*sic*] where the Lamps were sett, Cutting a dore way through a bourded p^{t}ition, putting up 2 dore posts And makeing & hanging a dore there & makeing a paire of staires there vp into ye gallery & bourding up a p̃ticõn at ye staires foote & hanging an old dore in it putting up & takeing downe railes att ye guard Chamber when ye play was Acted there." — *Ibid.*

September, 1675.
Carpenters: "Mending & putting ye Sceanes in there places at ye theatre in Whitehall." — Works 5/26.

November, 1675.
Carpenters: "takeing Downe y[e] Theatre where y[e] Kings throne stood & layeing y[e] halfe pace there agayne with a rayle round about it, Couering y[e] pitt with bourds & ioysts for Dancing and takeing downe y[e] formes from vnder y[e] Stage & placeing them vppon y[e] stage, takeing away two boxes from amongst y[e] Sceanes putting vp & takeing y[e] rayles at y[e] Dore of y[e] Theatre & in y[e] guard Chamber & y[e] guard Chamber Staires, takeing Downe y[e] Cloath Ceileing there." — *Ibid.*

Matlayer: "Mending y[e] old Matts vppon y[e] Staires in y[e] Theatre, putting a peece of New Matts before y[e] Throne there." — *Ibid.*

"October xxviij[th]. 1675
An agreement made then by the Officers of his Maj[ts] Workes on the behalfe of his Maj[tie] with M[r] Sell to erect a floore for a ceiling in the Hall according to the direction he hath already receiued and to finish all fitt (for the Plaist[rs]: to ceile the same) with slitt deale as shall be hereafter directed if it shall be required for which floore without the ceiling the said Sell doth agree to performe the same findeing all materialls workmanshipp and scaffolding at p̃ square three pounds tenn shillings & for the ceiling if the same be required he doth agree to receive p̃ square 25[s]. and to be allowed for anie mouldings if anie be and to finish all by the 12th. of December next ensueing the date hereof and if the same be not ceeled with slitt deale then to finish all by the seaven and twentieth day of November 1675." — Works 5/145, p. 101.

November and December, 1675.
Extraordinary Account.
"Theatre att Whitehall Nov[r]: 1675
To Iohn Cell Carpenter ffor eighteene squares and ninety five foote of new flooreing and bourding in the roofe of the Theatre and putting

vp a scaffold there to be lett standing for the Plaisterer to lath and plaister the ceiling at iij^{li}.x^s. the square by agreem^t lxvj^{li}.vj^s.vj^d. ffor ninety foure fo^t. of suffeete molding vnder the ceiling and ij scymores on each side of y^e brestsommer there at xv^d. the fo^t. running measure v^{li}. xvij^s.vj^d. ffor xx fo^t. of O.G. there at iij^d. the foote v^s. more to him for viij fo^t. of double quarter used for branches under the ceiling and $\frac{1}{2}$ a dayes worke of a man aboute putting it up ij^s.vij^d. ffor 100 foote of single quarters used aboute the hammer beames and three hundred of tennpenny nailes and one d̄s worke and halfe of a man about putting them vpp Seaventeene shillings and Sixpence ffor cutting ij l̄d of timber for scaffolding xij^s. lxxiiij^{li} xiij^d.

December 1675

To Iohn Grove M^r. Plaisterer ffor lathing and plaistering the ceiling of the Theatre containing one hundred and ninety yards being done with hart laths and floated at xvj^d the yard xij^{li}.xiij^s.iiij^d.
To Robert Streeter Serjant Painter for painteing timber colour in distemper twice in a place the new beames in the ceiling of the Theatre xij^s." (Total £87.6.5.) — Works 5/25.

December, 1675.
Carpenters: "helping to take Downe ye scaffold in ye Theatre at Whitehall and to Carry it into ye Yard & mending som of ye Seats there, Makeing and hanging a Little dore where ye Scaffolding stuff was taken in & putt out there." — Works 5/26.

Plasterer: "poynting of Eight lights in ye great window at ye end of ye Theater." — *Ibid.*

Matlayers: "new Matteing part of ye floore betwixt ye Sceanes in ye Theater at Whitehall Soweing peeceing & Mending ye Matts vppon ye Staires & seuerall other places there." — *Ibid.*

February, 1675/6.
Carpenters: "Setting vp and takeing downe ye rayles at ye guard Chamber Dores and for ye Theater dore, whene ye danceing was there, and makeing a ption betweene two boxes there 8 foo^t: Long: 3 foo^t high and Cutting way through a rayle into another box there, and putting a flapp to ye said rayle, And Makeing good ye Seates & Dore Commeing Into ye Theater & Carrying the Mewsicke Seat out of the Queenes presence into ye Theater, and Carrying them backe agayne." — *Ibid.*

May, 1676.

Carpenters: "taking vp ye stage[1] in ye Theater & Layeing vp ye stuff there, putting vp ye Survey^r of ye Works box there, putting vp ye backe bourd and ye Deske for ye Musicke there, putting vp ye Rayles with flapps to them" at the guard chamber and theatre doors, "Makeing 4 New formes for ye Musicke to Sitt on there."

Works 5/27.

June, 1676.

Matlayers: piecing and mending the mats. — *Ibid*.

November, 1676.

Carpenters: "layeing ye floore ouer ye pitt at ye Theater for ye Dancing at ye Queenes Birth Day, putting vp iio foo^t: of Benching for degrees With foo^t Steps to them, putting vp three barrs With flapps" at the Guard Chamber and Theatre doors, "takeing fower Mewsicke Seats out of ye Store & Carrying them into ye Theater . . . helping to Carry xxvij formes out of ye Theater into ye said Privie Chamber & Carrying them backe agayne into ye Theater." — *Ibid*.

Matlayer: matting several degrees and forms. — *Ibid*.

December, 1676.

Carpenters: "helping to Carry formes Seuerall times out of ye Theater vp to ye Duches of Yorks presence & Carrying them downe into ye Theater agayne." — *Ibid*.

January, 1676/7.

Carpenters: carrying forms several times from the theatre to the Duchess of York's privy chamber and back again, "Carrying three Mewsicke Seats out of ye Theater into ye Clockehowse, takeing Downe ye Degrees on both sides of ye pitt & takeing vp ye floore & ye Joysts ouer ye pitt & carrying it vnder ye Stage agayne putting vp ye Rayle for ye Musicke Cross ye pitt into there places agayne putting vp ye Deskes for ye Musicke to Lay there books vppon, putting vp ye Surveyo^r of ye Works box agayne." — *Ibid*.

Plumbers: mending a "drip" over the theatre. — *Ibid*.

February, 1676/7.

Carpenters: carrying forms from the theatre to the Duchess of York's privy chamber and back again several times. — *Ibid*.

---

1. Probably the floor over the pit.

May, 1677.

Carpenters: "pulling downe the Boxes the throne [*sic*] in ye Theater & bringing in ye Seate againe and laying itt downe againe as itt was before, makeing vpp seu'all dores as they were before and putting vp benches there againe, putting vpp the railes againe" at the guard chamber and theatre doors. — Works 5/28.

Plumbers: minor repairs to the roof of the theatre. — *Ibid.*

November, 1677.

Carpenters: "takeing downe pte of the musick seates and the Deskes where they lay there bookes in the Pitt in the Theatre and the Surveyour of the workes Box, takeing the bourds and joysts from under the stage and laying it even with the stage for the Danceing for the Queenes birth day at night; and putting upp the degrees on both sides of the stage; putting upp 2 long Railes before ye degrees with flapps to them both; placeing seuerall long formmes there fetching the musicke Seates out of the Queenes Presence and placeing them upon the Stage, puttingupp [*sic*] iij Railes with flapps to them" at the guard chamber and theatre doors, "carrieing the musicke Seates out of the Theatre into the Queenes presence, and takeing downe the rayles at the doores againe." — *Ibid.*

December, 1677.

Carpenters: "taking up the floor that was laid ouer the Pitt in the Theatre and carrieing it under ye stage takeing downe the degrees on each side of the Pitt where the floore lay and carrieing them under the said Stage: takeing away the fo^t: pace and raile where the kings chaire of state stood & carrieing it into the Lobby goeing into the kings Guardchamber & putting up the boxes and seates as it was before for the Italians, makeing a new box for his Maj^{tie}. tenn fo^t. long for awarder [*sic*] into the Pitt 8 fo^t. wide, laying a new floore with Ioysts and bourds on each side of the kings Box 8 fo^t. wide and tenn fo^t. long and putting up 5 benches on each side: and putting up 2 railes before the said benches, & bourding upp with slitt deale before the benches, lengthening the degrees in ye Lord Chamberlaines and Lord Treasurers lodgs [*sic*] 3 fo^t. ½ long^r. then they were before."
Ibid.

Plumber: "makeing 3 w^{tts}. for the curtaine ouer the stage in the Theatre." — *Ibid.*

November, 1678.

Carpenters: "raiseing and new boarding ye Ld Chamberlaines box in ye Theater, makeing 2 Portholes with 2 dores in them betweene ye Seeings each ii foote high & 4½ foote wide." — *Ibid.*

Matlayer: "peeceing & mending ye matts in severall places in ye Theater." — *Ibid.*

February, 1678/9.

Carpenters: "takeing away pte of the Kings Box and takeing away 2 other Boxes and carrieing them downe the stage at the Kings Theatre, setting up 2 seates in the Kings Box and setting up a new seate in the Dutchess of Richmonds Box there, takeing downe the backe of the Lord Chamberlaines box; and bringing it one seate nearer, to make it less, bourding up 2 sides of a paire of staires goeing downe in the passage that leads to the winesellar for to keepe ye house warme, putting up a long trough to sett the Lamps in, at the end of the staige against the Pitt there, altering a trapp doore, in the middle of the stage, and makeing it good againe as it was, setting up 2 rayles in ye gallery for the musick, and putting 2 flapps to them to keepe the people from the Musickque roome there, setting up a doore and doorecase that was broken downe one night under the degrees at the Theatre." — *Ibid.*

Matlayers: "takeing up the old mattes of the staires goeing out of the Kings guardchamb^r. downe into the Hall, driueing downe the nailes and cleaning the staire there, new matting ye Lord Chamberlaines box in the Theatre." — *Ibid.*

September, 1679.

Plasterers: "Washing Stopping & Whiteing ye Ceilling & Walls of ye Hall & ye Bottomes Coloured there." — Works 5/32.

November, 1679.

Carpenters: "Makeing a New Box at ye Kings Theatre for ye Suruaior of ye Workes & Setting vp 3 Rayles there & Takeing them Downe againe & Giuing attendance there att night." — *Ibid.*

Slater: "Cutting of Slates & Mending ye Slateing & Tileing on One Side of ye Roofe ouer the Greate Hall." — *Ibid.*

(The Accounts for 1680–81 are missing.)

November, 1681.

Carpenters: "making good the Degrees in the Hall and setting vp three barrs before the Doores to keepe off the croud of people and taking them downe againe and oyling the Scenes and cleansing the groves to make them slide and putting new ropes to them and setting on severall locks and attending in the night." — Works 5/33.

Matlayer: "new matting severall degrees and mending the rest of the Matts in the Theatre." — Ibid.

May, 1682.

Bricklayers: "mending broken tyling in severall places over the Theater in the old hall and mending the slating there."

Works 5/35.

November, 1682.

Carpenters: "taking downe severall boxes and carrying them under the stage in the Kings Theater and putting vp the Kings Throne in the place of them, and making it good and putting vp three barrs in the passage leading there making seu'all alterations vnder the stage, putting vp 3 slitt deales on one side of the Kings Throne and putting vp 3 benches there. In putting vp a new raile with a flap in it to the Vice Chamberlins Box and putting vp 2 leaves of slitt deale in the back of the L^d. Stewards box, mending and cleaning the Sceans and the Curtaine & taking Downe the three railes in the passage and bringing them into the Store." — Ibid.

Matlayer: "mending the matting in the Theater and new matting the Kings Throne." — Ibid.

January, 1682/3.

Carpenters: "taking the formes out of the hall and out of the Dukes Lodgings and carrying them into his Ma^ts. Eating roome and cutting and fitting them there, taking them from thence and carrying them into the Dukes Lodgings, removing them from thence and fitting and mending them for the Q^s. Presence and carrying them into the Hall againe." — Ibid.

February, 1682/3.

Carpenters: "laying a floore with joysts and boards over the pitt in the Theater for a ball and fitting and putting vp the Degrees on both sides the stage and putting up railes before the Degrees, putting vp two railes on each side the Kings Throne and raising another raile higher in the back making 8 new formes 4 fo^t. 10^{in}. long the others 5 fo^t. long there removing all the Formes out of the Hall into the Q^s. Presence and removing them back into the Hall and fitting and placing them there againe putting vp 3 barackado railes in the way leading to the Hall & taking them downe and carrying them into the Hall againe & putting vp 2 seats in a doorway there." — *Ibid.*

November, 1683.

Carpenters: "inlarging the musick seats and desks in the Theater, and putting vp 3 benches and 60 fo^t. of raile and taking downe an old doore there." — Works 5/37.

February, 1683/4.

Carpenters: "taking downe the musick seats at the Hall Theater and bring [*sic*] them into the store, and severall degrees & railes and ye floore of the pitt cont'. abo^t. 7 sq^r. and putting them vnder the stage, and taking downe the formes there, setting vp 2 short railes on each side the stage and 2 more in the pitt, boarding a sta^{r}case & putting seats in it and cleaning all the grooves and fitting the sceens there."

Ibid.

September, 1684.

Carpenters: "setting vp 40 fo^t. of raile in the hall Theater & 25 fo^t. of roofing [*sic*] before the Stage to set candles in & 20 fo^t. of Shelves cutting a hole & making a sight in ye doore putting a shelfe vnderneath to slide vp and downe setting a raile before the doore and a shelfe to lay books on for the Musick there." — Works 5/38.

October, 1684.

Carpenters: "fixing two large balks each 14 fo^t. long to fasten ye flying ropes in the Theatre and making two scaffolds there abo^t. 12 fo^t. long a peice and two foote wide." — *Ibid.*

November, 1684.

Carpenters: "taking out the timber and boards vnder the K^s. Throne in the Hall and laying them over the pitt for a floore for the ball, In taking out the formes vnder the stage and the degrees with railes before them, and setting them vp on each side that floore; In taking the Musick seats out of the store in Scotland yard and fitting & setting them vp on the Stage; In setting vp railes with flaps before three doores, In making vp one doore and barring vp three more, and in taking vp the flo^{rs}. & Degrees and formes &c' and placing them in theire severall places vnder the Throne and stage againe and waiting in ye night vpon the stage and looking after the scenes &c'." — *Ibid.*

January, 1684/5.

Carpenters: "taking downe and removing the Kings old Throne in the Hall & carrying it out and placing it over the enclosure in the Lobby and setting vp three boxes and seats in the place of the Throne and enlarging and setting vp a new flo^r. forward over the pit for his Ma^{ts}. Chairs 10 fo^t. long and about 8 fo^t. wide and enclosing it with railes and boards about 3 fot. ½ high and making two desk boards for the Musick 8 fo^t. long a peice, and setting vp two bearers for the Harpsicall In making a drip vpon the flat over that hall 8 fo^t. long 2 fo^t. wide for the plomber . . . carrying & recarrying formes to and from the hall." — *Ibid.*

Plumber: mending the leads over the hall. — *Ibid.*

June, 1685.

Carpenters: "enclosing a box in the Hall Theater to lay the books in that came from the Councell chamber with a Shutting window to it, and making the seats broader to lay the books on, making the seats broader in another box to lay papers on there." — Works 5/39.

July, 1685.

Carpenters: "raising the sides of two boxes in the Hall Theatre about 3 foote high 25 foote long for the Clarkes of the Councell and mending the boxes in severall places and fixing the screw for the Seale." — *Ibid.*

To Walter Wright, Matlayer: for 12½ yds. of bulrush mat, "in the Hall Theatre finding n^ts and packthread for the Clarkes of ye Councells seats." £0.12.6. — *Ibid.*

October, 1685.

Carpenters: "taking downe the K^s. Throne in the Theatre in the Hall and laying the floore with joysts and boards over the pitt for a Ball cont'. 5 square. In bringing in the old Throne againe & fixing it in its place, and putting vp severall degrees: In making and putting vp a new hatch, against a doore & setting vp the railes to keep people out, and in taking downe all the aforesaid worke againe, and putting it into the Store, and making the house ready for a play." — *Ibid.*

Walter Wright, Matlayer: "ffor taking vp the old matts in the Pitt in yᵉ Theatre knocking vp the nls and cleaning the said Pitt, and mending the seats with the best of the old matt finding nls and Labour — 00:6:00. ffor new matting the Degrees in the Pitt Cont'. 45 yards at xijᵈ. p yard — 02:5:00." — *Ibid.*

November, 1685.

Carpenters: "laying the floores with joysts & boards over the pitt in the Hall Theatre for a ball cont'. 5 sqʳˢ. and putting vp severall degrees on each side, setting vp the railes to keep people out and taking downe all tha'foresaid work againe and putting it into the Store & making the house ready for a play." — *Ibid.*

November, 1685.

Bricklayer: "attending by night in the Playhouse." — *Ibid.*

December, 1685.

Carpenters: "taking vp the floore of joysts & boards over the pitt and the degrees & laying them vnder the Theatre and making the house ready for a play, and taking out the stuff againe and laying downe tha'foresaid floʳ. & degrees to make it ready for a Ball, altering it againe and making it ready for a play, and making a raile with a flap at the Kˢ. doore." — *Ibid.*

Walter Wright, Matlayer: "taking vp the old matts of the staʳˢ. &
    Scenes knocking out the nls & cleering them"   0. 5.0.
96½ yds. of new bulrush mat   4.16.6.
6 lbs. of Candles   0. 3.0.
                                                                    Ibid.

January, 1685/6.

Carpenters: "putting vp two new benches each 3 foᵗ. long for the Gent. Vshers in the Theatre, & in setting vp the railes & taking them downe againe before 3 doʳˢ. to keep off the people, & attending 3 severall Nights in the playhouse vpon yᵉ Scenes and to looke after the Lights &c." — *Ibid.*

February, 1685/6.

Carpenters: "setting vp the railes and taking them downe againe severall times" at the guard chamber and theatre doors, "and attending 3 severall Nights vpon yᵉ Scenes and to look after the Lights &c." — *Ibid.*

Walter Wright: "new matting a paire of Staires & parte of two benches in the gallery in the Hall . . . taking vp the old matts of the Sta^{rs}. & sweeping them and making them clean & knocking downe the nailes." — *Ibid.*

September, 1686.

Carpenters: "laying the floore in the Theatre in ye hall with joysts and boards over the pitt for a Ball cont. 5 sq^{rs}., and putting vp 10 Degrees with railes before them, & mending severall formes there." — Works 5/40.

October, 1686.

Carpenters: "making 3 new Degrees for the Hoboyes in the Hall Theatre 8 fo^t. long a peice with a raile before them to be vsed when the Ball was and taking them away againe, taking vp the floore of joysts and Boards over the Pitt and the Degrees and laying them vnd^r. the Theater and making the house ready for a play, making a new raile with a flap to it in the K^s. Guardchamber to keep the people out 11:0 ⎰ with a returne, & boarding the foreside of it with 3:9 ⎱ slitt Deale. . . ." — *Ibid.*

November, 1686.

Mason attending 5 nights at the Theatre.

Carpenters: "laying the floore in the Theatre in the Hall wth: joysts and boards over the Pitt for a Ball cont'. 5 sq^{rs}. and putting vp ye Degrees on each side with railes before them, taking vp the floore of Ioysts and boards over the Pitt and the Degrees and laying them vnder the Theatre and afterwards making the house ready for a play, and setting vp ye railes and taking them downe againe 5 severall times." — *Ibid.*

Plasterer: pointing 6 stone lights in the window. — *Ibid.*

December, 1686.

Mason: "attending by Night the Plays and Balls in the Hall."
Ibid.

Carpenters: the same work as in November; the rails were set up and taken down four times. — *Ibid.*

Walter Wright: 107 yds. of new matting in the theatre, £5.7.0., and 97 yds. of old matting taken up and relaid in the galleries, £2.8.6.
Ibid.

January, 1686/7.

Mason: attending 5 nights for plays and balls. — *Ibid.*

Carpenters: the same work as in November; the rails were set up and taken down 5 times. — *Ibid.*

April, 1687.

Carpenters: "setting vp the Railes in the Theatre and taking them downe againe 3 severall times, putting vp a short bench in the pitt 3 fo^t. long, and attending by night the Playes there." — Works 5/41.

May, 1687.

Carpenters: "setting vp the Railes in the Theatre and taking them downe againe two severall times and putting vp another short bench: In enclosing a place within the Scenes for the plays 16 foot long 2 fo^t. ½ high and a flo^r: 3 fo^t: ½ by 3 fo^t. and taking them downe againe, and attending by night vpon the Plays." — *Ibid.*

July, 1687.

Robert Streeter:

436 yds. of work done in distemper at 6^d.	£11.11.6.
"mending ye cloth of ye clouds"	£ 0. 8.0.
	Ibid.

January, 1687/8.

Carpenters: "carrying of formes from the Hall Theater to Father Peters Lodgings for a ball in the Presence chamber there . . . making 11 new Steps of whole Deale over the old Sta^{rs}. going into the Hall Theatre for her Maties: Chaire to goe downe easily, and making 3 halfpaces there 7:6 by 6:6 and putting vp the Railes in the Guard-chamber and at the Stairhead and attending by Night." — *Ibid.*

Walter Wright: new matting the new stairs and halfpaces, 20 yds. at 12^d. a yard. — *Ibid.*

February, 1687/8.

Carpenters: putting up the rails 4 times and attending by night.
Ibid.

Mazerscourers: carrying forms from Father Peters' lodgings to the Theatre, and attending there. — *Ibid.*

October, 1688.

Masons: repairing 5 squares of slating over the Hall. — Works 5/42.

October, 1689.

Carpenters: "taking out the floore vnder the Stage in the Hall Theatre and laying yᵉ Ioysts and boards over the pitt for a Ball being all new nailed, fird, and made good, altering and setting vp the Seats on each side, in putting vp timber and boards for Seats for the Musick round the Sceens 11 foot high and placing the Sceens, making a place above the Sceens to sett the Lamps on with 3 Steps to it, making and hanging Three Doores with doorposts to them setting vp the Railes in the Theater, Guard chamber and at the top of the Staʳˢ. and attending by Night at the Ball." — Works 5/43.

Joiners: making 20 forms for the Hall, size not specified. — *Ibid.*

Alexander Fort, Master Joiner: 13 forms of deal for the theatre, "cont. 141:3" £7.13.0¼. — *Ibid.*

John Grosvenor, Plasterer: pointing 8 stone lights in the theatre.
                                                                                              Ibid.

November, 1689.

Carpenters: taking up the floor and degrees on each side of the pit, etc., "placing the boxes for the Lamps at the end of the Stage next the Pitt, & fitting the house for a Play and attending within the Scenes in the Nights during the Play's." — *Ibid.*

"To [*blank*] Latton man For Skonces vsed in the Theatre for the Ball

	li. s. d.
For a branch with 4 Lights	01:10:00
For 6 lesser branches at vjˢ. each	01:16:00
For 14 plates for 2 Candles at iiˢ.vjᵈ. each	01:15:00
For 40 plates at xijᵈ. each	02:00:00
For 9 Rundles at xvᵈ. each	00:11:03
For 72 little Lampes at ijᵈ each	00:12:00
For 28 bigger Lampes at iiijᵈ. each	00:09:04
For Covering the Degrees with white Latton	01:00:00
For 3 dozen ½ of little Candlesticks for the Musicians at ijˢ.vjᵈ. p dozen	00:08:09
	10:02:04 "

                                                                                              Ibid.

To Walter Wright: "For new matting the Throne in the Theatre and the great Sta^{rs}. and the Gallery and severall other benches with 100 square yds of bulrush matt at xij^d. p yard" 05:00:00.

For taking vp the old matt from the Throne and great Sta^{rs}. and sweeping it & carrying away the Dirt 00:03:06.

For mending the old matts of 4 pa^r. of Sta^{rs}. 00:05:00.

For 50 sq^r: yds: of Bulrush matt vsed in the pitt at xij^d p yard 02:10:00.

For mending the matts vpon the great Sta^{rs}. 00:02:06.

For taking vp the old matts from the Benches in the pitt & knocking downe the nʃs & sweeping it and carrying away the dirt 00:03:00."

Ibid.

April, 1690.

Carpenters: "sweeping & cleering the Stage & cleering the Grooves & putting the Sceens in theire places & fastning the braces in the Clouds, boarding vp the doorway by the Wine cellar, and putting vp Seats there, putting vp the Railes in the Guard chamber & the Railes at the Sta^r: head to keep out the people." — Works 5/44.

November, 1690.

Carpenters: "Searching the Scenes in ye Theatre, & nailing & mending the Braces and brushing the groves for them to slide & soping them, in Serching and mending the Seates and putting vp the Railes in Severall places, in Setting vp the Lights within the Scenes, and attending during the play and taking down the Railes againe."

Ibid.

June, 1691.

Walter Wright: mending the mats in the playhouse, £0.3.6.

Works 5/45.

November, 1691.

Carpenters: "taking out the old floore vnder the Stage and laying the Ioysts and boards over the Pitt for a Ball being all new nailed, fird, & made good, altering and Setting vp the Seats on each side, putting vp 6 Seats in degrees One above another wth. Strings and bearers and footboards, & boarding vp the back with boards 3 fo^t. high above the Seats and making two Steps at each end to go vp to those Seats, in putting vp the railes in the Theatre, Guardchamber, and at the top of the Sta^{rs}. and attending by night the Ball." —*Ibid.*

December, 1691.

Walter Wright: matting stairs and degrees in the theatre, 160 yds., £2.13.4. Taking up the old mats, sweeping and mending, £0.5.6.

Ibid.

(The Accounts for 1692–93 are missing.)

November, 1693.

Carpenters: "boarding vp a doore in the Hall Theatre & mending the Seats that were broken, & mending the railes going vp to the Guard-chamber and mending the boards above the Scenes and the floore where the Musick playes, and putting vp boards to keep people out of the Musick and nailing severall formes, & carrying vp the Musick Seats and railes in the Q^s. presence & the formes for the Ball to practise." — *Ibid.*

Plasterers: pointing 9 stone lights in the theatre. — *Ibid.*

December, 1693.

Walter Wright: newmatting the throne and stairs, and "other steps" in the theatre, 40 yards square, £2.2.6. — *Ibid.*

October, 1694.

Plasterers: "lathing & plastering parte of a wall in the Hall Theatre."

Works 5/47.

Richard Browne, Slater, for repairing the slating of the roof over the Hall, 49½ squares, £6.3.9. — *Ibid.*

November, 1694.

Carpenters: "mending the Musick Seats & formes in the Hall Theatre, boarding vp a doorway & making ready for the ball & carrying & recarrying ye musick Seats and forms into the Drawing roome and bringing them back into the Hall againe 2 Severall times."

Ibid.

Plasterer: pointing 8 stone lights in the Theatre. — *Ibid.*

July, 1695.

Bricklayers: repairing 3 squares of plain tiling over the Hall.

Works 5/48.

(The Accounts for 1696–97 are missing.)

October, 1697.
Robert Streeter: "For repairing the Scenes" £2.0.0. — Works 5/49.

November, 1697.
Carpenters: "Shooting and laying a new floore over the pitt in the Playhouse with joysts and two inch planks 28 foot by 18 foot and mortissing through the joysts against the joynt of every plank & mortissing the edge of every plank over the mortisses of the joysts for the irons to lay downe the planks, & Setting vp the degrees for the Lords and Ladys & mending the musick Seats & the desks. with other works there." — *Ibid.*

December, 1697.
Walter Wright; new matting the throne, stairs, other steps, benches and forms, 260 yards, £4.6.8.[1]

(The Accounts for 1698–99 are missing.)

ATTENDANCE AT PLAYS

In the Works Accounts, the description of each month's work is followed by a list of the workmen employed, with the number of days each worked, and the wages due him. The description often includes attending on the plays, or on the scenes and lights, and certain men are put down for so many nights. But sometimes night work is charged when there is no mention of the theatre. Again, it is impossible to tell, for example, when two men are charged for three nights and two men for two nights, whether three or five performances are represented. There is also the possibility that some attendances were for rehearsals. It therefore seems best, though far from satisfactory, simply to list the months in which theatre attendance is specified and give the number of workmen employed for each number of nights. It is impossible to tell how

1. Undoubtedly this was for the Theatre, but it is not mentioned in the entry.

many of these attendances were for balls, but I have marked with an asterisk months in which there are known to have been balls in the Hall Theatre. Attendance was generally assigned to the carpenters, but masons, bricklayers, and "mazerscourers" were sometimes called upon.

Works

November 1668: 8 men for 4 nights, 3 men for 3 nights. 5/11
December 1668: 11 men for 3 nights.   "
January 1668/9: 3 men for 2 nights, 8 men for 1 night. "
February 1668/9: 11 men for 4 nights.   "
February 1670/1: 1 man for 2 nights, 2 men for 1 night. 5/15
April   1673:   5 men for 6 nights.   5/21
January 1673/4: 1 man for 5 nights, 2 men for 4
                 nights, 1 man for 2 nights, 1 man
                 for 1 night.   "
January 1674/5: 1 man for 1 night.   5/24
February 1674/5: 1 man for 4 nights, 2 men for 3 nights,
                 7 men for 2 nights.   "
November 1679:   4 men for 1 night.   5/32
November 1681:   5 men for 1 night.   5/33
November 1685:   1 man for 6 nights.*   5/39
January 1685/6: 4 men for 3 nights.   "
February 1685/6: 3 men for 3 nights, 1 man for 2 nights. "
November 1686:   6 men for 5 nights.*   5/40
December 1686:   5 men for 4 nights.*   "
January 1686/7: 4 men for 5 nights, 1 man for 3 nights.* "
April   1687:   4 men for 3 nights.   5/41
May   1687:   4 men for 2 nights.   "
January 1687/8: 5 men for 1 night.   "
February 1687/8: 1 man for 5 nights, 3 men for 4 nights. "
October 1689:   1 man for 4 nights, 1 man for 3 nights,
                 3 men for 2 nights, 7 men for 1 night. 5/43
November 1689:   4 men for 5 nights, 1 man for 2 nights.* "
April   1690:   3 men for 2 nights.   5/44
November 1690:   3 men for 2 nights, 3 men for 1 night. "
November 1691:   1 man for 4 nights, 1 man for 3 nights,
                 4 men for 2 nights.   5/45

APPENDIX B

REVELS ACCOUNTS AND PAYMENTS

I

HERBERT'S first account (AO. 3/908/24) is a paper book consisting of a cover of coarse paper on which is written "ffrom j° Novem'. 1660 to .vlt° Octobr' 1661," and a folded sheet enclosing a half sheet. The account begins on fol. 2 and ends on 4: 4 verso is blank.

Fol. 2. The Accounts of the Office of the Reuells vizt. Beginning the first of Nouemb^r. 1660 Anno Regni Regis Caroli 2^{di} duodecimo And ending the last of Octob^r. 1661. being for one whole yeare. As well by meanes of Attendance, makeing Choyce peruseing, reformeing and altering of Playes, as were p^{r}pared, p^{r}sented and sett forth, before the Kings Ma^{ty}. in the tymes aforesaid, as allso the Officers, Boardwages, Journeying, charges, and other expences thereunto belonging, As allso for ffuell and Chaundryware, for the Masters Lodgeinges with such like ordinary Allowances as hath been Accustomed heretofore, As allso for the Officers extraordinary Attendance, being by the Lord Chamberlain thereunto Cõmanded The particulars whereof with the partyes names to whom and wherefore the same is due, hereafter followeth.

Fol. 2^v 1660   S^r. Henry Herbert K^{nt}. Master of His Ma^{ts}. Office of the Reuells demandeth Allowance as hath been accustomed for himself and 4 men for his Attendance, at the Court for His Ma^{ts}. Service in the Said Office from the last of Octob^r. 1660 till the Ashwednesday following being the 27th: day of ffebruary Amounting to 119. dayes and 40. nights, as allso for .4. dayes at Easter and 4 dayes at Whitsuntide, and 20 dayes at Sũmer at 8^s. p̃ diem, and totidem p̃ noctem Amounting alltogether to the number of

	ł.	s.	d.
187. —	74.	16.	00
ffor ffuell as hath been accustomed	08.	00.	00
ffor Greencloth cum pertinentijs	03.	00.	00
ffor Torchlights and Candles	03.	00.	00
ffor Boathire	03.	00.	00

for Engrosseing the Bookes and declareing them be-
fore the L^d. T̃rer and Chancellor of the Excheq^r.   05.00.00
ffor the ffees and Rewards to the Offic^{rs}. of the Re-
ceipts   05.00.00
ffor the ffees to the Signett and Priuy Seale   05.00.00
ffor Allowance for the Rent of his house as hath been
Accustomed   30.00.00
ffor the Rent of the Office as hath been accustomed   20.00.00

                                                In toto 156.16.00

Fol. 3. [*Blank*] Yeoman of the Revells demandeth for things layd
out by him   ł.   s.   d.

Imprimis for a Lanthorn	0.	3.	4
Item for Ayreing the Stuff	1.	0.	0
It' for Brush Blackthread and Cord	0.	6.	0
It' for Boathire for himself and the rest of the Officers	2.	10.	0

                                                in toto   3.19. 4

George Iohnson Groom and Purvey^r of the Office of the Revells
demands Allowance.

Imprimis for his yeares Attendance	6.	13.	4
Item for Rushes Sundry tymes for the Revells	0.	05.	00
It' for a great Earthen pann for fire to the Play^{rs}	0.	01.	06
It' for Carriage of the Iron table and Cradle to Court	0.	00.	06
It' for a Lock and Key to the Musick house	0.	02.	06

It' for Boathire being Sent to the Players diuers
tymes   0.05.00
It' for a Chamberpott for the Players   0.01.06
It' for diuers propertyes used about the Playes   0.05.00
It' for Bellowes, fire Shouell, tongues and other
Necessaryes used at the Cockpitt for the Players   1.00.00

                                                in toto   8.14.04

Fol. 3ᵛ [*Blank*] Clark Comptroller of His M̄aᵗˢ. Revells demandeth Allowance for Boardwages and dyett as hath been Accustomed for his Attendance from the last of Octobᵣ. till Ashwednesday and for

	}.	s.	d.
other Services	13.	06.	08

Iohn Green — Clark of His Maᵗˢ. Reuells demandeth Allowance for his Boardwages and Attendance within the same tyme   13.06.08

Also he demandeth Allowance for his house-Rent as hath been formerly Allowed him   15.00.00

ffurthermore as being Clark of the Office he demandeth Allowance for a desk, Paper, Ink, and Greencloth with other things thereto belonging as formerly hath been allowed him to make vp the Bills and Bookes for the Auditor, and a Leiger Booke for the Office   03.06.08

[*Blank*] Yeoman of His M̄aᵗˢ. Reuells demandeth the like Allowance for his Board-wages and Attendance wᵗʰin the same tyme   13.06.08

Allso hee demandeth Allowance for his house rent as formerly hath been Allowed him   15.00.00

in toto   73.05.08

Fol. 4. More the Master and Officers demand Allowance for their extraordinary Attendance from the last of Septemᵣ. till the last of Octobᵣ. being thereto Com̄anded by the Lord Chamberlayne vizᵗ. at 8ˢ. ꝑ djem, Which com̄eth to 12ˡ. the Clark Comptroller, Clark, and Yeoman att 3ˡ.6ˢ.8ᵈ. apiece, which Cometh to 10ˡ: And the

Groome 1ˡ.13ˢ.4ᵈ. which cometh in all to

	}.	s.	d.
	23.	13.	04

Sum' total'. 266.09.08

Iur' 8°. die Aprilͦ 1665 cora'
    Chr. Turnᵣ.

Henry Herbert
I: Loyd
Io Greene Clerke
Hen: Harris

Greene did not write the account, but he inserted his own name and Johnson's and added "Iur' 8°. die April 1665 cora'." The signatures are autograph: Sir Christopher Turnor was a Baron of the Exchequer.

The only point of interest in the subsequent accounts is to be found at the beginning of the Accounts for 1661–62. The clerk copied the 1660–61 book *verbatim*, including the date of Ash Wednesday and the number of days. This is queried in the margin in a hand which appears to be Turnor's, although one cannot be sure with so little writing to go on.[1] Apparently Greene has added the correction to 104 days and £68.16.0, but it is not carried through the book, and the corresponding Declared Accounts retains the original amount.[2] The Audit Office does not seem to have worried over trifles.

II

A table of payments to the Theatre-Keeper provides an interesting illustration of Household economy. These payments are charged on the Accounts of the Treasurer of the Chamber. (For the warrants for payment see LC. 5/137, p. 270; 5/140, p. 154; AO. 15/8, p. 800; LC. 5/143, p. 76; 5/12, p. 379; AO. 15/9, p. 336.) Some of the records are lost, but the gaps seem to be chiefly due to the principle that a new king made a fresh start in accumulating debts. Probably the Theatre-Keeper came off as well as any minor official.

1. In some of the later accounts, he wrote the "Iurat." as well as his signature. Dr. W. W. Greg agrees with me on this point.
2. AO. 1/2047/28.

PAYMENTS OF THEATRE-KEEPER'S WAGES OF £30 PER ANNUM

Reference	Name	Period	Ending	£	s.	d.
E. 351/546.		*Cockpit in Court*				
Acct. for 25 Dec. 1661 to 24 June 1663.	George Johnson	1 year, ending	Midsummer 1662	30	0	0
Acct. for 24 June 1663 to 29 Sept. 1664.	"	1/4 "	Michaelmas 1662	7	5	0
Acct. for 29 Sept. 1664 to 29 Sept. 1665.	"	3 1/4 years "	Christmas 1665	97	5	0
E. 351/547.		*Hall Theatre*				
Acct. for Mich. 1668 to Mich. 1669.	"	1 1/2 years, ending	Midsummer 1667	45	0	0
E. 351/548. Mich. 1669–Mich. 1670.	"	1 year "	" 1668	30	0	0
E. 351/549. Mich. 1670–Mich. 1671.	"	1/2 "	Christmas 1668	15	0	0
A.O. 1/398/90. Mich. 1671–Mich. 1672.	"	1 1/4 years "	Lady Day 1670	37	5	0
A.O. 1/398/92. Mich. 1672–Mich. 1673.	"	1 year, "	" " 1671	30	0	0
A.O. 1/398/95. Mich. 1673–Mich. 1674.	"	1 " "	" " 1672	30	0	0
A.O. 1/398/97. Mich. 1674–Mich. 1675.	Mary Johnson, Admin.*	1/2 "	Michaelmas 1672	15	0	0
" " " "	Philip Johnson	1/2 "	Lady Day 1673	15	0	0
A.O. 1/399/100. Mich. 1675–Mich. 1676.	John Clarke	1 "	" 1674	30	0	0
A.O. 1/400/103. Mich. 1676–Mich. 1677.	"	3/4 "	Christmas 1674	22	10	0
A.O. 1/401/106. Mich. 1677–Mich. 1678.	"	1/2 "	Michaelmas, 1678	15	0	0
A.O. 1/401/109. Mich. 1678–Mich. 1679.	"	1/2 "	Lady Day 1679	15	0	0
A.O. 1/402/115. Mich. 1680–Mich. 1681.	"	1/2 "	Michaelmas 1679	15	0	0
A.O. 1/403/118. Mich. 1681–Mich. 1682.	"	1 "	" 1680	30	0	0
A.O. 1/403/119. Mich. 1682–Mich. 1683.	"	1/2 "	Lady Day 1681	15	0	0
A.O. 1/404/121. Mich. 1683–Mich. 1684.	"	1/2 "	Michaelmas 1681	15	0	0
A.O. 1/404/124. Mich. 1684–Mich. 1685.	"	1/4 "	Midsummer 1685	7	10	0
A.O. 1/405/127. Mich. 1685–Mich. 1686.	"	1 "	" 1686	30	0	0
A.O. 1/405/130. Mich. 1686–Mich. 1687.	"	1 "	" 1687	30	0	0
A.O. 1/406/133. Mich. 1687–Mich. 1688.	"	1 "	" 1688	30	0	0
E. 351/550. Mich. 1692–Mich. 1694.	"	1 "	Michaelmas 1692	30	0	0
E. 351/551. Mich. 1694–Mich. 1698.	"	4 1/2 years, "	Lady Day 1697	135	0	0
E. 351/552. Mich. 1698–Mich. 1701.	"	2 3/4 "	Christmas 1699	82	10	0

* On 22 May 1675, the Lord Chamberlain signed a warrant to pay George Johnson's executrix on six bills, he having neglected to take out his warrants at the due time, and being now dead (LC. 5/141, p. 199).

APPENDIX C

A CALENDAR OF PLAYS ACTED AT COURT

THIS list probably represents only about one-fourth of the performances at Court from 1660 to the end of the century, and even so, much of it is conjectural. For about 135 of these 159 performances there is documentary evidence, a prologue or epilogue at Court, or a specific statement in the dedication or preface, or in a contemporary letter or diary. Then there are a number of what seem to me clear inferences, as, for example, when E. Gower writes "No more plays at Court after this night" (Hist. Mss., V, 202), which I have accepted as establishing a performance. But there remain a number of instances in which there are varying degrees of uncertainty: a warrant for provisions (bread, wine, etc.) usually betokens a play that night, but one cannot be sure that it always does, and some of the warrants for payment do not state where the performance took place (see pp. 298–299). Even more difficult to deal with are such phrases in contemporary accounts as "the Court attended a play," "acted before the King," and the like. There are also a number of cases which rest on a prologue or epilogue addressed to the King: it seems highly probable to me that most of these were written for Court, but it is quite possible that special ones were sometimes written for the King's visits to public theatres, particularly if the occasion was the opening of a play written by one of his friends. *The Black Prince*, for example, has an epilogue to the King, but the title-page refers only to performance at the Theatre Royal, and there is no other trace of it at Whitehall. And finally, there are several prefaces which either suggest the play was acted at Court or say it was acted before the King, but make no definite statement as to place. In all these uncertain cases, I have placed * before the title.

I have added the name of the company wherever possible, even when it is not given in the quoted sources, and the theatre or palace in which the performance took place; but here, too, there is some room for doubt. In the first place, there is no evidence that I know of as to the ownership of some old plays. *The Young Admiral*, for instance, does not occur in any list of plays claimed by Killigrew or Davenant, but we know the King's Company inherited a number of Shirley's plays, and I have therefore assigned it to them with a query. In general, one can be sure of the theatre, but in the winter of 1662–63, the Cockpit in Court was in use and there was also a new stage in the Great Hall (see pp. 25–27). It occurs to me that this may have been built for the production of *The Adventure of Five Hours*, but on the other hand, it may not have been for plays at all, but for music or other entertainments. I have also placed a query against the theatre in all cases where the performance may have been in a public playhouse. And I have questioned a few dates where the evidence is suspicious. Of the references given, usually only one or two name the play, and all too often it is not named at all. The symbol > means on or before the given date, < on or after.

Finally, I have thought it might be helpful to include approximate dates for the visits of Continental companies. These are taken chiefly from the *Calendar of Treasury Books* (see pp. 117–127, *passim*.) and in rare cases only denote the actual dates of performances.

1660

| 19 November | *The Silent Woman*
Pepys, 20 Nov.; Hist.
Mss., V, 200. | King's | Cockpit |

1660/1

| 26 February | a play
Hist. Mss., V, 202. | | Cockpit |

1661

20 April	*The Humorous Lieutenant*	King's	Cockpit
	Pepys.		
August <	French Comedians		
	Pepys, 30 Aug.		
16 December	a French comedy		Cockpit
	Evelyn.		

1661/2

16 January	*The Widow*	King's	Cockpit
	Evelyn.		
6 February	a play	King's	Cockpit
	LC. 5/137, p. 100.		
11 February	a comedy		Cockpit
	Evelyn.		

1662

22 September	a play	Duke's	Cockpit
	LC. 5/137, p. 389.		
2 October	*The Cardinal*	King's	Cockpit
	Pepys.		
8 October	puppet plays		?Queen's Guardchamber
	Pepys.		
16 October	*Volpone*	King's	Cockpit
	Evelyn.		
27 October	*The Villain*	Duke's	Cockpit
	Pepys.		
1 November	*Ignoramus*	?Duke's	Cockpit
	LC. 5/138, p. 91.		
17 November	*The Scornful Lady*	King's	Cockpit
	Pepys.		
20 November	* *The Young Admiral*	?King's	?Cockpit
	Evelyn.		
1 December	*The Valiant Cid*	Duke's	Cockpit
	Pepys.		
?15 December	*The Adventures of Five Hours*		
		Duke's	?Great Hall
	A. E. H. Swaen's edition, pp. xviii–xix.		
17 December	* *The Law against Lovers*	Duke's	?Great Hall
	Evelyn.		

1662/3

5 January	*Claracilla*	King's	Cockpit
	Pepys.		
5 February	*The Wild Gallant*	King's	?Great Hall
	Evelyn.		
9 February	a play	Duke's	?Great Hall
	LC. 5/137, p. 389.		
23 February	*The Wild Gallant*	King's	?Great Hall
	Pepys.		

1663

>1663	* *Cutter of Coleman-Street*	Duke's	?Cockpit
	Prologue and epilogue to		
	King in 1663 edition.		
>1663	* *The Slighted Maid*	Duke's	?Cockpit
	Prologue and epilogue to		
	King in 1663 edition.		
2 July	a masque		
	Evelyn.		
25 August <	French Comedians		
	SP. 29/79, no. 73.		
5 October	a play		Cockpit
	LC. 5/61, p. 63.		
>December	*The Step-mother*	Duke's	Cockpit
	Prologue at Whitehall, in		
	edition licensed 26 De-		
	cember 1663.		

1664

>1664	*Pompey the Great*	Duke's	St. James'
	Epilogues to King and		
	Duchess in 1664 edition.		
14 September	* *The General*	King's	?Cockpit
	Stowe Ms. 744, f. 81.		
17 October	a play		Cockpit
	Pepys.		
19 December	a play	King's	Cockpit
	LC. 5/138, p. 156.		

1665

20 April	a play Pepys.		Hall Theatre

1666

11 October	*Wit without Money* Rugge II, f. 179; LS. 8/6; Pepys, 15 Oct.	King's	Hall Theatre
18 October	*Mustapha* Evelyn; Pepys; LS. 8/6.	Duke's	Hall Theatre
29 October	*Love in a Tub* Pepys; LC. 5/139, p. 125; LS. 8/6.	Duke's	Hall Theatre
?5 November	*Mustapha* LC. 5/139, p. 125; LS. 8/6; Pepys.	Duke's	Hall Theatre
26 November	*Worse and Worse* LC. 5/139, p. 125; LS. 8/6.	Duke's	Hall Theatre
3 December	*The Adventures of Five Hours* LC. 5/139, p. 125; LS. 8/6.	Duke's	Hall Theatre
10 December	Either *The Scornful Lady* or *The Silent Woman* LC. 5/12, p. 17; LC. 5/139, p. 129; LS. 8/6.	King's	Hall Theatre
17 December	*Macbeth* LC. 5/139, p. 125; LS. 8/6.	Duke's	Hall Theatre
28 December	*Henry Fifth* (Orrery's) LC. 5/139, p. 125; LS. 8/6; Pepys.	Duke's	Hall Theatre

1666/7

1 January	*The Villain* LC. 5/139, p. 125; LS. 8/6.	Duke's	Hall Theatre
14 February	Either *Flora's Vagaries* or *Rule a Wife and Have a Wife* LC. 5/139, p. 129; LC. 5/12, p. 17; LS. 8/6.	King's	Hall Theatre

| 18 February (Shrove Mon.) | ? a masque Evelyn. | | Hall Theatre |
| 19 February (Shrove Tues.) | a comedy Evelyn. | | Hall Theatre |

1667

18 April	*The Maiden Queen* LC. 5/139, p. 129; 5/12, p. 17; LS. 8/6.	King's	Hall Theatre
2 May	*The Wits* LC. 5/139, p. 125; LS. 8/6.	Duke's	Hall Theatre
9 May	*Love Tricks or the School of Compliments* LC. 5/139, p. 125; LS. 8/6.	Duke's	Hall Theatre
16 May	*Aglaura* LC. 5/12, p. 17; LS. 8/6 as 17 May.	King's	Hall Theatre
28 August	*Volpone* LC. 5/139, p. 129.	King's	Hall Theatre

1667/8

13 January	*The Indian Emperour* Pepys, 14 Jan.	Amateurs	Hall Theatre
27 January	*The Maiden Queen* LC. 5/12, p. 17; LC. 5/139, p. 129.	King's	Hall Theatre
?3 February (Shrove Tues.)	*Sir Martin Marr-all* LC. 5/139, p. 125.	Duke's	Hall Theatre
3 February	? a masque Rugge II, f. 218ᵛ.		Hall Theatre
?4 February (Ash Wed.)	*Horace* Evelyn.	?Amateurs	Hall Theatre

1668

| 29 May | *She Wou'd if She Could* LC. 5/139, p. 125. | Duke's | Hall Theatre |
| 14 October | *The Queen of Arragon* Hist. Mss., XII, vii, 59; Pepys. | Duke's | St. James' |

9 November	*The Woman's Prize or the Tamer Tamed* LC. 5/12, p. 17; Hist. Mss., XII, vii, 60.	King's	Hall Theatre
16 November	* a comedy Hist. Mss., XII, vii, 60.		?Hall Theatre
21 November	*The Scornful Lady* LC. 5/12, p. 17.	King's	Hall Theatre
7 December	*The Usurper* LC. 5/12, p. 17.	King's	Hall Theatre

1668/9

8 February	*The Committee* LC. 5/12, p. 17.	King's	Hall Theatre
15 February	*The Adventures of Five Hours* Pepys.	Duke's	Hall Theatre
22 February	*Bartholomew Fair* LC. 5/12, p. 17; Pepys.	King's	Hall Theatre

1669

>1669 October <	* *The Black Prince* Epilogue to the King. French Comedians LC. 5/12, p. 252.	King's	?Hall Theatre

1670

6 April	a comedy Hist. Mss., XII, vii, 70.	Amateurs	St. James'

1670/1

6 February	The Queen's masque Hist. Mss., XII, v, 22–23; Evelyn as 9 Feb.; LS. 8/7.	Amateurs	Hall Theatre
10 February	*The Conquest of Granada Part I* Evelyn.	King's	Hall Theatre

11 February	*The Conquest of Granada*		
	Part II	King's	Hall Theatre
	Evelyn.		
20 February	The Queen's masque	Amateurs	Hall Theatre
	Hist. Mss., XII, v, 22–23;		
	SP. 44/25, ff. 195–196; LS. 8/7.		
21 February	The Queen's masque	Amateurs	Hall Theatre
	SP. 44/25, ff. 195–196;		
	LS. 8/7.		

1671

14 November	*Sir Salomon*	Duke's	Hall Theatre
	LC. 5/141, p. 2.		

1672

>March<	French Comedians		
	Lawrence, I, 142–143.		
17 December	French Comedians		
to 1 May	*Cal. of Treas. Books.*		
27 December	*Epsom Wells*	Duke's	Hall Theatre
	LC. 5/141, p. 2.		

1673

?c. March	*The Empress of Morocco*	Amateurs	Hall Theatre
	See pp. 183–186.		
>1673	*The Siege of Rhodes*	Duke's	
	Epilogue at Whitehall in 1673		
	edition of Davenant's Works.		
21 April to	Italian Comedians		
12 September	*Cal. of Treas. Books.*		
29 May	an Italian comedy		Hall Theatre
	Evelyn.		
Summer	French Comedians		
	Lawrence, I, 143.		

1673/4

5 January	Italian Opera		Hall Theatre
	Evelyn.		
14 January	* a play		Hall Theatre
	LC. 5/140, p. 407.		

1674

1 June to 19 August	French Comedians *Cal. of Treas. Books.*		
July <	Italian Comedians LC. 5/140, p. 509.		
3 November	*The Citizen Turn'd Gentle- man* LC. 5/141, p. 216.	Duke's	Hall Theatre

1674/5

15 February (Shrove Mon.)	*Calisto* See pp. 180–182.	Amateurs	Hall Theatre
16 February (Shrove Tues.)	*Calisto* See pp. 180–182.	Amateurs	Hall Theatre

1675

>1675	* *The Country Wit* Dedication of 1675 edition.	Duke's	?Hall Theatre
23 April <	*Calisto* See pp. 180–182.	Amateurs	Hall Theatre
7 June	*The Island Princess* LC. 5/141, p. 215.	King's	Hall Theatre
20 June to 4 October	Italian Comedians *Cal. of Treas. Books.*		
29 September	Italian Comedians Evelyn.		Hall Theatre

1676

>1676	* *Sophonisba* Dedication of 1676 edition.	King's	?Hall Theatre
18 May	* *Tyrannic Love or the Royal Martyr* LC. 5/142, p. 52.	King's	?Hall Theatre
29 May	*Aureng-Zebe* LC. 5/142, p. 52.	King's	Hall Theatre
4 December	* *Julius Caesar* LC. 5/142, p. 52.	King's	?Hall Theatre
5 December	* *The Maiden Queen* LC. 5/142, p. 52.	King's	?Hall Theatre

1676/7

12 January	* *The Destruction of Jeru-* *salem Part I* LC. 5/142, p. 52.	King's	?Hall Theatre
February to June	French Comedians LC. 5/141, p. 528; 5/142, p. 38.		

1677

>April	* *The Country Innocence* Dedication of edition licensed 6 April.	King's	Hall Theatre
29 May	*Rare-en-Tout* LC. 5/142, p. 38.	French Co.	Hall Theatre
30 November to 12 April	French Comedians *Cal. of Treas. Books*; LC. 5/142, p. 160.		
5 December	French Comedians LC. 5/142, p. 160.		Hall Theatre

1677/8

>January	*Sir Patient Fancy* Preface to edition licensed 28 January.	Duke's	Hall Theatre

1678

>June	*Friendship in Fashion* Preface to edition licensed 31 May.	Duke's	Hall Theatre
11 November to 12 Feb.	Italian Comedians *Cal. of Treas. Books.*		

1678/9

6 February	a play LC. 5/143, pp. 267, 435.	King's	Hall Theatre
March	a play LC. 5/143, p. 435.	King's	Hall Theatre

1680?/1

11 February	*The Rover* LC. 5/145, p. 120.	Duke's	Hall Theatre
13 February	*The Amorous Widow or the* *Wanton Wife* LC. 5/145, p. 120.	Duke's	Hall Theatre
17 February	*The Man of Mode or Sir* *Fopling Flutter* LC. 5/145, p. 120.	Duke's	Hall Theatre
20 February	*Epsom Wells* LC. 5/145, p. 120.	Duke's	Hall Theatre
27 February	*She Wou'd if She Could* LC. 5/145, p. 120.	Duke's	Hall Theatre
6 March	*The Feign'd Curtizans or* *A Night's Intrigue* LC. 5/145, p. 120.	Duke's	Hall Theatre

1681

15 November	*The Rival Queens or the* *Death of Alexander the* *Great* LC. 5/144, pp. 140, 141, 146; LS. 8/18; Hist. Mss., VI, 230.	King's	Hall Theatre

1682

15 November	*Rule a Wife and Have a* *Wife* LC. 5/144, pp. 303, 304.	United	Hall Theatre

1683

?20 May <	Italian Comedians Hist. Mss., VIII, ii, 458.

1683/4

11 February	*Valentinian* LC. 5/145, pp. 14, 17; LC. 7/1, p. 11.	United	Hall Theatre

1684

26 May to 11 December	French Players of Prince of Orange *Cal. of Treas. Books.*	
29 September	French Players LC. 5/145, p. 90.	Hall Theatre

1684/5

?2 January	a play LC. 5/145, p. 135.	Hall Theatre

1685

29 October	*The Rover*	United	Hall Theatre
	LC. 5/147, p. 68; LS. 8/22.		
4 November	*Rule a Wife and Have a Wife*	United	Hall Theatre
	LC. 5/147, p. 68; LS. 8/22.		
9 November	*Sir Courtly Nice*	United	Hall Theatre
	LC. 5/147, p. 68; LS. 8/22.		
16 November	*The City Politiques*	United	Hall Theatre
	LC. 5/147, p. 68; LS. 8/22.		
24 November	*The Moor of Venice*	United	Hall Theatre
	LC. 5/147, p. 68; LS. 8/22.		
30 November	*The Man of Mode or Sir Fopling Flutter*	United	Hall Theatre
	LC. 5/147, p. 68; LS. 8/22.		
14 December	*The Plain Dealer*	United	Hall Theatre
	LC. 5/147, p. 68; LS. 8/22.		

1685/6

13 January	*The Duchess of Malfi*	United	Hall Theatre
	LC. 5/16, p. 124; LC. 5/147, p. 125; LS. 8/22.		
20 January	*All for Love*	United	Hall Theatre
	LC. 5/16, p. 124; LC. 5/147, p. 125; LS. 8/22.		
27 January	*The Chances*	United	Hall Theatre
	LC. 5/16, p. 124; LC. 5/147, p. 125; LS. 8/22; Hist. Mss., XII, v, 102.		

3 February	*The Scornful Lady* LC. 5/16, p. 124; LC. 5/147, p. 125; LS. 8/22.	United	Hall Theatre
10 February	*The Humorous Lieutenant* LC. 5/16, p. 124; LC. 5/147, p. 125; LS. 8/22.	United	Hall Theatre
16 February (Shrove Tues.)	*The Mock Astrologer* LC. 5/16, p. 124; LC. 5/147, p. 125; LS. 8/22; Hist. Mss., XII, v, 104, as 17 Feb.	United	Hall Theatre

1686

30 April	*Hamlet* LC. 5/16, p. 124; LC. 5/147, p. 125; LS. 8/22.	United	Hall Theatre
20 October	*Sir Martin Marr-all* LC. 5/147, p. 260.	United	Hall Theatre
27 October	*The Rival Queens or the Death of Alexander the Great* LC. 5/147, p. 260.	United	Hall Theatre
3 November	*Sir Courtly Nice* LC. 5/147, p. 260.	United	Hall Theatre
10 November	*Othello* LC. 5/147, p. 260.	United	Hall Theatre
17 November	*The Committee* LC. 5/147, p. 260.	United	Hall Theatre
24 November	*The Humorous Lieutenant* LC. 5/147, p. 260.	United	Hall Theatre
1 December	*The Beggars* LC. 5/147, p. 260.	United	Hall Theatre
9 December	*A King and No King* LC. 5/147, p. 260.	United	Hall Theatre
15 December	*The Maiden Queen* LC. 5/147, p. 260.	United	Hall Theatre

1686/7

3 January	*The Fond Husband* LC. 5/147, p. 361.	United	Hall Theatre
10 January	*The Orphan* LC. 5/147, p. 361.	United	Hall Theatre
19 January	*The Rover* LC. 5/147, p. 361.	United	Hall Theatre
26 January	*The Bloody Brother or Rollo Duke of Normandy* LC. 5/147, p. 361.	United	Hall Theatre

1687

11 April	*The Spanish Curate* LC. 5/147, p. 361; LS. 8/23.	United	Hall Theatre
18 April	*Julius Caesar* LC. 5/147, p. 361; LS. 8/23.	United	Hall Theatre
25 April	*The Island Princess* LC. 5/147, p. 361; LS. 8/23.	United	Hall Theatre
9 May	*King Lear* LC. 5/147, p. 361.	United	Hall Theatre
16 May	*Valentinian* LC. 5/147, p. 361.	United	Hall Theatre
December	*The Emperor of the Moon* LC. 5/148, p. 59.	United	Hall Theatre

1687/8

31 January	*The Villain* LC. 5/148, p. 145; LS. 8/24, 8/25.	United	Hall Theatre
6 February	*The Double Marriage* LC. 5/148, p. 145; LS. 8/24, 8/25.	United	Hall Theatre
13 February	*Beggars' Bush* LC. 5/148, p. 145; LS. 8/24.	United	Hall Theatre

| 20 February | *King Lear* United LC. 5/148, p. 145; LS. 8/24. | Hall Theatre |
| 27 February | *The Humorous Lieutenant* United LC. 5/148, pp. 121, 145; LS. 8/24. | Hall Theatre |

1688

| 9 August to 22 September | French Comedians *Cal. of Treas. Books.* | Windsor |

1689

| >1689 | * *The Princess of Cleve* United Prologue in 1689 edition. | ?Hall Theatre |
| 15 November | *The Jovial Crew* United LC. 5/149, pp. 321, 368; LS. 8/26, pp. 370–371, 381; LC. 5/68, f. 151ᵛ; LC. 5/124; LC. 5/149, p. 318. | Hall Theatre |

1690

30 April	*Sir Courtly Nice* United LC. 5/150, pp. 72, 73, 74; LS. 8/27, pp. 94, 99.	Hall Theatre
4 November	*The Rover* United LC. 5/150, p. 156; LC. 5/151, p. 369; LS. 8/28, f. 24; LC. 5/69, f. 1ᵛ; LC. 5/123; LC. 5/150, p. 164.	Hall Theatre
c. November	* *Circe* United LC. 5/150, p. 170.	?Hall Theatre

1691/2

| c. March | * *The Orphan* United LC. 5/151, p. 30. | ?Hall Theatre |

1693

c. June   * *Caius Marius*   United | ?Hall Theatre
         LC. 5/151, p. 242.

1694

c. April   * *The Old Bachelor*   United | ?Hall Theatre
         LC. 5/151, p. 352.

1696

>1696   * *Cyrus the Great*   ?Betterton's | ?Hall Theatre
         Dedication and Prologue to
         Princess Anne in 1696 edition.

1696/7

6 February   a play   Hall Theatre
         LC. 5/151, p. 458; LC. 5/69,
         f. 132^v.

1697

4 November   a play   "both Companies" | Hall Theatre
         LC. 5/152, pp. 202, 220.

APPENDIX D

PAYMENTS FOR PLAYS AT COURT

(1)   Warrant dated 19 February 1661/2, including £700 for 35 plays at Court from 19 November 1660 to 6 February 1661/2, payable to Theophilus Bird, Charles Hart, Michael Mohun, and Walter Clun, or any of them for the Company.

LC. 5/137, p. 100.

The same warrant, made payable to Thomas Killigrew, was repeated on 14 April 1662. — *Ibid.*, p. 110.

Entry of payments in the Accounts of the Treasurer of the Chamber for 25 December 1661 to 24 June 1663.—E. 351/546.

(2)   Warrant dated 16 April 1662, including £140 for 7 plays at Court, no dates, payable to Sir William Davenant.

LC. 5/137, p. 110.

The same warrant was repeated on 3 September 1662.

Ibid., p. 228.

Entry of payment in the Acct. of the Treas. of the Chamber, as above. — E. 351/546.

(3)   Warrant dated 4 April 1663, including £540 for 27 plays at Court from 31 March 1662 to 20 March 1662/3, payable to Thomas Killigrew. — LC. 5/137, p. 421.

(4)   Warrant dated 16 June 1663, for £300 for 15 plays at Court from 22 September 1662 to 9 February 1662/3, payable to Sir William Davenant. — *Ibid.*, p. 389.

(5)   Warrant dated 17 October 1663, for £20 for *Ignoramus* at Court on 1 November 1662, payable to John Rhodes.

LC. 5/138, p. 91; Nicoll, pp. 278, 316.

(6)   Warrant dated 24 January 1664/5, for £253 for plays at Court and the theatre on and before 19 December 1664, payable to Thomas Killigrew. Deleted. — LC. 5/138, p. 156.

(7)   Warrant dated 7 February 1664/5, for £813 for plays at Court and the theatre from 31 March 1662 to 29 December 1664, payable to Thomas Killigrew, with note that the last two warrants were cancelled. — *Ibid.*, p. 157.

(8)   Warrant dated 5 June 1665, for £150 for plays at Court and the theatre from 14 August 1663 to 3 April 1665, payable to Sir William Davenant. — *Ibid.*, p. 171.

Entry of payment of £450 by 2 warrants (see no. 4) in the Acct. of the Treas. of the Chamber for 29 September 1665 to 29 September 1666.[1] — E. 351/546.

(9)   Warrant dated 24 November 1666, for £1050 for plays at Court and the theatre from 31 March 1662 to 20 November 1666, payable to Thomas Killigrew. Deleted.

LC. 5/138, p. 222.

Warrant dated 24 November, to the Signet Office for a privy seal for payment of this amount out of the Receipt of the Exchequer. — *Ibid.*, p. 275.

The docquet of the privy seal is in SP. 38/23. (See no. 14.)

(10)   Warrant dated 29 August 1668, including £100 for 5 plays at Court from 10 December 1666 to 14 (should be 31) July 1668, payable to Thomas Killigrew.

LC. 5/139, p. 127; Nicoll, p. 305.

(11)   Warrant dated 31 July (should be August) 1668, including £220 for 11 plays at Court from 29 October 1666 to 7 August 1668, payable to Sir William Davenant.

LC. 5/139, p. 125; Nicoll, p. 308.

Entry of payment, to Lady Mary Davenant, in the Acct. of the Treas. of the Chamber for 1670–71. — E. 351/549.

(12)   Warrant dated 4 June 1669, including £200 for 10 plays at Court from 10 December 1666 to 6 May 1669, payable to Thomas Killigrew. — LC. 5/12, p. 16; Nicoll, p. 305.

(13)   Warrant dated 18 November 1670, for £340 for plays at Court and the theatre from 5 June 1669 to 12 September 1670, payable to Thomas Killigrew. — LC. 5/13, p. 445.

---

1. Thereafter the Accounts run from 29 September to 29 September, and I shall give only the years.

(14)   Treasury letter dated 14 December 1670, authorising payment of £800 to Thomas Killigrew, by virtue of the privy seal of 29 November 1666 (no. 9), in full satisfaction for plays from the Restoration to 19 September 1669. — T. 51/28, p. 44.

Payment ordered out of the loans on the farm of the customs, 20 May 1671. — T. 11/2, p. 160.

Entry of payment by the Exchequer, 22 May 1671, with note that the Lords Commissioners of the Treasury have ordered the Officers of the Exchequer to take acquittances for this sum in full of the above privy seal and of all claims of the Comedians to 29 September 1670. — E. 403/1778, p. 44.

(15)   Warrant dated 3 January 1670/1, for £300 for plays at Court and the theatre from 16 November 1668 to 20 June 1670, payable to Lady Davenant. — LC. 5/13, p. 446.

(16)   A series of warrants, all dated 30 April 1674, payable to Thomas Killigrew:

For £90 for plays at Court and the theatre from 12 December 1666 to 6 March 1666/7,
For £260 for plays at Court and the theatre from 15 April 1667 to 2 March 1667/8,
For £340 for plays at Court and the the theatre from 18 May 1668 to 23 March 1668/9,
For £270 for plays at Court and the theatre from 17 April 1669 to 12 March 1669/70,
For £330 for plays at Court and the theatre from 12 May 1670 to 25 March 1671,
For £320 for plays at Court and the theatre from 9 April 1671 to 23 March 1671/2,
For £260 for plays at Court and the theatre from 25 March 1672 to 3 March 1672/3,
For £60 for plays at Court and the theatre from 8 March 1672 to 9 June 1673. — LC. 5/140, pp. 473–474.

Entry of payment of £60 in part payment of no. 3 above, and of £350 for the first two of these warrants, in Acct. of Treas. of the Chamber for 1672–73: it is impossible to say when the payments were actually made. — AO. 1/398/90.

(17)   Warrant dated 11 September 1674, including £40 for 2 plays at Court from 9 March 1670/1 to 12 March 1672/3,[1] payable to Lady Davenant. — LC. 5/141, p. 2; Nicoll, p. 309.

(18)   Warrant dated 14 June 1675, including £20 for 1 play at Court from 25 January 1674/5 to 7 June 1675, payable to Thomas Killigrew. — LC. 5/141, p. 215; Nicoll, p. 307.

Entry of payment of £60 for plays from 8 March 1672/3 to 9 June 1673 (see above, no. 16), and of this warrant in the Acct. of the Treas. of the Chamber for 1674–75.
AO. 1/399/97.

(19)   Warrant dated 14 June 1675, including £20 for 1 play at Court from 3 July 1673 to 2 March 1674/5, payable to Lady Davenant. — LC. 5/141, p. 216; Nicoll, p. 310.

(20)   Warrant dated 1 June 1677, including ?£100 for 5 plays at Court from 19 June 1675 to 5 May 1677, payable to Charles Killigrew. — LC. 5/142, p. 52; Nicoll, p. 307.

Entry of payment of £1520 to Thomas Killigrew for plays in 1668, 1669, 1670, 1671, and 1672, by 5 warrants dated 30 April 1674 (see above, no. 16), and of this warrant to Charles Killigrew, in the Acct. of the Treas. of the Chamber for 1676–77. — AO. 1/400/103.

(21)   Warrant dated 27 December 1679, for £20 for 2 plays at Court in February and March 1678/9, payable to Charles Killigrew. (Note that this is only £10 per play.)
LC. 5/143, p. 435.

Entry of payment in the Acct. of the Treas. of the Chamber for 1680–81. — AO. 1/402/115.

In the Secret Service Accounts (published by the Camden Society), this money is entered on 19 October 1681, as paid to the Treas. of the Chamber to be paid over to John Lacy, assignee of Charles Killigrew.

---

1. These are not the dates of the plays, but the dates covered by the warrant, and so throughout.

(22)   Warrant dated 10 January 1684/5, including £120 for
6 plays at Court from 5 November 1677 to 2 January 1684/5,
payable to Charles Davenant.
                          LC. 5/145, p. 120; Nicoll, p. 311.

(23)   Warrant dated 28 December 1685, including £140 for 7
plays at Court from 13 January 1684/5 to 14 December 1685,
payable to Charles Davenant and Betterton.
                          LC. 5/147, p. 68; Nicoll, p. 312.
Entry of payment of £270 by 2 warrants dated 19 and
28 December 1685, in the Acct. of the Treas. of the Chamber
for 1685–86. — AO. 1/405/127.

(24)   Warrant dated 15 May 1686, including £140 for 7 plays at
Court from 30 December 1685 to 10 May 1686, payable to
Betterton.[1] — LC. 5/16, p. 124; 5/147, p. 125; Nicoll, p. 312.
Entry of payment in the Acct. of the Treas. of the Chamber
for 1686–87. — AO. 1/405/130.

(25)   Warrant dated 30 December 1686, including £180 for 9
plays at Court from 6 October to 15 December 1686, payable
to Charles Davenant, Betterton, and Smith.
                          LC. 5/147, p. 260; Nicoll, p. 313.
Entry of payment in the Acct. of the Treas. of the Chamber
for 1686–87. — AO. 1/405/130.

(26)   Warrant dated 30 June 1687, including £180 for 9 plays at
Court from 3 January 1686/7 to 16 May 1687, payable to
Charles Davenant and Betterton.
                          LC. 5/147, p. 361; Nicoll, p. 313.

(27)   Warrant dated 20 December 1687, for £20 for *The Emperor
of the Moon*, payable to Mrs. Barry as assignee of the Company. — LC. 5/148, p. 59; Nicoll, p. 318.
Entry of payment in the Acct. of the Treas. of the Chamber
for 1687–88. — AO. 1/406/133.

---

1. A warrant dated 8 May 1686, for payment of £40 to Mrs. Barry seems to
be for plays at the theatre, attended by both King and Queen. So with
a similar warrant dated 21 April 1687. LC. 5/147, pp. 136, 321;
AO. 1/405/130.

(28)   Warrant dated 3 April 1688, for £100 for 5 plays at Court
from 31 January to 27 February 1687/8, payable to Charles
Killigrew and Thomas Davenant.
                        LC. 5/148, p. 145; Nicoll, p. 313.

Entry of payment in the Acct. of the Treas. of the Chamber
for 1687–1688. — AO. 1/406/133.

(29)   Warrant dated 2 January 1689/90, including £20 for 1 play
at Court from 28 May to 4 December 1689, payable to
Charles Killigrew and Thomas Davenant.[1]
                        LC. 5/149, p. 368; Nicoll, p. 314.

(30)   Warrant dated 7 November 1670, for £25 for *Circe*, acted
for the Queen, payable to Mrs. Barry as assignee for the Company. — LC. 5/150, p. 170; Nicoll, p. 319.

(31)   Warrant dated 3 March 1691/2, for £25 for *The Orphan*,
payable to Mrs. Barry as assignee of the Company.
                        LC. 5/151, p. 30; Nicoll, p. 319.

(32)   Warrant dated 10 June 1693 for £25, for *Caius Marius*, payable to Mrs. Barry. — LC. 5/151, p. 242; Nicoll, *loc. cit.*

(33)   Warrant dated 16 April 1694, for £25 for *The Old Bachelor*,
payable to Mrs. Barry. — LC. 5/151, p. 352; Nicoll, *loc. cit.*
Entry of payment for these 3 plays, to Mrs. Barry for herself
and the rest of the Comedians, in the Acct. of the Treas. of the
Chamber for 1692–94. — E. 351/550.

(34)   Warrant dated 20 June 1694, including £40 for 2 plays at
Court from 16 January 1689/90 to 13 January 1692/3, payable
to Charles [*sic*] Rich. — LC. 5/151, p. 369; Nicoll, p. 314.

(35)   Warrant dated 8 June 1699, for £30 in part payment for
1 play at Whitehall on 4 November 1697 and 2 at the theatre,
payable to Christopher Rich. — LC. 5/152, p. 202.

---

1. A warrant dated 8 June 1689, for £25 for *The Spanish Friar* acted before
the Queen, payable to Mrs. Barry, is probably a mistake, for the same
item is included in a bill for plays at the theatre, where it was acted on
28 May. See LC. 5/149, pp. 154, 368, and Nicoll, pp. 314, 318. Nos. 30
to 33 may also be for plays at the theatre.

APPENDIX E

GREEN BAIZE FOR THE STAGE

THE COCKPIT IN COURT

		£.	s.	d.	
24 November 1660	Warrt. for baize lined with canvas, to cover the stage	13.	0.	0.	LC. 5/60, p. 63; 5/118.
Mich. 1660–1*	Bill for 120 yds. of baize	6.	13.	4.	LC. 9/104; 9/378.
Mich. 1660–1	Bill for 100 ells of canvas	4.	13.	4.	LC. 9/104; 9/377.
Mich. 1660–1	Upholsterer's bill including "other worke"	11.	12.	6.	LC. 9/104; 9/378; 9/381.
Mich. 1661–2	Bill for 93 yds. of Manchester baize				LC. 9/105; 9/378; 9/381.
4 Nov. 1661	Upholsterer's bill, including other work				LC. 9/105; 9/380.
4 Feb. 1661/2	Warrt. for baize to cover stage				LC. 5/60, p. 245.
26 Aug. 1662	Warrt. for baize to cover stage				LC. 5/60, p. 344.
Lady Day–Mich. 1662	Upholsterer's bill including other work				LC. 9/105; 9/380.
13 Nov. 1662	Warrt. for baize to cover stage and hang over the doors there				LC. 5/60, p. 385; 5/137, p. 175; Nicoll, p. 341.
25 Nov. 1662	Warrt. for green cotton or baize to cover the stage	(no amount)			LC. 5/60, p. 389; 5/118.
Mich. 1662–3	Bill for 76 yds. of green baize				LC. 9/106.
Mich. 1662–3	Upholsterer's bill, including other work				LC. 9/106.
5 Oct. 1663	Warrt. for baize to cover stage				LC. 5/61, p. 63.
Mich. 1663–4	Upholsterer's bill, including other work				LC. 9/107.

* Most of the Wardrobe Accounts run from Michaelmas to Michaelmas, without individual dates.

THE HALL THEATRE

		£.	s.	d.	
22 Jan. 1662/3	Warrt. for baize to cover the stage				LC. 5/60, p. 404; 5/118.
Mich. 1662–3	Bill for 156 yds. of green baize	20.	16.	0.	LC. 9/106.
Mich. 1662–3	Upholsterer's bill for covering stage and seats *	5.	10.	0.	LC. 9/106.
Mich. 1664–5	Bill for 80 yds. of baize, "to Couer the stage and Imployed about other places"	10.	13.	4.	LC. 9/108; 9/382.
Mich. 1664–5	Upholsterer's bill for covering stage and dais with canvas and baize	3.	10.	0.	LC. 9/108; 9/378; 9/382.
17 Oct. 1666	Warrt. for green cloth and canvas to cover the stage "for her Maties. Daunceinge"				LC. 5/138, p. 74.
Mich. 1666–7	Bill for 108 ells of canvas	9.	18.	0.	LC. 9/375; 9/382.
Mich. 1666–7	Bill for 69 yds. of French green cloth	29.	6.	6.	LC. 9/375; 9/382.
Mich. 1666–7	Upholsterer's bill for making a "falce Cover" for the stage, to fasten with iron buttons	6.	3.	0.	LC. 9/375; 9/382.
31 Jan. 1667/8	Warrt. for green baize to cover stage				LC. 5/139, p. 9.
3 Feb. 1667/8	Warrt. for green baize to cover stage				LC. 5/62, f. 16; 5/118; 5/139, p. 9.
3 Feb. 1667/8	Warrt. for green baize to cover "turning door"				LC. 5/62, f. 16^v; 5/118; 5/139, p. 9.
10 Feb. 1667/8	Bill for 76½ yds. of Manchester baize	8.	18.	6.	LC. 9/271. f. 15^v.
10 Feb. 1667/8	Bill for 12 yds. of broad green baize, for the turning door	1.	13.	0.	LC. 9/271, f. 15^v.
5 Feb. 1667/8	Upholsterer's bill for covering stage and turning door	1.	0.	0.	LC. 9/271, f. 20; 9/379.
1 Nov. 1670	Warrt. for 100 yds. of baize to cover the stage				LC. 5/62, f. 117^v.
11 Jan. 1670/1	Warrt. for baize to add to that on the stage, 3 yds. broad and the length of the stage				LC. 5/62, f. 119^v; 5/63, p. 85.
14 Feb. 1670/1	Warrt. for baize for the Queen's attiring room				LC. 5/62, f. 121; 5/63, p. 91.
19 Feb. 1670/1	Warrt. for baize to cover stage				LC. 5/62, f. 121^v.

* These three items refer to a temporary stage erected in the Hall.

THE HALL THEATRE (*continued*)

		£.	s.	d.	
Mich.1670–Lady Day 1671	Upholsterer's bill for covering the stage, the the addition to the stage (twice), the tiring rooms and stage again	5.	12.	0.	LC. 9/272, f. 111v-12; 9/381.
Mich.1670–Lady Day 1671	Bill for 44½ yds. of baize	5.	3.	10.	LC. 9/272, f. 94.
Mich.1670–Lady Day 1671	Bill for 68 yds. of baize for the Queen's attiring room, and 30 yds. for the Ladies' attiring room	11.	0.	6.	LC. 9/272, f. 98v.
Mich.1670–Lady Day 1671	Bill for 143¾ yds. for the stage, hangings, and forms	16.	3.	5¼	LC. 9/272, f. 99v.
13 Nov. 1671	Bill for 120 yds. of "grasse green" Manchester baize, and 80 yds. of the same	25.	0.	0.	LC. 9/109; 9/273.
12 Oct. 1671/2 (*sic*)	Upholsterer's bill for covering the stage and and "the dancing Roome"	1.	10.	0.	LC. 9/273; 9/110 (where amount is given as £15).
14 Nov. 1672	Warrt. for green baize to cover stage and forms				LC. 5/64, f. 51.
Winter of 1672/3	Bill for 43 yds. of baize				LC. 9/110; 9/273.
13 Nov. 1673	Warrt. for baize to cover stage	5.	0.	4.	LC. 5/64, f. 79v.
15 Feb. 1682/3	Warrt. for baize to cover forms, for the dancing				LC. 5/144, p. 364.
28 Nov. 1685	Warrt. to cover stage with "strong course greene cloth"				LC. 5/147, p. 24.
Mich. 1688–9	Upholsterer's bill for covering stage		12.	6.	LC. 9/279.
13 Nov. 1689	Warrt. for baize to cover stage				LC. 5/68, f. 151v; 5/124. LC. 5/147, p. 318 as 15 Nov.; and so Nicoll, p. 341.
Mich. 1689–90	Bill for 48 yds. "lati viridis panni villosi"	7.	4.	0.	LC. 9/124.
Mich. 1695/6	Bill for 42 yds. of broad baize and work	8.	3.	6.	LC. 9/377; 9/380.
4 Feb. 1696/7	Warrt. for baize to cover stage				LC. 5/69, f. 132v; 5/151, p. 458.

APPENDIX F

THE COSTUMES FOR *CALISTO*

THE bills for one hundred and sixty-one costumes for *Calisto* are to be found in two Wardrobe books in the Public Record Office,[1] the Annual Account for 1674–75,[2] and a book into which the original bills submitted by tradesmen were copied.[3] In the former, which is in Latin, the masque bills are grouped and labelled; in the latter, they are scattered and are not always marked for the masque, but they are more detailed and are, of course, in English. I have checked the totals in the Annual Account, but have used the Bill Book for the following descriptions, and give references to it alone.

Valuable as these Accounts are, it does not seem desirable to reproduce them *in extenso*. There is a vast deal of repetition, quantities and amounts are seldom given concisely or uniformly, and in order to assemble a complete costume, the pertinent items have to be extracted from half a dozen bills. Fortunately, this last is an easy task, for nearly every item is marked for such and such a costume.[4] I shall, therefore, take up each character in the masque, in the order of appearance, and give first the tailors' description of the costume, quoted *verbatim*, then a summary of materials and accessories, and finally, any relevant information from other sources. In listing the materials, I have omitted the occasional description as "rich" or "broad" where there is no change in price, and have itemised the tailors' findings — called "small" or "petty furniture" — only once, since they are much the same for all costumes.[5]

---

1. See also pp. 214–215.
2. LC. 9/112. Nicoll (p. 322) mentions this book but makes no use of it.
3. LC. 9/274.
4. Only two bills, the glover's and the shoemaker's, present difficulties, and these I shall summarise separately.
5. See Europe on pp. 307–308. At the end of the appendix will be found a glossary of terms occurring in the Accounts.

Handling the material this way eliminates all mention of the tradesmen, all of whom, I think, were regular purveyors to the Great Wardrobe, and as they may be of interest, I list them here:

Nicholas Fownes, mercer
Daniel Deive, draper
William Gosling or Gostling, laceman
John Eaton, laceman
William Rutlish and George Pinckney, embroiderers
Thomas Templer, hosier
William Terry, hatter
John Pate, shoemaker
Thomas Hawley, ribbonman
Lawrence Verryer, glover
John Allen and William Watts, tailors
Richard Chace, featherman
Abraham Downing, skinner
Jay Devoe, maker of properties
Edward Younger, cutler.

VIOLINS (20)
"ffor makeing a taffaty gowne Laced with gawes downe before round the bottome round the neck and the sleeves with all small ffurniture"   10. 0
for making 19 more   9.10. 0 ·
        (LC. 9/274, p. 278.[1])

31½ ells cherry taffeta   20. 9. 6
31½ " sky taffeta   17. 6. 6
27 ells yellow taffeta   14.17. 0
150 " narrow silver gauze   7.10. 0
        (p. 263.)

20 garlands   5. 0. 0
        (p. 273.)   _____

                                                                75. 3. 0

_____

1. Except where otherwise noted, all the following entries are from LC. 9/274, and I shall give only the page reference.

"Hoa Boyes" (2)
"ffor makeing a gowne of greene Avinnion printed with silver with
all small ffurniture"   8. 0
for making a gilt leather cap, lined and stiffened   4. 0
gilt leather   4. 0
for making another   16. 0
    (p. 278.)

18 yds. green avinnion printed with silver   5.17. 0
4   "   narrow silver gauze   4. 0
    (p. 263.)

2 prs. fine grey worsted hose   12. 0
    (p. 260.)
                                                        ─────────
                                                        8. 5. 0

"Kittars" (4)
"ffor makeing a taffaty gowne Laced with gawes downe before round
the sleeves and neck and bottome with all small ffurniture"
                                                        10. 0
making a gilt leather cap with feathers   4. 0
gilt leather   4. 0
for making 3 more   2.14. 0
    (p. 278.)

18 ells white taffeta   9.18. 0
16 yds. broad gold gauze   1.12. 0
2   "   broad gold gauze   4. 0
    (p. 263.)

"Gytar: Master 14 falls [*of feathers*] of severall collours" 2.16. 0
    (p. 294.)
                                                        ─────────
                                                        18. 2. 0

Trumpetters and Drummer (5)
"ffor makeing a [gowne] vest: with hanging sleeves of Cherry cŏll
taffaty lined with Callicoe sleeves ffaced with taffaty laced with
silver gawes in every seame and round the hanging sleeves bottome
of the vest and a banner of red taffaty laced round with silver
gawes"   18. 0
findings   11. 6
making a cap of gold gauze   5. 0
for making 4 more   6.18. 0
    (p. 278.)
                                                        ─────────
                                                        8.12. 6

23 ells cherry Florence taffata	14.19. 0
140 yds. narrow silver gauze	7. 0. 0
9 yds, broad silver gauze	18. 0
2½ yds. broad gold gauze	5. 0
2½ " false silver tabby	17. 6
(p. 264.)	

5 prs. grey worsted hose   1.10. 0
(p. 260.)

2 pcs. & 18 yds. cherry 8^d ribbon   2.10. 0
(p. 271.)

                                    36.12. 0

THAMES (Mrs Davis)
No bills for costume
a ship   4. 4. 0
a silver oar   9. 0
(p. 272.)

"For a Shipp: ffor one fine and white feather 20 falls 4
fine red falls and 4 red spriggs"   10. 0. 0
(p. 294.)

                                    14.13. 0

PEACE (Mrs Knight)
"ffor makeing a habbit of silver tabby covered all over with silver
and gold lace and embroidered with steyes and all small furniture"
—(p. 289.)   4.10. 0

21¼ yds. white silver tabby   15.18. 9
*"ffor a petticoate and Lace — agreed for"¹   15. 0. 0
(p. 268.)
1¼ yds. white lutestring   (8. 9)
(B. M. Add. Ms. 27588, f. 16.)

"Gold & silver lace for a Pettycoate for Mrs Knight, and
to trim cloathes for her to wear in a Masque perform'd
at Whitehall"   256.14. 3
(AO. 1/2053/25. Master of Robes.)

---

1. I have marked with an asterisk all items of which the allocation is doubtful.

18 yds. cherry 10^d ribbon   12. 0
    (p. 271.)

1 feather, 33 falls, white   6.12. 0
    (p. 293.)

an olive branch   15. 0
an olive cap   15. 0
    (p. 271.)
                                     301. 5. 9

PLENTY (Mrs Butler)
"ffor makeing a habbit of gold tabby with steys and all small furniture and sarsnet to line it"   3. 0. 0
"ffor makeing along petticoate of fflowred silver stuffe
being lengthned with pockets and all small ffurniture"   15. 0
    (p. 290.)

18 yds. gold tabby   13.10. 0
"ffor a petticoate and Lace — agreed for"   15. 0. 0
$\frac{3}{4}$ yd. sky lutestring   5. 3
$\frac{3}{4}$ ell white Florence sarsenet   8. 3
    (p. 268)

1 yd. cloth of silver
1$\frac{1}{4}$ yds. pink lutestring   } no prices
9$\frac{1}{2}$ "   flowered silk and silver stuff
    (B. M. Add. Ms. 27588, ff. 4 and 16.)

18 yds. green 10^d. ribbon   12. 0
    (p. 271.)

1 feather, 24 falls, cherry and white   4.16. 0
    (p. 293.)

a cornucopia   1.10. 0
a cap of flowers and leaves   10. 0
    (p. 272.)
                                     40. 6. 6

EUROPE (Mr Hart)
"ffor makeing the body baces and sleeves of silver tabby and longets
of gold gawes scollops round the wast and sey of silver tabby laced
with gold fringe the bace sleeves and garters laced with gold Lace the

body scollups and Hellmet adorned with Iewells and spangles the
body sleves and bace lined with deamoty the hellmet adorned with
ffeathers and apaire of white taffata drawers   2.10. 0[1]
ffor Canvas buckeram stifning and whalebone   6. 0
ffor fustian to line bace body sleves and Longets   8. 0
ffor silke thread and two silke Laces tagged   6. 0
ffor hookes and Eyes   1. 0
ffor 20 dō: of small round Iewells of seṽ collours att 12ᵈ   1. 0. 0
ffor 2 grosse of spangles at 2ˢ:2ᵈ   4. 4
ffor makeing a scarlet paragon robe lined with white
printed lutestring with silke and all small ffurniture"   15. 0
    (p. 280.)
12 yds. scarlet paragon   1.16. 0
14 "   white lutestring "printed with Silver and black
Ermin"   7. 0. 0
10 yds. false silver tabby   3.10. 0
3½ "   broad gold gauze   7. 0
1¼ ells white taffeta   13. 9
    (p. 264.)

12 yds. broad lace, 7 fingers wide   3.12. 0
12   "   gold fringe   1. 1. 4
    (p. 257.)

1 pr. pearl silk hose   14. 0
    (p. 260.)

1 pc. scarlet 8ᵈ taffeta ribbon   1.13. 0
    (p. 270.)

1 feather, 24 falls, red and white   4.16. 0
1 herne top   5. 0
    (p. 293.)

a headpiece with jewels and pearls   2. 0. 0
    (p. 271.)   _____
                                                          32.18. 5

Europe's Attendants
First Attendant
"ffor makeing body scollups and Longets of gold gawes: baces sleves
of sky sattin scollups round the waste and sey all Laced with gold

_____

1. The figures are given in the original in the form 002 10.

fringe body sleeves and bace lined with ffustian the bace sleeves and
garters laced with gold gawes the waste and Sey adorned with
Iewells spangles, and drawers"   2. 0. 0
findings   1. 1. 0
8 doz. small round jewels & 1 gross spangles   10. 2
making a gilt leather cap with feathers   4. 0
gilt leather   4. 0
    (p. 280.)

Second and Third Attendants
"ffor makeing the body and Longets of silver Gawes the
sleeves and scollups of Cherry sattin lined with ffustian
bace sleeves and garters laced with silver gaws and a
paire of drawers"   2. 0. 0
findings   1. 1. 0
making a gilt leather cap with feathers   4. 0
gilt leather   4. 0
for making another   3. 9. 0
    (p. 280.)

Fourth Attendant
"ffor makeing a doublet of ffalse silver tabby cloake and
truncks of Cherry Avinnion printed with silver the Cloake
lined with sky Avinnion the doublet and truncks lined
with ffustian: the sleeves and Round the truncks laced
with silver gawes and a paire of taffatae drawers"   1. 5. 0
findings   12. 0
3 doz. small silver buttons   3. 0
making a gilt leather cap with feathers   4. 0
gilt leather   4. 0
"ffor makeing his doublet and truncks into a Roman habbitt with silke and all small furniture"   15. 0
    (p. 281.)

First Attendant
4½ yds. sky Florence satin   2.14. 0
5½ " broad gold gauze   11. 0
7   " broad gold gauze   14. 0
1¼ ells white taffeta   13. 9
    (p. 265.)

Second and Third Attendants
10 yds. cherry Florence satin   7. 0. 0

11 yds. broad silver gauze	1. 2. 0
28 " narrow silver gauze	1. 8. 0
2½ ells white taffeta	1. 7. 6
(p. 265.)	

Fourth Attendant

8 yds. cherry avinnion printed with silver	2.16. 0
6 " sky avinnion	18. 0
2 " false silver tabby	14. 0
9 " narrow silver gauze	9. 0
1¼ ells white taffeta	13. 9
(p. 265.)	

6 yds. cherry and silver lace, 7 fingers wide	1.16. 0
4 doz. gold fringe	3.17. 7
(p. 257.)	

4 black felt hats	1. 0. 0
"ffor Laceing them and buttons and Loopes"	6. 0
(p. 261.)	

4 feathers, 10 falls each, of several colours	8. 0. 0
(p. 293.)	

4 prs. pearl silk hose	2.16. 0
(p. 260.)	

3 pcs. cherry 8^d taffeta ribbon	3. 0. 0
1 pc. sky taffeta ribbon	18. 0
(p. 270.)	
	56.14. 9

Asia (Mr Richardson)
"ffor makeing avest of sky printed Avinnion and scarlet serge breeches: the vest laced downe before round the bottome and sleeves with 3 laces: the one of gold: sky silver and grydeline: 5 fingers broad: the 2^d: of a silver lace 4 fingers broade: and the third a gold lace 3 fingers broade: lined with Callico and innerlñd with Callicoe adorned with colloured Iewells the breeches lined with Callicoe"   3. 0. 0

findings	1. 9. 0
34 doz. small coloured jewels	1.14. 0
9½ " big round jewels, several colours	2. 7. 6
6 " "bigg round and trebble Iewells"	1. 4. 0

4 doz. square and long jewels	1. 8.	0
1½ " big jewels "with ared in the midle"	7.	6
8 " treble jewels, several colours	2. 0.	0
16 strings of pearl	4.	0
2⅓ gross spangles	5.	5
"ffor makeing a roabe of gold colloured printed Avinnion lined with a pincke avinnion silke and all small furniture"	15.	0
"ffor makeing a Turbunt adorned with Iewells and pearles with lineing silke and all small furniture"	1. 0.	0
(p. 283.)		

8 yds. sky avinnion printed with silver	2.12.	0
3½ " scarlet rateene	1.15.	0
14 " gold avinnion printed with silver	4.11.	0
14 " yds. pink avinnion	2. 9.	0
(p. 266.)		

16 yds. gold silver & pink lace, 7 fingers	4.16.	0
16 " ditto, 5 fingers	3.12.	0
44 " ditto, 2½ fingers	6.12.	0
48 " gold galloone	1.16.	7
3 " "great gold Loope Lace"	7.	4
18 doz. cherry and silver roses	1.10.	0
(p. 258.)		

1 pr. scarlet worsted hose	7.	6
(p. 260.)		

12 yds. gold 8ᵈ ribbon	6.	0
(p. 270.)		

1 herne top	10.	0
(p. 293.)		

a "semiter"	10.	0
(p. 254.)		

	47. 8.10	

ASIA'S ATTENDANTS
First and Second Attendants

"ffor makeing a vest of gold colloured Avinnion lined and innerlined with Callicoe and laced with silver gawes downe before round the bottome and sleeves with a gold gawes as a lace: apaire of red Padua breeches lined with Callicoe"	2. 0.	0
findings	1. 8.	0

"ffor makeing a turbunt with areath of painted Callicoe
silke and all small furniture" 4. 0
for making another 3.12. 0
 (p. 284.)

Third Attendant
"ffor makeing a vest of Cherry Avinnion Lined and innerlined with Callicoe laced with silver gawes and gold fringe
downe before round the bottome and sleeves the breeches
of Red Padua serge Lined with Callicoe" 1.10. 0
findings 1. 2. 0
"ffor makeing a Turbunt with a reath of painted Callico
with all small furniture" 4. 0
 (p. 284.)

Fourth Attendant
"ffor makeing avest of greene Avinnion lined and innerlined with Callicoe laced with gold gawes and a silver lace
downe before round the bottome and sleeves and a paire
of red Padua breeches lined with Callicoe" 2. 0. 0
findings 1. 8. 0
turban, as above 4. 0
 (p. 285.)

First and Second Attendants
16 yds. gold avinnion 2. 8. 0
6½ " red serge 19. 6
30 " broad gold gauze 3. 0. 0
 6 " " " " 12. 0
 (p. 267.)

Third Attendant
8 yds. green avinnion 1. 4. 0
3¼ " red serge 9. 9
7½ " broad gold gauze 15. 0
 (p. 267.)

Fourth Attendant
6 yds. cherry avinnion 1. 1. 0
3¼ " red serge 9. 9
14 " broad silver gauze 1. 8. 0
 (p. 267.)

4 prs. scarlet worsted hose	1.10. 0
(p. 260.)	
1 pc. gold 8ᵈ taffeta ribbon	18. 0
(p. 270.)	
4 scimitars	2. 0. 0
(p. 254.)	
	30. 7. 0

AFRICA (Mr Marsh, Jr)
"ffor makeing body and longets of gold tinsell the sleeves and gorget
of black sattin bace and scollups of scarlett sattin scollups round the
waste and Sey the longets sleves and bace shammaired with white
pearle and two bands of scarlet sattin round each sleeve and Edged
with silver gawes and a band of black sattin round the bottome of
the bace shammaired with white pearle Iewells and spangles the
body bace and sleeves lined with ffustian and a Capp of gold Gawes
faced with black sattine adorned with Iewells and twelve ffalls of

ffeathers with a pʳ of white taffaty drawers"	2.10. 0
findings	1. 1. 0
a black perriwig	1. 0. 0
making a cap	6. 0
2 "messes of pearle"	1. 0. 0
24 doz. small round jewels	1. 4. 0
24 " spangles	4. 4
(p. 281.)	
5½ yds. broad gold gauze	11. 0
4½ " scarlet satin	3. 3. 0
3 " black Florence satin	1.16. 0
3 " broad gold gauze	6. 0
1¼ ells white taffeta	13. 9
(p. 265.)	
1 pr. black silk hose	14. 0
(p. 260.)	
1 pc. scarlet 8ᵈ taffeta ribbon	1.13. 0
(p. 270.)	
1 feather, 12 falls, red and white	2. 8. 0
(p. 293.)	
	18.10. 1

Africa's Attendants
First and Second Attendants
"ffor makeing the body of sky Avinnion the Gorgett of black sattin
the sleeves and bace of gold Colloured Avinnion the body bace and
sleeves lined with ffustian and two bands of scarlet sattine round
each sleeve and one about the bottome of the bace edged with silver
gawes and pearle about the waste and gorget and apaire of white
taffaty drawers"   2. 0. 0
findings   1. 1. 0
24 strings of pearl   6. 0
making a cap of gold gauze   4. 0
for making another   3.11. 0
      (p. 282.)

Third Attendant
"ffor makeing the body of black Avinnion bace and sleeves
of sky Avinnion the body bace and sleeves lined with
ffustian the bands of yellow sattine edged with white
gawes two about each sleeve and i about the bottome of
the bace the gorget and waste shammaired with white
pearle and a paire of white taffata drawers"   2. 0. 0
findings   1. 1. 0
24 strings of pearl   6. 0
making a cap   4. 0
      (p. 282.)

Fourth Attendant
"ffor makeing the body of red Avinnion the gorget of
black sattin the bace and sleeves of silver gawes the body
sleeves and bace lined with ffustian and bands of red sattin
edged with gold gawes two about each sleeve and one
about the bottome of the bace the gorget and waste
shammaired with white pearle and a paire of taffaty
drawers"   1.10. 0
findings   18. 6
20 strings of pearl   5. 0
making a cap   4. 0
      (p. 283.)

First and Second Attendants
3 yds. sky avinnion   9. 0
10 "   gold avinnion   1.10. 0

3 yds. scarlet satin	1.10. 0
1 yd. black satin	12. 0
6 yds. broad silver gauze	12. 0
2 " " gold gauze	4. 0
2½ ells white taffeta	1. 7. 6
(p. 265.)	

Third Attendant

1½ yds. black avinnion	4. 6
5 " sky avinnion	15. 0
1½ " yellow satin	12. 9
½ yd. black satin	6. 0
3 yds. broad silver gauze	6. 0
1 yd. " gold "	2. 0
1¼ ells white taffeta	13. 9
(p. 266.)	

Fourth Attendant

1½ yds. cherry avinnion	5. 3
6½ " broad silver gauze	13. 0
1½ " cherry satin	16. 6
½ yd. black satin	6. 0
2 yds. broad gold gauze	4. 0
1 yd. " " "	2. 0
1¼ ells white taffeta	13. 9
(p. 266.)	

4 prs. black silk hose	2.16. 0
(p. 260.)	

1 pc. & 12 yds. scarlet 8^d ribbon	2. 4. 0
(p. 270.)	
	30.15. 6

AMERICA (Mr Ford)

"ffor makeing the body of silver tinsel sleeves and bace of pincke colloured sattin covered all over with colloured ffeathers and 3 rowes of Iewells and spangles about the bace: and 3 about the body: and the gorget shammaired with Jewells and spangles and white pearle: the body bace and sleeves lined with fustian the sleeves faced with silver gawes and gold gawes round the sleeves and bottome of the bace and a paire of taffaty drawers"   3. 0. 0

findings   1. 1. 0

30 doz. jewels, several colours   1.10. 0
36   "   spangles   (no price)
25 strings of pearl   6. 3
12 yds. black 4^d ribbon "to sett the Iewels on with"   3. 0
"ffor makeing a Capp of silver gawes with lineing and
stifning adorned with Jewells and 12 falls of ffeathers
with one long sprigg"   6. 0
jewels and spangles for the cap   8. 0
    (p. 285.)

2 yds. false silver tabby   14. 0
5   "   pink satin   2.15. 0
1 yd. false silver tabby   7. 0
1¼ ells white taffeta   13. 9
7 yds. broad gold gauze   14. 0
    (p. 267.)

1 pr. scarlet silk hose   16. 0
    (p. 260.)

1 pc. green 10^d ribbon   1. 4. 0
    (p. 270.)

1 feather, 12 falls, red   2. 8. 0
1 Indian shape, 6000 swan's feathers of several colours   1.10. 0
* 1 herne top and 1 cock's tail   10. 0
    (p. 293.)
                                                         ─────────
                                                         18. 6. 0

AMERICA'S ATTENDANTS
First Attendant
"ffor makeing the body bace and sleeves of greene Avinnion done over with bands of Colloured ffeathers and
lined with fustian and a paire of taffaty drawers"   2. 0. 0
findings   1. 1. 0
making a cap of silver tinsel with feathers   4. 0
    (p. 286.)

Second and Third Attendants
"ffor makeing the body bace and sleeves of yellowe Avinnion lined with fustian and Covered over with colloured
feathers and apaire of drawers"   2. 0. 0
findings   1. 1. 0

Making a cap of white gauze with feathers   4. 0
for making another   3. 5. 0
   (p. 286.)

Fourth Attendant
"ffor makeing the body bace and sleeves of black Avinnion lined with ffustian and covered over with colloured
feathers and apaire of taffaty drawers"   1.10. 0
findings   17. 0
making a cap of white gauze with feathers   4. 0
   (p. 287.)

First Attendant
7 yds. green avinnion   1. 1. 0
1¼ ells white taffeta   13. 9
1 yd. broad silver gauze   2. 0
6 yds. broad gold   "   12. 0
   (p. 267.)

Second and Third Attendants
14 yds. yellow avinnion   2. 2. 0
2½ ells white taffeta   1. 7. 6
14 yds. broad silver gauze   1. 8. 0
   (p. 267.)

Fourth Attendant
6 yds. black avinnion   18. 0
1¼ ells white taffeta   13. 9
6 yds. broad silver gauze   12. 0
   (p. 267.)

4 prs. scarlet silk hose   3. 4. 0
   (p. 260.)

1 pc. green 10^d ribbon   1. 4. 0
   (p. 270.)

4 feathers, 6 falls each   4.16. 0
4 Indian shapes, 24000 swan's feathers, several colours   6. 0. 0
   (p. 293.)
                  ————
              37. 0. 0

CALISTO (Princess Mary)
No bills for costume.

Nyphe (Princess Anne)
No bills for costume.

Attendant Nymphs (Countess of Derby, Countess of Pembroke,
Lady Katherine Herbert, Mrs Katherine Fitzgerald, Mrs Carey
Fraizer)
No bills for costumes.

6 plain quivers and arrows "for the Ladys"	15. 0
(p. 272.)	

Shepherds (Duke of Monmouth, Viscount Dunblaine,
Lord Deincourt, Mr Trevor, Mr Lane)
Probably they supplied their own costumes, but see below.

a velvet cap for the Duke of Monmouth, "to Dance in"	18. 0
(B. M. Add. Ms. 27588, f. 33.)	

The Genius of England (Mr Turner)
"ffor makeing the body and longets of gold gawes bace
sleeves and scollups of Cherry sattin the bace longets and
scollups laced with anarrowe silver lace and a broad
silver lace on the top of it: on the bace with 2 silver laces
round each sleeve with a gold silver and silke lace in the
midle adorned with great silver scollups small silver and

purle roses Iewells and spangles: and apaire of drawers"	3.10. 0
findings	1. 3. 0
10 gross spangles	1. 1. 8
6½ gross small jewels, several colours	3.18. 0
4 doz. round jewels with 7 stones	1. 4. 0
6½ doz. big round white jewels	1.12. 6
(p. 288.)	
6 yds. broad gold gauze	12. 0
5½ " cherry satin	3. 0. 6
1¼ ells white taffata	13. 9
(p. 268.)	
18 yds. silver lace, 4 fingers wide	3. 3. 0
4 " gold and silver point lace, 7 fingers	1. 4. 0
80 " silver lace, 1½ fingers	6. 0. 0
12 " gold, silver and pink lace, 4 fingers	1.10. 0
18 doz. silver and cherry roses	1.10. 3
(p. 257.)	
1 pr. pearl silk hose	14. 0
(p. 260.)	

1 pc. cherry 8ᵈ ribbon (p. 271.)	1.	0.	0
1 feather, 20 falls, red (p. 293.)	4.	0.	0
a headpiece with jewels and pearls	2.	0.	0
a trunchion (p. 271.)		1.	0

37.17. 8

HERO OF THE SEA (Mr Harpc)
"ffor makeing the Body bace and breeches of greene printed Avinnion shammaired over with red bands the body and bace lined with Callicoe and pufted round the bottome in forme of a shell and a band of Cherry sattin puft round the bottome of the bace and the sleeves hands cherry sattin scollups round yᵉ waste and Knees of the breeches shammaired with white pearle and a paire of taffatae drawers" 3. 0. 0

findings	1.	7.	0
for making a cap adorned with feathers, jewels and spangles		8.	0
3 gross spangles		6.	6
10 doz. small round jewels, several colours		10.	0
4 " big round jewels	1.	4.	0
1½ mess false red coral	1.	4.	0
20 strings white pearl (p. 276.)		6.	8
12 yds. green avinnion printed with silver	3.	18.	0
3 " cherry satin	2.	2.	0
1¼ ells white taffeta (p. 263.)		13.	9
1 pr. fine mixed silk hose (p. 260.)		14.	0
green ribbon (see next costume) (p. 271.)			
1 feather, 24 falls, red and white (p. 294.)	4.	16.	0
a vizard (p. 272.)		5.	0

20.14.11

SEAGODS (4)

"ffor makeing a doublet and Breeches of greene printed Avinnion Lined With Callicoe and interlined with ffustian the doublet and Breeches embroidered all over with Red pearle and ffinns of green printed Avinnion round the waste sey Gorget sleeves and Knees of the Breeches stifned with horne Buckerome Lined with Cherry Avinnion and silver tabby and a paire of taffaty drawers"

	2.10. 0
findings	1. 3. 0
making a cap trimmed with feathers	6. 0
1½ mess false red pearl	1. 1. 0
for making three more	15. 0. 0
(p. 277.)	
40 yds. green avinnion printed with silver	13. 0. 0
8 " cherry avinnion	1. 8. 0
12 " false silver tabby	4. 4. 0
5 ells white taffata	2.15. 0
(p. 263.)	
4 prs. fine mixed silk hose	2.16. 0
(p. 260.)	
2 pcs. green 8ᵈ ribbon (shared with Hero of the Sea)	1.16. 0
(p. 271.)	
4 feathers, 32 falls, green and white	6. 8. 0
(p. 294.)	
4 vizards	1. 0. 0
(p. 272.)	
	53. 7. 0

TRITONS
No bills for costumes.

HERO OF THE LAND (Duke of Monmouth)
* "A Roman habitt being a shape for the Body wᵗʰ: scollups & furniture for the same wᵗʰ: a black Velvett Capp & white Plume of ffeathers"   18. 4. 6
    (AO. 1/2052/25. Acct. of Master of Robes.)

"a Combatants Capp foʳ the Duke of Monmouth"
(The price, £1.5.0, is, I suppose, included in the above.)
    (B. M. Add. Ms. 27588, f. 33.)

ROMAN COMBATANTS (6)

"ffor makeing a Roman habbit body sleeves and Cuffes of silver tabby lace half sleves gorget and faceing of the hellmet of green sattin the Hellmet scollops and barrs of the body of gold tabby edged with gold galloone the Longest [*sic*] turning up of the Cuffs and faceing the helmet of scarlet sattin edged with a gold galloone the bace and upper sleves bordered with a silver tabby with a deep gold fringe and a gold galloone adorned with Roses Jewells and spangles the body and Longetts adorned with gold scollops gold purle rosets Iewells and spangles the hellmet adorned with pearle roses Iewells ffeathers and spangles edged with galloone with a paire of white taffaty drawers." [1]

drawers." [1]	3. 0. 0
findings	1. 0. 0
making the helmet	6. 0
5 doz. big white jewels	1.10. 0
32 " round jewels, several colours	1.12. 0
24 gross white spangles	2.12. 0
for making 5 more	50. 0. 0
(p. 273.)	
9 yds. rich gold tabby	7. 4. 0
21 " " silver tabby	15.15. 0
18 " green Florence satin	11. 5. 0
12 " scarlet Florence satin	8. 8. 0
7½ ells white taffeta	4. 2. 6
(p. 261.)	
132 doz. gold roses & silver roses	16.10. 0
24 gold scollops	11. 0
39 doz. scarlet and silver roses	3. 5. 0
6 " silver buttons	12. 0
11 " silver and scarlet galloone	4. 8.10
2 " silver galloone	14. 0¾
24 " gold galloone	7.14. 8¼
30 " deep twisted gold fringe	8. 0.10½
6 gold vellum buckles for the girdles	12. 0
(p. 255.)	

---

1. This was the noblest Roman of them all! *Cf.* the print of Quin as Coriolanus.

6 prs. large cherry silk hose	4.10. 0
(p. 259.)	
2 pcs. scarlet 8ᵈ taffeta ribbon	3. 6. 0
(p. 270.)	
6 hats	1. 4. 0
(p. 273.)	
6 feathers, 12 falls each	14. 8. 0
(p. 293.)	
7 vizards	15. 0
(p. 271.)	
6 swords	3.12. 0
(p. 254.)	

$$176.17.11\tfrac{1}{2}$$

RURAL GODS
No bills for costumes; probably the satyrs (see below).

Two who sing a song
No bills for costumes.

CARPENTERS (12)
"ffor makeing a red Padua serge Wastcoate and gray cloth breeches
the wastcoat lined with ffustian and laced with silver tinsell galloone
two in aseame the breeches laced with a gold tincell galloone 4 about
each Knee and 6. up each side"   18. 0
findings   7. 6
3 doz. silver tinsel buttons   2. 0
for making 11 more   15. 2. 6
(p. 289.)

27 yds. scarlet serge   4.14. 6
18   "   gray cloth   6. 6. 0
(p. 272.)

25 doz. gold galloone   4. 9. 1
20½ "   silver galloone   3.15.11
(p. 256.)

12 prs. fine gray worsted hose   3.12. 0
(p. 259.)

4 pcs. "Coronation" 8ᵈ taffeta ribbon   4. 0. 0
   (p. 270.)

12 coloured felt hats, and "for Laceing them: for makeing buttons and Loopes and furring them up with scutts" 3.12. 0
   (p. 261.)

12 aprons   18. 0
   (p. 273.)

12 vizards   3. 0. 0
   (p. 271.)
                                   50.17. 6

JUPITER (Henrietta, Baroness Wentworth)
No bills for costume.[1]

Lightning   5. 0
   (p. 272.)

MERCURY (Sarah Jennings)
No bills for costume.

a caduceus   1.10. 0
   (p. 272.)

DIANA (Margaret Blagge)
"ffor makeing her habbit richly laced with gold and
silver lace with steys and all small furniture 6.0.0."
"ffor makeing a Long petty coate richly Laced with
all small furniture 2.0.0"   8. 0. 0
   (p. 289.).[2]

24 yds. gold brocade   100. 0. 0
   (p. 241.)

---

1. Lady Philadelphia Wentworth imported a parcel of Flanders lace on
   5 February 1674/5 (Cal. of Treas. Books); it is not inconceivable that it
   was for Jupiter.
2. B. M. Add. Ms. 27588, f. 21 gives the following version of this: "Pour
   madame blake pour Vn habict de diane le corps Et les manche toneler
   doublure dantredeaux fason Et fourniture 03–10–00 pour la grande Jupe
   couuerte de dantelle boullonee pour la fason Et fourniture 02–00–00 por
   la Jupe courte couuerte de dantelle por la fason Et fourniture 01–05–00
   pour la coyfure Et monter les plume 01–05–00."

8 yds. broad gold and silver lace	14. 8. 0	
16 " broad gold lace	19. 4. 0	
16 " broad silver lace	25.12. 0	
40 " narrow gold lace	19. 0. 0	
40 " narrow silver lace	16. 0. 0	
20 " other narrow silver lace	7.10. 0	
6 " "midlesize" silver lace	5. 2. 0	
12 " narrow silver lace for gloves	4.10. 0	
(p. 242.)		

6½ yds. "poynt de Espayne"	16.18. 0	
1½ " fine "poynt de Espayne"	3. 7. 6	
3 " fine "poynt de Espayne"	12. 0. 0	
"ffor the Allowance of 2ˢ:6ᵈ: apound"	4. 0. 8	
(presumably customs duty or a tax)		
(p. 252.)		

"ffor the Allowance of 2^s:6^d: apound"

"one Plume of scarlet and White q^t: 40 ffalls"   25. 0. 0
   (p. 293.)

a quiver   1.18. 0
16 bows and arrows   2. 0. 0
   (p. 272.)
                                                    ─────────
                                                   284.10. 2

PSECAS (Lady Mary Mordaunt)
No bills for costume.

SHEPHERDS AND SHEPHERDESSES
There are costumes for Daphne and Sylvia, and also for four more
shepherdesses who do not appear in the text; for shepherds, there
are nine costumes, two of which I take to be for Strephon and
Corydon, and another set of six "for the Chorus." Some of these
were probably for the first version and discarded in the second,
although one shepherd was then added to the chorus (see p. 341).

STREPHON AND CORYDON (Mr Hart and Mr Turner)
"ffor makeing a ffour skirted doublet of silver Tabby the bagg
strings and breeches of Cherry sattin the hatt covered with a silver
tabby and ffaced with Cherry taffatae adorned with ffeathers and
Edged with a broad silver Lace the doublet body and sleeves Lined
with Callico the shirts [sic] and sleeves with Cherry taffaty the
breeches with deamoty laced with 3 silver laces and 3 silver ffringes

round each: Knee: the bagg Laced with a Cherry and silver Lace: the stringes with a silver ffringe: the doublet sleeves and gorget of striped gawes and 3 silver Laces: the body with 2 laces Cherry and silver: adorned with roses Jewells and spangles: the breeches, bagg and strings with Jewells and spangles and a paire of taffaty

drawers "	2.10. 0
findings	19. 0
covering, lacing and lining the hat	4. 0
32 doz. small round jewels	1.12. 0
4 gross spangles	8. 8
for making another	5.13. 8

(p. 275.)

10 yds. rich silver tabby	7.10. 0
6 " cherry satin	3. 6. 0
10 " pink, green and white taffeta	2.12. 0
2½ ells white taffeta	1. 7. 6

(p. 262.)

54 yds. cherry and tinsel lace	8. 2. 0
27 " narrower cherry & silver lace	2. 0. 6
28 " silver tinsel lace	6. 6. 0
22 " silver tinsel fringe	1. 1. 0
4 doz. cherry and silver roses	6. 8
8 " silver buttons	16. 0

(p. 255.)

2 prs. pearl silk hose	1. 8. 0

(p. 259.)

2 pcs. cherry 6^d taffeta ribbon	1. 8. 0

(p. 270.)

2 coloured castors	1. 8. 0

(p. 261.)

2 feathers, 18 falls each, cherry and white	7. 4. 0

(p. 293.)

                                                    56. 3. 0

SYLVIA (Mrs Davis)
"ffor makeing a sheppherdesses habbit with steyes and all petty furniture"   (no price)
(p. 289.)

No bills for materials.
1 pr. pearl silk hose   12. 0
   (p. 260.)

green ribbon (see below)
1 fine white straw hat lined with red silk   6. 0
   (p. 261.)

½ ell cherry taffeta to face the hat   6. 0
   (p. 269.)

1 crook   8
   (p. 272.)
                                             ——————
                                           1. 4. 8

DAPHNE (Mrs Knight)
"ffor makeing a shepherdesses habbit of tinsell covered all over with silver lace and embroidered with steys and all small furniture"
   (p. 290.)   3. 10. 0

9 yds. broad silver gauze   18. 0
2 "   broad gold gauze   4. 0
1¼ "   white lutestring   8. 9
¾ yd. cherry satin to face a hat   8. 3
¾ "   cherry satin for a bag   8. 3
   (p. 268 and B. M. Add. Ms. 27588.)

1 pr. pearl silk hose   12. 0
   (p. 260.)

green ribbon (see below)
1 fine white straw hat lined with red silk   6. 0
   (p. 261.)

1 crook   8
   (p. 272.)
                                             ——————
                                         6. 15. 11

OTHER SHEPHERDESSES (Mrs Butler, Mrs Hunt, Mrs Masters, Mrs Peirce)
Mrs Butler
"ffor makeing a shepherdesses habbit the gowne of sky colloured sattine the body of a cherry colloured sattin the pettycoate of silver tinsell with Bullions on it, the bace and sleeves of silver tinsell lined

with a Cherry colloured sarsnet the Lambricans on the baces and
sleeves of gold tincell with steys and all small furniture"

	4. 0. 0
6 strings of pearl	1. 6
(p. 290.)	

Mrs Hunt
"ffor makeing a shepherdess habbit with steys and all
small furniture"   4. 0. 0
6 strings of pearl   1. 6
"ffor makeing a petticoate of greene Avinnion all richly
laced with all small furniture"   1. 0. 0
   (p. 290.)

Mrs Masters and Mrs Peirce
"ffor makeing a shepherdesses habbit the body of Cherry
sattin the petticoate of greene tabby with silver gawes
and Bullions on it the bace of silver gawes with sleeves
of the same lined with Cherry Avinnion the Lambricans
on the bace and sleeves of gold gawes"   4. 0. 0
6 strings of pearl   1. 6
for making another   4. 1. 6
   (p. 291.)

Mrs Butler and Mrs Hunt
3 yds. sky satin   1. 5. 6
9 " broad cherry tabby   3.16. 6
6 " cherry avinnion   1. 1. 0
17 " broad silver gauze   1.14. 0
5 " green damask   2. 5. 0
   (p. 268.)

Mrs Hunt
24 yds. cherry and silver lace, 4 fingers wide   4. 4. 0
   (p. 258.)

Mrs Masters and Mrs Peirce
3 yds. cherry satin   1.13. 0
12 " broad green tabby   3.18. 0
4 " cherry avinnion   14. 0
17 " broad silver gauze   1.14. 0
   (p. 269.)

4 prs. pearl silk hose	2. 8. 0
(p. 260.)	
2 pcs. & 18 yds. green 8ᵈ taffeta ribbon (shared with Sylvia and Daphne)	2. 5. 0
(p. 270.)	
4 fine white straw hats lined with red silk	1. 4. 0
(p. 261.)	
2 ells cherry taffeta to face the hats	1.10. 0
(p. 269.)	
4 crooks	2. 8
(p. 272.)	

47. 0. 8

SHEPHERDS FOR THE CHORUS (6)
"ffor makeing a gold tinsell wastcoat and greene taffaty breeches the wastcoate Lined with Callico the colloured sleeves faced with greene taffatye and Laced with a broad silver tincell Lace and one in Every seame the breches lined with Callico: — and Laced with two laces of gold and silver downe Each mid thighe and two round Each Knee: the bagg and strings of greene taffatae laced with gold fringe and a paire of drawers"   1. 5. 0
findings   15. 0
3 doz. breast buttons   1. 0
for making 5 more   10. 5. 0
     (p. 277.)

27 yds. broad gold gauze   2.14. 0
15 ells green taffeta   8. 5. 0
7½ ells white taffeta   4. 2. 6
     (p. 263.)

111 yds. silver lace, 5 fingers wide   19. 8. 6
57 "   gold and silver lace, 3 fingers wide   8.11. 0
30 "   gold fringe   2.12.10
     (p. 257.)

6 prs. pearl silk hose   4. 4. 0
     (p. 260.)

6 pcs. cherry 6^d taffeta ribbon   4. 4. 0
   (p. 270.)

6 coloured castors and "ffor Lyneing them with green
silke and tinsey and buttons and loopes"   4.13. 0
   (p. 261.)

6 crooks   4. 0
   (p. 272.)   ─────────

                             71. 4.10

OTHER SHEPHERDS (7)
The tailors' bill has already been quoted for Strephon and Corydon
(see p. 324).
for making 7 more   39.15. 8
   (p. 275.)

35 yds. false silver tabby   12. 5. 0
21 " cherry satin   11.11. 0
35 " silk gauze   8.15. 0
25 " cherry avinnion   4. 7. 6
8¾ ells white taffeta   4.16. 3
   (p. 262.)

189 yds. cherry and tinsel lace   28. 7. 0
94½ " narrower cherry & silver lace   7. 1. 9
98 " silver tinsel lace   22. 1. 0
77 " silver tinsel fringe   3.13. 6
14 doz. cherry and silver roses   1. 3. 4
28 " silver buttons   2.16. 0
   (p. 255.)

7 prs. pearl silk hose   4.18. 0
   (p. 259.)

7 pcs. cherry 6^d taffeta ribbon   4.18. 0
   (p. 270.)

7 coloured castors   4.18. 0
   (p. 261.)

7 feathers, 18 falls each, cherry & white   25. 4. 0
   (p. 293.)   ─────────

                            186.11. 0

BASQUES (7)

"ffor makeing a paire of breeches and a six skirted doublet the body of ffillamort printed avinnion the sleeves longets and breeches of Cherry printed Avinnion shammaired with black lace and ffillamort paspoyles on the breeches and sleeves and Cherry paspoyles on the Body the sleeves faced with a cherry printed Avinnion and Laced with a broad silver tinsell lace: and apaire of taffaty drawers"

	1.10. 0
findings	16. 0
3 doz. black breast buttons	1. 0

"ffor makeing a bonnet of sky printed Avinnion Laced wth: black lace and paspoyles and buckerome to Line it"   5. 0
for making 6 more   15.12. 0
       (p. 276.)

45½ yds. cherry avinnion printed with silver	15.18. 6
24½ yds. gold avinnion printed with silver	7.19. 3
7 " sky avinnion printed with silver	2. 5. 6
8¾ ells white taffeta	4.16. 3

       (p. 262.)

287 yds. black colbertine lace, 3 fingers wide	9.11. 4
21 " broad silver lace, 7 fingers	6. 6. 0

       (p. 258.)

7 prs. cherry silk hose	5. 5. 0

       (p. 260.)

3 pcs. cherry 10^d taffeta ribbon	3.12. 0

       (p. 270.)

7 "white Towers round the Capp with 3 ffine falls curled" (feathers)   10. 0. 0
       (p. 293.)

8 tambors de baskes	3. 4. 0
8 vizards	2. 0. 0

       (pp. 271–272.)
               ————
              89. 1.10

WINDS (8)

"ffor makeing the Body of silver tabby the bace and sleeves of Cherry colloured sattin the Longetts of gold tabby the body capp and Longets all Embroidered a band of silver Tabby plated on the

bottome of the bace and a deep silver and Cherry ffringe att the
bottome of all and anarrowe silver ffringe downe the backsides
sleeves and paspoyles with silver and Cherry purle roses att the
topp of every Longet, the Longets lined with a cherry colloured
Avinnion with a paire of taffatae drawers"   3. 0. 0
findings, included "wyre to forme the Longet and wings" 1. 2. 0
making a cap   6. 0
for making 7 more   30.16. 0
    (p. 275.)

"ffor Embroidering eight habbitts and Capps with garters and shoestrings and for stuffe and other workeman-
shipp: each habbitt att 11 ¹ᶦ:"   88. 0. 0
    (p. 253.)

24 yds. rich silver tabby   18. 0. 0
34 " rich gold tabby   27. 4. 0
25 " mixed avinnion   3.15. 0
28 " cherry Florence satin   19.12. 0
 4 " musk colour tabby   1. 6. 0
10 ells white taffeta   5.10. 0
    (p. 262.)

20 yds. scarlet and silver fringe   2.11. 9
44 " silver fringe   2.18. 6
 4 doz. silver galloone   15.11¼
56 " cherry and silver roses   4.13. 4
 8 " silver buttons   16. 0
    (p. 256.)

8 prs. mixed silk hose   5.12. 0
    (p. 259.)

2 pcs. cherry 8ᵈ ribbon   2. 0. 0
    (p. 270.)

8 hats   1.12. 0
    (p. 273.)

8 garlands   1.12. 0
8 vizards   2. 0. 0
    (p. 272.)
                          ─────────
                      223. 2. 6¼

Cupids (2)

"ffor makeing a doublet and breeches of white sattin both lined with ffustian the scollups of pink coll^d: sattin laced with a pincke and silver Lace round the wast and Knees of the breeches: the wings made of ffeathers and a Capp of white tinsell"   15. 0
findings   9. 0
2½ doz. breast buttons   8
making a cap of white tinsel with a peak lined and stiffened   4. 0
for making another   1. 8. 8
          (p. 288.)

12 yds. white satin   5. 2. 0
1½ " pink satin   16. 6
2 " broad silver gauze   4. 0
4 " pink avinnion   14. 0
          (p. 268.)

20 yds. silver lace, 3 fingers wide   3.10. 0
          (p. 257.)

2 prs. pearl silk hose   1. 4. 0
          (p. 260.)

24 yds. white ribbon   12. 0
          (p. 271.)

2 prs. of wings of "Estridge" feathers, 80 falls, red and white   4. 0. 0
36 falls, pink and white, for 2 caps   5. 0. 0
          (p. 293.)

8 quivers and arrows   1. 8. 0
8 vizards   2. 0. 0
          (p. 272.)
          _____
          27. 7.10

Juno (Countess of Sussex)
No bills for costume.

Airy Spirits (4)
"ffor makeing two pincke Colloured gownes and 2 purple gownes laced with gawes downe before round the bottome sleeves and neck with silke and all small ffurniture"   2. 0. 0

making 4 caps of silver gauze   12. 0
"ffor making apincke colloured Coate and Spannishe
breeches coate laced with gawes downe before round the
bottome and sleeves with silke and petty ffurniture"   10. 0
2 doz. gold buttons   2. 0
making 3 more   1.16. 0
     (p. 279.)

5 ells purple taffeta   2.15. 0
5 " rich pink taffeta   3. 5. 0
40 yds. narrow silver gauze   2. 0. 0
     (p. 264.)

4 prs. pearl silk hose   2. 8. 0
     (p. 260.)
                           ————
                           15. 8. 0

Possibly the "Heavenly spirits" belong here too; see below.

GYPSIES
No bills for costumes.

SATYRS (8)
"ffor makeing the doublet and Breeches of muske collour taffatae
the breeches shammaired with gold and muske colloured fringe:
bands and Leaves of greene sattin on the breeches and doublet and
Capp the mantle and Longet of Doeskinn lined with Cherry collour
Taffaty silver fringe round the sleeves and Knees of the breeches:
gold fringe round the Knees of the breeches the Capp being shammaired all over with muske colour and gold fringe"   2. 0. 0
findings   18. 0
making the cap   6. 0
"Silke: Cotton for breasts in the doublet"   2. 0
     (p. 274.)

96 "Lustred sea batts to make the shapes for eight
Satirs"   24. 0. 0
"yellow and white spotts for the eight shapes"   2. 0. 0
"sewing in the spotts and makeing the Skinns fitt to the
shapes"   5. 0. 0
     (p. 252.)

32 ells musk colour Florence taffeta	17.	2.	0
16 " cherry Florence taffeta	10.	8.	0
16 yds. green Florence satin	10.	0.	0
(p. 262.)			

80 yds. deep gold and musk fringe	16.	14.	1
44 " silver fringe	2.	17.	4
12 " gold fringe	1.	1.	4
32 doz. silver buttons	3.	4.	0
(p. 256.)			

8 prs. fine mixed silk hose	5.	12.	0
(p. 259.)			

2 pcs. green 8^d ribbon	1.	16.	0
(p. 270.)			

8 hats	1.	12.	0
(p. 273.)			

8 clubs with flowers and leaves	8.	0.	0
8 vizards	2.	0.	0
3 ingots of gold		7.	0
3 ingots of silver		6.	0
a box of gold sand		5.	0
a casket of pearls and jewels	1.	0.	0
(p. 271.)			
	116.	10.	9

"BACCHUSES"
No bills for costumes for first production; see p. 339.

Two AFRICAN WOMEN (Mrs Butler and Mrs Hunt)
Mrs Butler
"ffor makeing an African habbit of Black sattin Cutt upon gold
tinsell: the longets on the sleeves and Bace of silver tinsell with all
petty furniture"　　　　　　　　　　　　　　　　2. 0. 0
24 strings of pearl　　　　　　　　　　　　　　　6. 0
"ffor Cutting an African habbit"　　　　　　　　12. 6
"ffor makeing a black lambskin Capp lined and stifned
with pearle"　　　　　　　　　　　　　　　　　4. 6
　　　(p. 290.)

Mrs Hunt
"ffor makeing an African habbit of black sattin Cutt
upon gold tinsell the Lambricans on the bace and sleeves
of silver tincell with all small furniture"   2. 0. 0
the rest as above   1. 3. 0
   (p. 291.)

8 yds. black satin   4.16. 0
17 " broad gauze   1.14. 0
   (p. 269.)

2 prs. fine silk hose   1. 4. 0
   (p. 260.)

4 black lambskins   4. 0
   (p. 252.)

* 2 vizards   10. 0
   (p. 272.)
                                                    _____
                                                        14.14. 0

THIRD AFRICAN WOMAN (?Mrs Blake)
No tailors' bill.

* The following items are marked "Mrs Blake the goddess of hunt-
ing," but obviously belong to the third African Woman.

14 ells black taffeta   7.14. 0
5 yds. black trilby   15. 0
2 " black 3-piled velvet   2. 4. 0
4 " white flowered gauze   2. 0. 0
   (p. 269.)

* 2 black lambskins   2. 0
   (p. 252.)

1 vizard   5. 0
   (p. 272.)
                                                    _____
                                                        13. 0. 0

AFRICAN KINGS (4)
"ffor making the body bace and sleeves of Black sattin Cutt all in
borders and shammaired with white pearl in waves betweene each
border the scollups of scarlet sattin round the waste and a Cherry
and silver lace on the scollups: the bands of scarlett sattin edged with
gold gawes two about each sleeve and one about the bace edged with
silver gawes the scollups and bands done round with white pearle
and innerlined with Cherry Avinnion the bace body and sleeves

lined with fustian and innerlined with gold gawes and a paire of
taffaty drawers"   3. o. o
findings   1. 1. o
80 strings white pearl   1. o. o
"Cutting the body and baces"   15. o
a periwig   1. o. o
making 3 more   20. 8. o
        (p. 287.)

28 yds. black satin   16.16. o
 8 "   pink avinnion   1. 8. o
16 "   broad gold gauze   1.12. o
 8 "   cherry satin   4. 8. o
 5 ells white taffeta   2.15. o
        (p. 268.)

24 yds. cherry and silver lace, 7 fingers wide   7. 4. o
        (p. 258.)

4 prs. black silk hose   2.16. o
        (p. 260.)

1 pc. & 12 yds. scarlet 8^d ribbon   2. 4. o
        (p. 271.)

4 feathers, 90 falls, several colours   18. o. o
        (p. 293.)

4 crowns   8. o. o
* 4 vizards   1. o. o
        (p. 272.)
                                                           ─────────
                                                           93. 7. o
African Slaves (6)
"ffor makeing awastcoate and breeches of black trilby the wastcoat lined with fustian the breeches with Callicoe and a Collar with
a band of silver gawes and one about each arme and an apron of
silver gawes"   10. o
findings   9. o
4 doz. black silk buttons   1. o
"ffor makeing a black lambskinn Capp with a reath of
silver gawes lineing to it"   2. 6
for making 5 more   5.12. 6
        (p. 287.)

39 yds. fine black trilby	5.17. 0
12 " broad silver gawes	1. 4. 0
(p. 269.)	
6 prs. black silk hose	4. 4. 0
(p. 260.)	
12 black lambskins	12. 0
(p. 252.)	
6 sticks	6. 0
6 vizards	1.10. 0
(p. 272.)	
	20. 8. 0

BOYS IN THE CLOUDS (6)
"ffor makeing two Cherry Avinnion gownes laced with silver gawes
downe before round the neck sleeves and bottome with all small
furniture" 14. 0
"ffor makeing two greene Avinnion gownes printed with
silver and two yellowe Avinnion gownes printed wth:
silver with all small ffurniture" 1. 4. 0
(p. 278.)

10 yds. pink avinnion	1.15. 0
10 " green avinnion printed with silver	3. 5. 0
10 " yellow avinnion printed with silver	3. 5. 0
16 " narrow silver gauze	16. 0
8 " " " "	8. 0
(p. 264.)	
6 prs. fine white worsted hose	1.10. 0
(p. 260.)	
	12.17. 0

HEAVENLY SPIRITS (4)
"ffor makeing a white taffatae gowne laced with gold gawes downe
before round the neck: sleeve and bottome with silke with all small
ffurniture" 10. 0
making a cap of gold tinsel 3. 0
"ffor makeing two sky gownes laced with gold gawes and
one white gowne with all small ffurniture" 1.10. 0
making 3 more caps 9. 0
(p. 279.)

"ffor makeing awhite taffaty Coate and Spannishe:
breeches the Coate laced with gawes downe before round
the bottome sleeves and neck with silke thread Canvas
buckeram and stiffning"   10. 0
2 doz. gold breast buttons   2. 0
making 3 more   1.16. 0
    (p. 279.)

5½ ells white taffeta   3. 0. 6
5½ " sky taffeta   3. 0. 6
22 yds. broad gold gauze   2. 4. 0
    (p. 264.)

4 prs. pearl silk hose   2. 8. 0
    (p. 260.)
                                   ————
                                  15.13. 0

There is also a bill for 127 pairs of perfumed gloves for men
and women, costing £12.14.0, but it is not itemised.[1] And
finally, the shoemaker put in a bill for £26.4.6, for 93 pairs of
shoes,[2] in which he stated whom they were for but not what
costume, and as many of them are for dancers, who required
several pairs apiece, they cannot be assigned very satisfactor-
ily. They range in price from five to eight shillings a pair, but
most of them are five shillings and sixpence.

All of the above-mentioned bills are dated in February or
are among those so dated. The costumes then provided also
served in most cases for the second production, but a few new
ones were required, the bills for which are dated April. Several new hand properties were needed for the leading ladies:
Lightning for Jupiter   1. 0. 0
Calisto and Nyphe
2 darts   16. 0
2 quivers with pearls and jewels   4. 0. 0
2 bosses with pearls and jewels   2. 0. 0
    (p. 322.)

2 falls of feathers for the darts   8. 0
    (p. 327.)
                                   ————
                                  8. 4. 0

————

1. LC. 9/274, p. 273.   2. *Ibid.*, pp. 311–312.

Satyrs (4)

"ffor makeing Body sleeves and Breeches of Pincke colloured taffaty lined with Dimoty the bodyes stiffned with bone and Buckerome and Canvas with a halfe Belly made out with Cotton and Callicoe: the breeches covered with sad-coloured worsted ffringe: the habbit garnished with greene vine leeves made of Parchment: with bunches of grapes annexed thereunto: with taffaty drawers"   1. 5. 0
findings, including "Cotton and Callicoe for the Belly"   1. 0. 6
silver buttons and loop-lace   1. 6
making a cap of gold gauze   4. 0
for making 3 more   7. 13. 0
 (p. 322.)

12 ells pink and white taffeta   6. 12. 0
 5 " white taffeta   2. 15. 0
 2 yds. broad gold gauze   4. 0
 2½ ells green taffeta   1. 7. 6
 (p. 320, marked for "Bacchusses.")

6 yds. worsted fringe "for 4 Satir backnesses"   2. 6. 7
 (p. 324.)

4 prs. coloured silk hose   2. 16. 0
 (p. 332.)

cherry taffeta ribbon — see next costume

4 prs. cordivant gloves   8. 0
 (p. 330.)

4 prs. shoes   1. 2. 0
 (p. 398.)

4 caps with grape leaves and hair   3. 0. 0
4 satyr's vizards   1. 0. 0
           ————————
vine leaves and grapes — see next costume   31. 15. 1
 (p. 322.)

Bacchants (4)

"ffor makeing Body sleeves and skirt of Isabella Lutestring stiffned with Buckerome bone and Canvas and garnished all over with spangles and greene grape leeves branched with grapes annexed

thereunto: the bottome of the skirt garnished with silver gawes: in
scollups with a paire of taffaty drawers"   1. 5. 0
findings, including cotton and calico for the belly   16. 6
silver buttons and loop-lace   1. 6
6 gross spangles   13. 0
making a cap   4. 0
for making 3 more   9. 0. 0
    (p. 323.)

32 yds. broad rich aurora & white lutestring   11. 4. 0
  5 ells white taffeta   2.15. 0
  2 yds. broad gold gauze   4. 0
24   "   narrow silver gauze   1. 4. 0
    (p. 320.)

4 prs. coloured silk hose   2.16. 0
    (p. 332.)

3½ pcs. cherry 12^d taffeta ribbon (shared with the
satyrs)
    (p. 337.)   5. 5. 0

4 prs. cordivant gloves   8. 0
    (p. 330.)

4 prs. shoes   1. 2. 0
    (p. 398.)

21 "Sprigges of ffalls of Corall Each haveing five branches
to trimme the Capps Instead of ffeathers"   2.12. 6
    (p. 339.)

4 bachant's vizards   1. 0. 0
4 great tambors with bells   4. 0. 0
4 "long sticks with pine Apples and bells att the End"   1.12. 0
4 caps, "with grape leaves and a greadle of Curled haire"   4. 0. 0
6½ gross vine leaves made of parchment (shared with
satyrs)
48 bunches of grapes (shared with satyrs)   4.18.11
    (p. 322.)   2. 8. 0

                                                       57. 9. 5

The last two costumes were:

A SHEPHERD ADDED TO THE CHORUS.[1]
"ffor makeing a gold tinsell wastecoate greene taffatae Breeches:
the wastecoate lined with callicoe the Culler sleeves ffaced with
greene taffatae and laces with a broad silver lace: one in Every
seame: Breeches lined with Callicoe and laced with gold and silver
Laces downe Each mide thigh and two round the Knee: the bagg
and strings of greene taffatae: laced with a gold ffringe and taffatae

drawers"	1.	5.	0
findings		15.	0
3 doz. coloured breast buttons		1.	0
(p. 323.)			
2½ ells green taffeta	1.	7.	6
4½ yds. broad gold gauze		9.	0
(p. 320.)			
18 yds. white tinsel lace, 4 fingers wide	4.	1.	0
9 " gold tinscl lace, 4 fingers	2.	0.	6
5 " gold tinsel fringe		11.	3
(p. 350.)			
1 pr. cherry silk hose		16.	0
(p. 332.)			
1 coloured castor trimmed with green silk and tinsel, with a gold button and loop		15.	6
(p. 321.)			
	12.	1.	9

PLENTY
"ffor makeing and ffurniture for the habbit Plenty being made as a
gowne of gold collor' and silver tabby haveing points buske and

Case and all other necessăr"	3.	0.	0

"ffor makeing and ffurniture for a Petticoate of pointed
Transilanway lutestring haveing pocketts ribbon and

all other necessar' "		15.	0
(p. 324.)			
16 yds. gold and (blank) tabby	12.	0.	0
7½ yds. green silver printed lutestring	3.	15.	0
(p. 320.)			

1. Warrant in LC. 5/141, p. 556.

1 feather, 30 falls, several colours   6. 0. 0
   (p. 327.)
a cap with flowers and silvered corn   12. 0
   (p. 322.)
                                                        26. 2. 0

And finally, 6½ yds. "Pentuan Prunella," price £1.15.9, was supplied "To Twist about 4 Turbat Capps," presumably those worn by Asia's attendants.[1]

GLOSSARY

Avinnion: not in the N. E. D. or Larousse; apparently a thin silk like sarsenet, perhaps first made in Avignon.

Bace: usually plural; a plaited skirt appended to the doublet and reaching to the knee, the skirt of a woman's outer petticoat or robe, an apron.

Bonelace: lace, usually of fine linen thread, made with bobbins on a pattern marked on a cushion with pins.

Bullion: an ornamental fringe of twists of gold or silver thread, a single twist of such thread.

Busk: the stiffening in the front of a woman's stays, a corset.

Calico: any cotton cloth imported from India, sometimes printed.

Camlet: a light stuff, made of wool or the hair of the Angora goat mixed with silk, cotton, or linen.

Castor: a hat of beaver or rabbit's fur.

Colbertine: a kind of lace with a square ground resembling net.

Cordivant: Spanish leather.

Damask: a rich silk with an elaborate woven design.

Deamoty (dimity): a stout cotton fabric, woven with raised stripes or figures.

Doublet: a close-fitting garment with or without sleeves.

Ermin: "printed with ermin" apparently means printed with black spots.

Fillamort (filemot): the colour of a dead or dry leaf, here described as gold.

Fustian: a coarse cloth made of cotton and flax.

Gawes (gauze): a transparent stiffened material, sometimes tinsel.

Gorget: a collar, an article of dress covering the neck and breast.

---

1. LC. 9/274, p. 320, and see pp. 309–310.

Grydeline (gridelin): pale purple or grey violet, sometimes pale red.

Lace: a string, cord, or tie, ornamental braid, a delicate open-work fabric of silk, linen, cotton, or metal thread.

Laced: trimmed with lace, braid, or cord.

Lambrican (lambrequin): "nom des bandes d'étoffe qui pendaient au bas de la cuirasse, dans l'imitation théâtrale du costume antique" (Littré). Here the same as longet, q. v.

Longet: not in N. E. D. or Larousse; apparently a trimming consisting of large shaped portions of silk or gauze, hanging from the elbows or hips, or both.

Loop-lace: an ornament consisting of a series of loops, lace consisting of patterns worked on fine net.

Lutestring: a glossy silk fabric.

Mess: a mess of pearls = 40 strings.

Paragon: a kind of double camlet, used for clothing and hangings.

Paspoyles (passe-poil): "liseré de soie, de drap, etc., qui borde certaines parties d'un habit, d'un gilet, etc., ou qui règne le long d'une couture" (Littré).

Pentuan: not in N. E. D.

Point: a piece of lace used as a kerchief, a tagged lace or cord.

Prunella: a strong stuff, originally silk, later worsted.

Rateene: a thick twilled cloth, frieze.

Sarsenet: a very fine, soft silk fabric.

Sea batt: a flying fish, the flying gurnard or swallow of the sea.

Sey: the opening into which the sleeve is inserted.

Shammair: a corruption of chammarrer (garnir).

Tabby: silk taffeta, waved or watered.

Taffeta: a plain glossy silk fabric.

Tambor de Baskes: tamborine.

Tincell, tinsell: wool or gauze interwoven with metal thread.

Transilanway: not in N. E. D. or Larousse; apparently a shade of green.

Truncks: trunk-hose.

Trilby: not in N. E. D. or Larousse; apparently a kind of cloth.

Vest: a general term used for any sleeveless garment, sometimes reaching nearly to the knee.

Wastecoat (waistcoat): a garment with or without sleeves, reaching to or below the hips.

APPENDIX G

NOTES ON SOME DIVERTISSEMENTS AT
WHITEHALL

IT MAY well be urged that the amusements here discussed do not properly belong to the history of the stage. But apart from their significance for Court life and Court tastes, they have definite associations with the stage: an account of the Cockpit in Court demands at least brief mention of cock-fighting, and the building of the Hope forever linked the bear-ring and the theatre. My apologia for the note on rope-dancing has, indeed, little to do with the Court, but in the public theatres the end of the Restoration period marked the rapid development of inter-act variety. Doubtless Betterton and the actors of legitimate would have scorned the association, but I believe the Master of the Bears, the Cockmaster and the rope-dancer contribute to a thorough understanding of the Court stage.

Bears at Whitehall

Among the royal sports and entertainments revived immediately upon the Restoration, bear- and bull-baiting at once assumed a fairly important place. The history of "His Majesty's Game of Bears, Bulls and Mastiffs" remains to be written, and when it is undertaken, there will be no lack of material for the second half of the seventeenth century: there are abundant lists of the Officers of the Bears,[1] the game was considered fit entertainment for ambassadors and visiting royalty,[2] the Master, like others of the same rank in the Household, received his New Year's gift of plate,[3] and there are, in addition to the regular salaries and wages, annual war-

1. LC. 3, *passim.*   2. LC. 5, *passim.*   3. *Ibid.*

rants for payment for "makeing ready" the game for His Majesty at Whitsuntide, warrants which discreetly omit to mention whether the King actually attended or not.[1] But most of these entries of appointments, payments and performances refer to the Bear Gardens in Clerkenwell and on the Bankside, and I must therefore, however regretfully, exclude them.

Bears and bulls appeared at Whitehall only in the first four years after Charles' return. The earliest baiting there to which I have found reference took place on 13 November 1660. Among the important events of that month, as recorded by Thomas Rugge, was a bull- and bear-baiting in the Tiltyard — an ancient custom in times of peace, he calls it[2] — and the inference that this was the first performance of the kind is borne out by an entry in the Works Account for that month, where the carpenters' work included "making & setting vp posts and rayles for bears bulls & doggs at ye tiltyard & setting vp seuerall stands & scaffolds there."[3]

It seems to have been part of the ancient custom alluded to by Rugge for the King to have his bear-baiting at Whitsuntide,[4] and that continued to be the regular procedure throughout the Restoration period. In the very next year, there was a baiting in the Tiltyard on Whit-Tuesday (4 June 1661). In that month, carpenters were employed in "making & setting vp scaffolds for ye master of ye Reuells & others for the bare-baiting in ye tilt yard," and[5] there is a warrant for payment of the usual £10 for sports on that date.[6] In 1662, the annual performance took place at Hampton Court,[7] but 1663 provides us with the fullest account we have of preparations in the Tiltyard. The carpenters were called upon to make degrees and scaffolds, set up posts to tie the bulls and bears to

1. *Ibid.* Payments of salaries and for baitings will be found in the Accounts of the Treasurer of the Chamber.
2. Rugge, I, f. 134ᵛ.
3. Works 5/1. The exact date is given in a warrant for payment of £10, quoted in E. 351/546.   4. Chambers, II, p. 453.
5. Works 5/2.   6. E. 351/546.   7. LC. 5/137, p. 227.

and set up a rail across the Tiltyard, while the more humble labourers known as "mazerscourers" carried the boards and dug the holes, and to them also fell the task of "wheeling of sand there and spreading it about the stake shoueling it vp together againe for the pauiors vse."[1] The ironmonger's bill for the same month includes "a stronge hoope of Iron to put on ye bearestake."[2]

After this baiting the scaffolds were taken down again, and a few months later was begun the construction of buildings in the Tiltyard for the Horse and Foot Guards,[3] which presumably so diminished its extent as to render it unsuitable for games. This last appearance of the bears in the yard where Prince Henry had tilted with his knights took place on a Whit-Tuesday, 9 June 1663, and was rewarded with the customary £10.[4] Thereafter, all baitings by royal command seem to have taken place at the public Bear Garden, with one remarkable exception. Luttrell tells us that on 19 January 1693/4, Prince Louis of Baden was entertained with a bull-and bear-baiting in St. James' Park.[5] The Royal Cockpit there must have been too small for this sport; there was no other building available. Unless a special amphitheatre was built for the occasion, which does not seem likely, there must have been only a temporary rail between the bears and the spectators. I hope Prince Louis enjoyed it.

Cockfighting

That Charles took great interest in this sport is abundantly clear from accounts of his sojourns at Newmarket, where he seems to have devoted much time to the mains, and even William allotted some of his scant leisure to them. But the letters which tell us of this royal patronage invariably refer to Newmarket, and the King seems to have considered the game

1. Works 5/4.
2. *Ibid.* It cost one shilling and sixpence.
3. *Ibid.*   4. E. 351/546.
5. Luttrell, III, 257.

more suitable for the country than the Court. Nevertheless, cockfighting is closely associated with Whitehall and no little confusion among stage historians has resulted from that one word, "cockpit."

The original Cockpit at Whitehall was built by Henry VIII for cockfighting, but it was later converted into a theatre, and the name came in time to be applied indiscriminately to the whole congeries of buildings between "the Street" and the park, and south of the Holbein Gate. I have already attempted to show that the Cockpit playhouse (as, to avoid confusion, it is usually called in the records) was never used for cockfighting after the Restoration.[1] But as early as November, 1661, a Cockmaster was appointed, and it would be unreasonable to suppose that his duties did not include the arrangement of mains for His Majesty's diversion.

The Cockmaster has a story of his own, which is not without interest. On 26 November 1661, Henry Browne, Esq., was sworn "Master of the Game of Cockfiteing in Ordinary."[2] The Establishment Books from which this entry is taken do not say on what authority this was done, but one would like to know, for the office had already been secured, as he thought, by someone else. An entry book among the State Papers records that on 13 November a warrant was signed for a Great Seal for Sir Richard Hubbert, the Groom Porter, as Cockmaster for life, with a salary of £20 *per annum* payable out of the Exchequer, as well as all profits, etc., arising out of the office.[3] Browne, however, seems to have enjoyed the post for the better part of a year, and then, on 30 August 1662, the Lord Chamberlain signified to him the King's pleasure that he forbear "to giue Commissions for any Cockfights or to authorize any to sett vp Cockpitts or Cockfighteings," until further notice, the Groom Porter having claimed these privileges as

1. See p. 20.
2. LC. 3/24, p. 153; 3/25, p. 119; 3/26, p. 159.
3. SP. 44/5, pp. 45–46. In SP. 38/20 there is a docquet of it, dated 30 November 1661, with the note, "Subscribed by Mr. Atturney by warrant vnder his Ma^te. Signe Manuall procured by Mr Secretary Nicholas."

belonging to his office.[1] On 3 September, the Lord Chamberlain wrote again, forbidding Browne to execute his office until further order, and added that it was the King's pleasure that the Groom Porter enjoy the post.[2]

When Thomas Offley became Groom Porter in 1667, he obtained a separate patent as "Prefect' Gallorum pugnan' nͬorum."[3] One would expect this to settle the matter, but not at all! In August, 1678, Offley being dead, the Lord Chamberlain signed the following warrant to the Gentlemen Ushers:

Whereas Our Late Soveraigne Lord King Charles by His Letters Patent dated the second of September in the seaventh yeare of His Reigne did for him his heires & Successors grant vnto S͏ͬ Henry Browne his Heires & Assignes the Office of His Ma͏ᵗᵉˢ Cockmaster within the Kingdome of England with Power to make a Deputy to Exercise the same: And Since the said Patent & office are lawfully come vnto & invested in Benedicta Browne Widdow and Relict of Henry Browne heire of S͏ͬ Henry Browne Which said Bendicta Browne hath made Iohn Archer Esq' her Lawfull Deputy These are therefore to require you to sweare and admitt the said Iohn Archer in the Place & quality of Deputy Cockmaster in Ordinary to His Ma͏ᵗᵉ for the Kingdome of England To Enjoy the same place with all rights Proffitts Priviledges & advantages thereto belonginge And this shall be yo͏ͬ Warr͏ᵗ.[4]

To return to the Cockpit, I think there can be no reasonable doubt that the Royal Cockpit on the south side of St. James' Park, at the end of Dartmouth Street, was in use in the days of Charles II. An account of the building and a picture of it will be found in Adams' *Shakespearean Playhouses*,[5] and it has also been described in Boulton's *Amusements of Old London*. It is there said to have been built about 1670,[6] but I have discovered one bit of evidence which suggests it was considerably older. On 8 March 1665/6, a Treasury warrant was

1. LC. 5/137, p. 351.   2. *Ibid.*, p. 352.
3. C. 66/3089, no. 18.
4. LC. 5/143, p. 142.   5. Pp. 408–409.
6. I, 177, 179; no authority is quoted.

signed for the payment of £454.14.11½ to Jervase Price, Under-Keeper of St. James' Park, "for reparations of the Cockpit, And the lodges in the said Park."[1] Unfortunately for us, both the building under discussion and the Cockpit playhouse were in, or at least adjoining, the park, and both were referred to as "the Cockpit in Sᵗ James Park"; but in 1666 the theatre had been abandoned, and I cannot imagine why Price should be paid for work on the Cockpit section of the palace. The word "reparations" certainly betokens a building already in existence, and I venture the suggestion that it was built in the 1630's, when the Cockpit in Court was remodelled.[2]

For the later use of the Dartmouth Street Cockpit, there are various notices. It is clearly shown on a map of St. Margaret's parish in Strype's edition of Stow's *Survey*,[3] and indeed, its location may still be traced by Cockpit Steps. Its flourishing condition in 1700 is attested by an advertisement quoted by Boulton, as follows:[4]

At the Royal Cockpit, on the South side of St. James' Park, on Tuesday, the 11th of this instant February, will begin a very great cock match, and will continue all the week, wherein most of the considerablest cockers in England are concerned. There will be a battle down upon the pit every day precisely at 3 o'clock, in order to have done by daylight. . . .[5]

It stood until 1816, when the Governors of Christ's Hospital refused to renew the lease of the ground.

"The Dancing of the Ropes"

Charles may have acquired his taste for rope-dancing while he was abroad; at any rate, he was not slow to introduce it in his restored Court. On 12 August 1660, William Smith

1. *Cal. of Treas. Books, 1660–67*, p. 719.
2. See p. 11. But cf. also Chambers, I, 217, note.
3. No. 38 on the key.
4. Boulton, I, 179; again he gives no source.
5. The rest relates to a match in Red Lion Fields.

wrote to John Langley that on Thursday the King had "had divertissement of dancing on the ropes before him in the great hall at Whitehall" at night.[1] For this entertainment, the first of any kind, I believe, to be held in the hall after the King's return, special preparations were necessary, and masons and carpenters were called upon to put up timbers for the ropes and degrees for the spectators.[2]

Who the stars of this performance were I do not know, but in 1663, Charles added to his Household three official acrobats. On 22 February, Jacob Hall, Thomas Cosby or Crosby, and William Fuller were sworn His Majesty's servants as "Valters & Dancers on ye Rope and other agillity of Body."[3] Hall was by far the most famous of the trio and is noticed in various memoirs of the Court, for his handsome face and magnificent figure made him a favourite with the ladies. Charles, it is said, once advised Castlemaine to be his mistress rather than Jermyn's, and she promptly took his advice.[4]

But all three were popular, and performed in public booths as well as at Court, as witness two permits preserved among the Lord Chamberlain's records. One reads:[5]

I doe hereby giue leaue vnto Thomas Cosbye his Maties servant to erect a Booth in Little Lyncolnes Inn fields for Danceing & Vaulting on the roope. Dat' Octo: 24th 1667.

The other is a similar licence for Hall and Fuller to put up a booth near the Maypole in the Strand, dated 26 March 1667.[6] In 1669 the troupe was augmented by the appointment of Stephen Scudamore, apparently on Tom Killigrew's recommendation;[7] and Fuller, Hall, and Scudamore reappear once more among the King's servants whose certificates were renewed by the Earl of St. Albans when he became Lord Chamberlain.[8]

1. Hist. Mss., V, 174.   2. See p. 241; E. 351/3274.
3. LC. 3/24, p. 197; LC. 5/138, p. 435.
4. Gramont's *Memoirs*, ed. by Vizetelly, II, 127.
5. LC. 5/138, p. 343.   6. *Ibid.*, p. 369.
7. LC. 3/24, p. 197.   8. LC. 3/27, p. 88.

It is remarkable that there are no entries relating to rope-dancing in the Works Accounts from 1660 until 1674. In September of that year, carpenters were employed in setting up timbers in the Banqueting House "for the Dancing of yᵉ ropes there," and making other necessary provisions.[1] The construction of the Hall Theatre in 1665 had evidently made the Hall impracticable for rope-dancing, and the Banqueting House afforded the only adequate space.

This stately apartment was the largest and finest in the palace.[2] Completed by Inigo Jones in 1622, it had been used for the Court masques until 1635, when the ceiling paintings by Rubens and Jordaens were put into place and the King, concerned for their preservation from smoke, transferred the masques and pastorals, first to the Great Hall and then to the "new masking house" hastily constructed for the Christmas season of 1637–38. Whether the Banqueting House was used for musical or other entertainments after 1635, I do not know, but it escaped injury during the Commonwealth, and one would expect to find Charles II prompt in making use of it. And, indeed, it was put to great variety of uses by him and his two successors, for here the King received ambassadors and Parliament, here he performed his Maundy and displayed his New Year's gifts, and here, if he did not go to Windsor, he celebrated the magnificent orgy of St. George's Feast. But there is no mention of a single play there. Charles, however, was not restrained by the memory that his father had walked through this room to the scaffold, for it now came to be used frequently for exhibitions of rope-dancing and acrobatics.

Two years later, elaborate preparations were again made there, described as

takeing downe yᵉ Rayles in yᵉ Banquetting howse for yᵉ Dancing on yᵉ Rope & Setting them vp againe Setting vp two long peeces of timber for yᵉ fastening of yᵉ Slacke Rope there and braceing them,

---

1. Works 5/24.
2. The inside dimensions are 112 by 60 feet.

putting vp peeces of timber in ye windows to fasten ye greate rope to dance on, laying a floore with baulks & bourds to tumble about 40 foo^t long & 10 foo^t wide.[1]

The last and most interesting entry is in the following May, for

takeing downe ye Rayles in ye Banquetting house before the Chaire of State, Laying downe 2 peeces of timber one in ye East window ye other in ye West window & shooreing them downe from ye windowes Downe to ye Stone worke of each side of ye windowes for to fasten ye Rope to Dance on trussing out 2 Scaffolds in the gallery one on ye one side ye other on ye other side to fasten the Slacke rope on, Nayling 2 bourds together with leadges and raised a yard high att one End for them to Vault vppon."[2]

A Drollery for the Queen

In October, 1666, preparations were made in the Queen's Presence Chamber for a show which is otherwise, I believe, unrecorded. The Works Accounts describe making a dais and enclosing a place for a drollery,[3] the only one ever mentioned in the records as acted at Whitehall. It is interesting, as indicative of the trend of fashion, to note that the Clerk of the Works first described the entertainment as a puppet-show, and then corrected the error.[4]

A Show in the Banqueting House

The Works Accounts tell us that in November, 1664 carpenters made a stage in the Banqueting House and "other provisions for a show there,"[5] and from Henry Muddiman we learn the occasion and something of the entertainment. In a newsletter dated 16 November, he writes:[6]

1. Works 5/27, September, 1676.
2. Works 5/28, May, 1677.   3. See p. 57.
4. For puppets at Whitehall see pp. 57, 116.
5. Works 5/5.   6. SP. 29/104, no. 146.

Yesterday being Her Maj^s. birthday, the affternoon was spent in several divertisements in ye Banqueting house, among w^h. was a Chariot, w^h. ran severall times about ye room the motion onely being forced by one & then by 2. men.

This scarcely sounds like a piece of clock-work, but I do not know what else it can have been.[1]

1. There are three entries in the Works Accounts which suggest *divertisse-ments* of some kind in the Banqueting House, although it is quite possible they should not be so interpreted: July, 1660. making and setting up 154 ft. of rails, and dividing the gallery with a partition 10 ft. high and 5 ft. broad (Works 5/1).

April, 1661. "makinge a box in ye banquetting house 10 fo^t. longe wth 3 degrees in it for ye Dutchesse of Yorke, & a nother [*sic*] box there for the Lord Chamberlaine wth a floore Joysted & bourded" (Works 5/2).

May, 1685. "cutting the raile cross my L^d. Chamb^r.lins box in the Banquetting house; putting vp a flight of Sta^{rs}. of 5 Steps wth. a hand-raile, & taking downe the railes there severall times" (Works 5/39).

After the fire of 1698, the Banqueting House was converted into a chapel, and it has never been restored to the purposes for which it was built.

INDEX

INDEX

Tнıs index is selective and omits casual, non-informative references. Names of musicians, dancers, tradesmen, craftsmen and attendants are not indexed separately except in important cases, but references to them are grouped under the general heading. A list of the persons whose letters are quoted is given under the heading "Letters." Appendix A is not indexed in detail, since full references to it are given in the footnotes. References to especially important material are indicated by italic figures.